THE INVASION

THE INVASION

A Narrative of Events Concerning the Johnston Family of St. Mary's

Janet Lewis

Michigan State University Press
East Lansing

∞ The paper used in this publication meets the minimum requirements of
ANSI/NISO Z39.48-1992 (R 1997) (Permanence of Paper).

Michigan State University Press
East Lansing, Michigan 48823-5202

Printed and bound in the United States of America.

07 06 05 04 03 02 01 00   1 2 3 4 5 6 7 8 9 10

Library of Congress Cataloging-in-Publication Data

  Lewis, Janet, 1899-1999
The invasion: a narrative of events concerning the Johnston family of St.
Mary's / Janet Lewis.
    p.   cm.
    Originally published: Denver: A. Swallow, [196, c1932], in series: The American
    fiction library.
    ISBN 0-87013-495-7
    1. Ojibwa Indians—Michigan—History—Fiction. 2. Indians of North
America—Michigan—History—Fiction. 3. Irish Americans—Michigan—Fiction.
4. Sault Sainte Marie (Mich.)—Fiction. I. Title.
    PS3523.E866 I58 1998
    813'.52-dc21   99-055796

Cover design by Heidi Dailey.
Book design by Michael Brooks.

Michigan State University Press wishes to acknowledge the invaluable assistance
of Doug Peterson in bringing this work to a new generation of readers.

Visit Michigan State University Press on the World-Wide Web at:
                    www.msu.edu/unit/msupress

for

The Red Leaf
Anna Maria Johnstone
Born October 25, 1844
Died August 13, 1928

and

Little Red Leaf
Joanna Winters
Born April 3, 1931

The Author wishes to thank the following persons for their invaluable assistance: Mr. William M. Johnstone, Miss Minnie Trempe, Miss Alice B. Clapp, Mr. Chase S. Osborn, Mr. and Mrs. Edwin Herbert Lewis, Mr. Yvor Winters, Mrs. Dorothea Brande, Mr. Achilles Holt, Mrs. Ulysses Guidoux, Mrs. T. U. Carlson, Miss Mabel Slocum, Mrs. Walter Richardson, and especially Mr. and Mrs. Howard Lewis Johnstone.

John Johnston of County Antrim, Ireland
    married
The Woman of the Glade, Ozhah-guscoday-wayquay,
    daughter of
Waub-ojeeg, the White Fisher,
    granddaughter of
Ma-mmongazid, the Big Foot, *friend of* Montcalm.
Later she is called Neengay, My Mother, and still later,
    Susan Johnston.

Their children:

Lewis Saurin
George
Jane *married* Henry Rowe Schoolcraft
Eliza
Charlotte *married* the Rev. William MacMurray
William
Anna Maria *married* James Schoolcraft, brother of Henry Rowe
    Schoolcraft
John MacDougall (sometimes written McDooal) *married* Justine
    Piquette

Their children:

Anna Maria (the Woman of the Red Leaf, Miss Molly)
Charlotte Jane (Miss Charlotte)
Eliza Susan (Mrs. Anthony)
Howard Lewis (the Black Hawk)
William Meddaugh
Wayish-kee, the First-Born, *brother of* Neengay
Ah-deek, the Deer, *youngest brother of* Neengay

The children of Henry Rowe Schoolcraft and Jane Johnston:
William Henry (Penaysee, the Bird)
Jane Susan Anne
John Johnston

Justine and her daughters, Charlotte (standing), Eliza or Mrs. Anthony, and Miss Molly

Howard Lewis Johnston and Miss Molly Johnston

Howard Lewis Johnstone

Anna Maria Johnstone (The Woman of the Red Leaf, Miss Molly) on her cabin porch at NeeGish Island. Photograph by Irwin Rosenfels, August 1926.

THE PLAINS OF ABRAHAM

1759

That September day the English appeared so suddenly that they seemed to have dropped from the sky; appeared, and fired. A warm rain fell now and again upon the troops, and the smoke from the rifles lay in long white streamers, dissipating slowly. The noise of the rifles, reflected from the running water and from the cliffs, was something like thunder, but the rain was too quiet. And running, for the French, had become almost more important than fighting. The head of Montcalm lay upon the breast of Ma-mongazid, the young Ojibway, the dark sorrowful face, with its war paint of vermilion and white, intent above the French face graying rapidly. Presently they took the Marquis to the hospital at St. Charles, where he died. Ma-mongazid with his warriors in thirty bark canoes returned to La Pointe Chegoimegon through the yellowing woods and the increasing storms of autumn. The rule of the French was over, the Province of Michilimackinac had become the Northwest Territory. The Ojibways called the English Saugaunosh, the Dropped-from-the-Clouds, and regretted the French.

I

Manibush ran in the woods, sometimes as a rabbit, sometimes as a young Indian. The sand point at Chegoimegon was the remnant of the great beaver dam which he built generations ago. The wild rice, the short, blunt ears of maize, the fire, curling in narrow tongues about the birch logs in the center of the wigwam floor, were the gift of Manabozho.* Because of him the gull was white, the kingfisher was barred and crested, the woodpecker red-headed, the sap in the maple trees thin, instead of thick as formerly, the helldiver a red-eyed bird with crooked legs, the squirrel little, the bear big and eating only berries unless attacked, the bark of the red willow good to smoke. Because of him, likewise, the Mide lodge was built yearly on the shore of the Bay St. Charles and ceremonies were performed to heal the sick and even, in the old days, to raise the dead, to enjoy again, in some place far off, their earthly bodies. There was nothing in the woods with which he had not tampered, and the stories told of him were of all varieties, ludicrous, obscene, grave, or sacred. The earth was his grandmother, the west wind his father, the Indians his uncles. The bear, lumbering obscurely through the wet leaves and grasses, was versed in the Mide mysteries, and full of unknown, if beneficent, power. The otter was the first of the Mide initiates; the wolf was the brother of Manabozho and conducted the dead in safety to the Lodge of Reindeer.

In her father's lodge was the Mide pole surmounted by the carved wooden figure of Kokokoho, the Owl, which spun with the wind, and which was never allowed to be seen unless her father was at home. The lodge was narrow but long, "an egg cut in two," an egg sixty feet from end to end and perhaps ten feet wide. It was constructed of cedar poles, thongs, and bark, and a tall man could stand upright in it easily. In a row down the center were three or more fires, above which, in the opening of the smoke holes, corn, meat, and fish were hung to dry, and skins which had been previously scraped and boiled in a solution of wood ash and animal brain. These skins, once tanned, were almost translucent and had a sweet, tarry odor. They were soft, and remained so even after being wet through. The floor of the lodge was earth, trampled and swept, and around the entire wigwam, next the wall, ran a low platform of cedar and balsam boughs covered with skins, furs, or woven cedar mats. A deerskin hung across the entrance.

---

* The zh in this word and in other Ojibway words is the best English orthography I can devise for the French *j*, or the *s* in pleasure. Chegoimegon is purely French orthography, and should be pronounced so.

On the mild spring night after the corn-planting, her mother left the lodge, alone, and walked in the soft darkness naked about the borders of the cornfield, trailing after her upon the freshly turned earth her deerskin garment full of fertility. The girl, lying in her place on the balsam boughs near the lodge door, saw her go, stepping quietly through the diminished firelight, and heard her return softly and lie down beside her husband on the far side of the lodge. The corn had been planted in hills, and in each hill a fish, or part of a fish, had been buried, since life comes from life. As they lay there, all of them, in the fragrance of wood smoke and evergreen boughs, in the odor of burnt fish and the warm familiar odor of their own bodies, often as not the sharp, light patterings of the spring rain would grow distinct through the noises of the trees and of the lake, and they would fall asleep feeling the powers of earth and air beneficent. After the bitterness of winter it was profoundest happiness.

Her father's first wife slept near the girl on the women's side of the lodge. Her brothers and half brothers and sisters were there, eight of them in all, and sometimes her grandfather with his two wives, an uncle and a daughter who had married a French Canadian after the death of her first husband, and been deserted by him. Sometimes there were also guests. Her father was Waubojeeg, the White Fisher, hereditary chieftain of the Ojibway nation, her grandfather, Ma-mongazid, the Big Foot, who had fought for Montcalm; she herself was Ozhah-guscoday-wayquay, the Woman of the Glade, but her mother called her Nindanis, My Daughter, and her father said "Equay-zonse, Little Woman." She was fourteen years of age.

The wigwams about Chegoimegon were all Ojibway now, save for a few visiting Potawatamis, or Ottawas, or Menominees. No man could remember when they had not been Ojibway, and the Sioux had been driven by her father beyond the Mississippi. Lake Superior and all the surrounding territory was Ojibway, and the center of the Ojibway power was Chegoimegon.

In some remote way her father acknowledged a British jurisdiction over and above the Ojibway. He did not think of the land as being British, but of the Ojibways as being bound by treaty to the English as they were to the Ottawas, Potawatamis, Illinois, and Menominees. He expected to punish an Ojibway who transgressed against an Englishman, and he expected the English to do justice for the Ojibways upon French or English. He granted the English the right to trade in his territory; he admitted that the day of the French was over. This man, Waub-ojeeg, had the greatest dislike for all white men, although he tolerated a Frenchman. His

2

father had fought for the French, and had been honored by the English. He had wasted his time and his strength in battles that were not his own, and he had been given whiskey to drink.

After the last desperate effort of Pontiac to maintain the French supremacy in America, which resulted in the massacre of 1763 at Old Fort Mackinac, the French traders were forbidden the Lake Superior territory, and the English traders were afraid to venture among such bitter enemies. Meanwhile the Indians, who had become accustomed to European kettles and guns and blankets, and who had neglected their own industries for hunting and trapping in order to possess these foreign articles, were suffering want. Moreover, once the musket was extensively introduced into the country, the Indian who had to rely upon bow and arrow was considerably at a disadvantage, and the Iroquois, old enemies of the Ojibways, were well supplied with bullets and powder. Therefore, two years later, Chegoimegon sent Ma-mongazid to Sir William Johnson at Johnson Hall in the Mohawk Valley with peace offerings and the request that a trader might be sent among them soon. The offerings were accepted, Ma-mongazid was treated with great honor, and a silver gorges and a belt of blue and white wampum were bestowed upon him—blue sky, white clouds, fair weather. The trader was promised. But Waub-ojeeg, some eight or ten years later, undid the blue and white belt, shell by shell, and, making it into war messages, sent out his runners to all the Ojibway villages to organize his nation against the Sioux. When the belt was reassembled and returned to the old man, many Ojibways were dead, many more Sioux; and the people of the lake villages, for the first time in generations, went about their daily business without fear. Thus did Waub-ojeeg turn his back on the white man and fight the battles of his own people. He had no gifts from either French or English, and he had never tasted whiskey.

Father Allouez had been at Chegoimegon in 1665, the first priest, and almost the first white man, to visit the place. He had found there a village of eight different nations, chief among them the Ottawas and Hurons, and he had built there a small chapel of bark. He named the lake Lac du Tracy, in honor of the then governor of New France, and the islands about the Red Cliff Point the Apostle Islands. Bay St. Charles he had named, and Ile St. Michel; and Chegoimegon itself, the Sandy Lowland, he had named La Pointe du St. Esprit. It was now called by the French La Pointe Chegoimegon, or simply La Pointe. He was the first man to write down the word, inscribing it with his square-tipped quill Chagouoimegong. He said, "They are here to the number of eight hundred men bearing arms," and again, "They are licentious and superstitious. I have thought fit to baptize only the children and the dying." Neither the Devil nor the Ottawas had desired the presence of this priest at Chegoimegon. The Devil caused his box of medicines and letters, his precious theriacs compounded of opium and sweet spices, cardamon, cinnamon, mace, to be left behind at a portage; the Ottawas, finding it, plundered it, left it open to the rain, and finally, fearful of the white devils in it, brought what was left of it to its owner. While the priest implored St. Anthony for the sake of his box, Shingwauk, the Pine, in the next shelter, made a prayer and offerings to the Bear to soften the obstinate temper of this white man's mind, and make him wish to return to Montreal, that he might not be a burden on the Ottawas forever. The Devil caused the priest's canoe to be wrecked; the Ottawas thereafter, not unreasonably, took him into their canoes under the condition that he should also paddle. Asceticism and contemplation had not prepared him for this trial, and day after day he suffered torture at the humble occupation, many times continuing in an actual physical daze, many times fainting under his load at the portages. Even so, in passing up "a river which united two great lakes and ended in a rapids two and a half leagues in length," he lifted his eyes to the islands, the wooded shores and trim bays, and said, touched by their beauty, "So God gives us always some little grace to sweeten our days."

This patient man continued with the Ottawas for two years; then, returning to Quebec for help, stayed there but two days before embarking again for La Pointe. He labored that winter among the Hurons at Red Cliff, witnessed their sacred dances, was abused, converted a few savages, preached the gospel to those who would listen and to those who would not listen, and at last, after one more winter, re-embarked for Quebec, never to return. He took with him two Iroquois whom he had ransomed. He stepped into the canoe barefooted, in order not to damage with his heavy French shoes the fragile floor; he was bareheaded in order that the brim of his hat might not inconvenience the Ottawa paddlers; his black skirts were gathered up, not to carry sand into the craft. Blanket he had none; it had been stolen from him long before. The holy pyx he carried in his arms, and letters for his superior at "Kebec." So after four years of semi-starvation, of a diet of tripe de rockier—that small, shell-shaped fungus, often covered with cobwebs and spiders, of which the Indians made a thin black soup—of powdered fishbones and spoiled corn, after four years of hardships encountered day and night, and parted; and when, in the year 1791, the Woman of the Glade woke at night and heard the rain falling upon the bark roof and upon the new corn, not even the oldest man in the Ojibway tribe, who kept the records, incised on birchbark or on native copper, who renewed them every ten years and buried them, wrapped in bird down and soft skins, in a secret place, had ever heard of Father Claude Allouez or of his chapel.

In the late summer Chegoimegon was filled with visitors come to observe or to participate in the Mide ceremonies. Runners were sent out weeks beforehand, with bundles of painted sticks, and presently many light shelters sprang up along the shore of Bay St. Charles, built of saplings thrust into the ground in a circle, the unremitting labor and gentleness, the ends tied together at the top and the framework covered with rush or cedar mats, or with pieces of bark. Walking between the tall leafy clusters of cornstalks, the girl who was known as the Woman of the Glade heard the sound of the Mide drum and the voices from the great Mide shelter in the center of the village. The corn was ripe for eating but not for harvesting. She broke the green ears from the stalks, the leaves rustling heavily and crisply about her, and dropped them on her outspread blanket, and the beat of the Mide drum, small, remote, powerful, traversed the wall of leaves, entered the wood and the cornfield, spread outward upon the water of the bay, and became a part of the weather and the still sunshine. She gathered the ends of the blanket together, and swinging the bundle over her shoulder, came from the cornfield by the trail through the aspen wood to the village. The ground was soft, it sprang under her feet a little at each step. Through her moccasins she felt the texture of it, twig and leaf and moss, and the thin moccasins, in summer, lasted a long time upon this gentle earth; it was the ice of winter that cut them. She wore leggins of red cloth, and a short-sleeved buckskin tunic, and a buckskin skirt reaching to her knees and fringed about the bottom. Her hair was in two braids, but she wore no feather, being a woman. She came from the aspens at early dusk, and saw beyond the wigwams and the people the quiet shore of the bay and the far-away shape of La Pointe, and, beyond it, Ile St. Michel, all wooded shapes.

People were making their fires, many of them out of doors. She passed near the high green lattice wall of the Mide lodge. A group of Ottawas with bundles of things to trade were waiting for the ceremonies to be over. An Ottawa woman seated on the ground, her feet drawn up to one side of her, half kneeling, was nursing a baby bound to a cedar frame. The men, crouching on the balls of their feet, their buttocks on their heels, were smoking. The bowls of the long pipes rested on their knees. She knew they were Ottawas because of their curious clipped speech. The drumming and the singing from the Mide lodge was loud and distinct. "Into thy body I shoot the spirit. Into thy body. How beautiful it is, our

5

Mide shell. Drifting snow, it is the drifting snow is why I sing." Any one might hear it because, unless one had been instructed, no one might understand it. People were standing at the entrance looking in, and her oldest brother was there, wandering about with an apparent aimlessness. He had been stationed as a guard to make sure that no careless Ottawa constructed a lodge between the Mide wigan and the small, dome-shaped sudatory lodge opposite its eastern entrance. "It is the drifting snow is why I sing." She went on to her father's lodge.

That evening the Mide priests came to call upon her father. He was dressed in white buckskin, with fringes over his shoulders and down the outside of his arm, and down the outer seam of the leggins which reached from his thighs to his ankles. Diagonally across his breast and shoulders were hung two beaded belts, which crossed each other, and from these hung his Mide bag of otter skin and his embroidered tobacco pouch. He sat cross-legged on the platform beyond the fire. His face was painted red with a narrow green stripe running from the base of the right ear across the cheek and nose to the left forehead. His pipe, beautifully decorated with the red scalps of woodpeckers and green and burnished feathers of the humming bird, lay across his knees.

All evening the visitors kept coming—old Mide, newly initiated Mide, Mide who had been advanced to a second or, rarely, a third degree. All were dressed in new blankets and in their finest clothes. Some of the faces were painted the lower half red, the upper half green, the division in color coming in a horizontal line across the center of the bridge of the nose. A young man with a band of green across the eyelids and the root of the nose, above that a narrow red line, and then a green line again until the forehead was barred red and green in narrow alternate stripes, wore about his shoulders a blanket of white rabbit skins sewed together. The pipe was offered to each visitor in turn, and each smoked once to the east, once to the south, to the west, to the north, once to the earth, Nokomis, the Grandmother, once to the sky, Gitche Manido, the Master of Life. Then her mother and the old woman, the first wife, and herself brought food to the guests, basswood bowls of fish soup, square birchbark dishes of parched corn and maple sugar, deer meat boiled with corn, dishes of smoked rice, dishes of meenin, the small sweet blueberry.

Very late that night when every one had gone and the village had become quiet she heard her father and mother talking together on the other side of the fire, and laughing a little.

She went the next day with her mother and the old woman up La Riviere Mauvaise to cut rushes. In the shallows the round green water reeds grew outward toward the river channel in long points, and they went among them in a small canoe, kneeling and reaching down into the cold water to cut them as long as they could. The old woman, kneeling in the stern to paddle, guided them here and there with deft and tranquil strokes. Her mother began to tell them about Tchweetchweesh-keway, the Plover. The worse his luck at hunting, the more strongly he had desired to become a Mide, in hopes that he might change it. The night before, having paid many furs and kettles to his preceptors, and many blankets to the society itself, he had been initiated. Now, Waub-ojeeg had said, he was very likely to starve before the hunting season began unless his relatives should feed him. The old woman, her face wrinkled with laughter, leaned backward on her paddle, swinging the bow around. She said, "He has good medicine now; he will have to eat his medicine."

They took the rushes home, and laid them in a pit of water, and tumbled hot stones in upon them. When they were bleached, they took them out and dried them, and later wove them into flexible, light mats, using a cord of basswood fiber for the warp. A few reeds stained with hickory were worked into a border.

The great Mide assembly had begun to disperse the morning after the final ceremonies. All day long, canoes were moving off into the lake, wigwams being dismantled, pitch being heated to mend canoes. The ashes of the fires, the stakes from which the kettles had been hung, the trampled grass, a few bones that the dogs had not devoured, were left, and the sixty or more wigwams of the regular village. Soon even these began to disappear. Early in September her grandfather and his family left to gather wild rice, ascending the Mauvaise with many portages. The poverty-stricken Plover took his family and went to his accustomed trapping ground, having borrowed from one of his Mide brethren an extra blanket and an ax. She was very busy husking and parching corn, and storing it in big birchbark hampers. The openings in the woods were full of goldenrod; going to the river for water one early morning she broke the first skim of ice. Maples were turning scarlet overnight, and the wind, blowing from the north, was sharp and breath-taking. She liked to go inland a little way and lie in the deep grass like the deer, sunning herself, out of the confusion and vigor of the weather. Before the month was over they too were dismantling their lodge, taking it apart, piece by piece, and packing it, with other possessions, in the canoes. Some of the poles they left behind them, hidden in a safe place. On the morning of the twentieth they left Chegoimegon and went north, rounding the Red Cliff peninsula, and coasting the shore until they came to the Wisakoda, or Burntwood River.

This they mounted, and went inland until they reached good beaver country, and before snow fell three smaller lodges were erected from the stuff of the large one. Waub-ojeeg and Wayishkee, the First Born, were setting their traps. The solitary life of the winter months had begun.

At night, after a day among the traps, the men returned to the lodges, told the women how much game there was and where to find it, and the women went after it to bring it home. While the women were gone the men ate the food which had been prepared for them, and rested. Some meat was smoked, some dried and pounded into short fibers and mixed with bear grease as pemmican. In November, while the ground was yet clear of snow, Wayishkee took his sister on a deer hunt. When they came to the deer run, and the Indian was satisfied that the tracks were fresh, he knelt and dropped into one hoofprint a small quantity of powdered vermilion and tobacco. He then drew the outline of a deer upon the ground and, marking the heart with a pointed stick, dropped there also a pinch of vermilion. Having thus assured himself that the quarry would grow faint and wait for him, he nodded to his sister, and they went forward softly. They came to a good ambush among low cedars, where the trail ran into a glade, and waited there, and when the deer came, a yearling buck, stepping delicately through the long seeded grass, it was the girl who pulled Wayishkee's bow and sent an arrow into its side behind the shoulder. Wayishkee said: "Very good. Now you can marry. If your husband won't hunt, still you won't be hungry." He cut up the animal and put the pieces in the skin, and his sister carried it home.

Waub-ojeeg was a good hunter. His children could not remember a winter when there had not been plenty of meat in the lodge, although other families often suffered. At the end of the season he had usually four packs of furs to trade at the Sault Ste. Marie for powder and bullets, traps, kettles, calico, and tobacco. Each bundle was valued at forty pounds sterling, and although the trader, having a monopoly of the market, charged extravagant prices for his goods, one hundred and sixty English pounds bought a great deal. For food and raiment, lodging and transportation, Waub-ojeeg paid nothing. His women were industrious and strong, and his family lived well. He had, moreover, a virtue which few white men shared with him. He knew when he had enough.

Winter was the season for story-telling. At night, the animals hidden away in thickets, in hollow trees, in holes in the earth, the birds gone south, the chickadee ruffled into a ball, asleep with his head under his wing, the plants covered with snow, the fish locked under ice, the little flies and insects gone no one knew where, this animistic universe was earless, and it was safe to gossip. In the winter the innumerable stories of Manabozho were repeated, together with stories of the warpath, all the legendary history of the tribe. The dance drum, larger than the Mide drum but with a softer beat, was taken to the fire and tuned by warming it, and Wayishkee and his father took turns at singing, accompanying the song with a light throbbing of the drum. Snow fell upon the snow. Bare branches rubbed together, creaking in the wind as on the day when Manabozho lost his moose; ice and snow broke from the trees and fell upon the lodge, and slid to the snow-covered ground with a light scraping, and Ozhah-guscoday-wayquay swept the ashes into the edge of the fire with a balsam branch. The noise of the wind was soft and lonely.

II

About the middle of August of that same year, 1791, a canot du nord, or canot du maître, a birch canoe of the largest size—which meant that it was anywhere from thirty to thirty-six feet long and six feet wide at its widest—left Michilimackinac and came by slow stages up the St. Mary's River, past the Sault, past Les Grands Sables, past the Pictured Rocks, and so on along the south shore of Lake Superior. It was laden with bundles of scarlet cloth, bundles of calico, strouds, blankets, little packages of powdered vermilion, traps, wormers, awls, bullets, powder, muskets, corn, pork, nets, axes, tobacco, and rum, and it was propelled by four Canadian voyageurs. It carried two passengers, one a young Canadian who had been added to the party largely in the capacity of an interpreter, the other the bourgeois or trader, an Irishman. These two sometimes spelled the canoemen at the paddles, the interpreter doing so far more frequently than the bourgeois.

They spent two weeks in the river; in September they entered the lake. The weather was very bad, given to sudden squalls, and on the sixth of the month it snowed for over two hours. They were forced to put ashore frequently. At the Pictured Rocks they waited a day and a half for calm water in which to pass that dangerous shore, and finally set out at three in the morning in a cold white mist beneath which the water lay as still as a mill pond on the surface, yet undulating with a slow, powerful, and almost secret movement. They traveled, when the weather permitted, until eight or half-past eight in the evening. They always rose before dawn and traveled three or four hours before pausing for breakfast. They camped, without putting up a shelter, by their overturned canoe, which had to be unloaded at every stop, and sometimes repaired with hot balsam gum and fresh bark. The pitch bubbled thickly as it was melted, sending forth a pungent fragrance which mingled with the odor of their food—corn, boiled with pork or with bear tallow. They slept on the ground, waking with a haze of frost on their blankets, on their packs, on the leafy earth. The regular rations for each man per diem were a quart of corn which had previously been boiled with a small amount of lye to soften the husk and make more mealy the center, and a small portion of salt pork or other fat. A quart of tallow to a man per month was the standard. When they had done a very hard portage or when the weather was particularly inclement the trader portioned them out a cup of rum or shrub apiece; they called it a regale, and were pleased, and made no complaints about the monotony of their usual diet. It was the time-honored menu of their calling. While they were traveling there was no time for hunting, but they knew that when they reached their winter camp the fare would be varied according to their own skill, with fish, deer meat, bear meat, and other game.

At Kewenaw Point they made the portage, climbing through the woods to the height of land from which they looked down upon the tranquil beaches. The weather was calm, but the water came in heavy continuous swells, breaking upon the sand like the waves of a quiet ocean. The lake was intensely blue, the shores Persian-colored, shot with lines of regularly pointed dark green conifers, the beaches the color of wheat. The last day of September they reached the group of islands about the Red Cliff Point known to them as the Apostle Islands, and La Liberté, the steersman, pointing with his hand, the palm held vertical and knifelike for an instant, said, "Ile St. Michel." His hand went back to the shaft of his paddle, turning the blade expertly in the water, and moving with it at the same rate at which the water fled past the side of the canoe. They coasted down the heavily wooded shore, past the thick growth of hickory, walnut, oak, and pine, and as they came in sight of what was apparently another island, lying parallel with St. Michel and separated from it by only half a mile of water, La Liberté said again, "La Pointe." They had arrived. The canoe swung to the right, rounding the southern tip of St. Michel, and was brought ashore there in a small sandy cove formed by a projecting sandbar.

The men stepped overboard in the shallow water, and two of them, taking the bourgeois on their shoulders, set him ashore dry-shod. The canoe still floated, and they unloaded it before they lifted it by the narrow cedar thwarts and brought it up the beach to a high grassy spot. They were gay; their feet started showers of crystal as they waded about, and they shouted to each other with a heavy resonance and stridency, the words breaking into sudden flat noises, like hands clapped together. They were all hivernants, these men, that is to say, they were old-timers, each of them

10

having spent several or many winters in the bush. They were Canadians with French fathers and Indian mothers—Ojibway, Potawatomi, Huron, Ottawa—a combination of the volatile and the solid, yet not so curious a blending as might be supposed, certain tenacities, loyalties, and superstitions merging indistinguishably; it was often impossible to say which was French and which was Indian.

The steersman, and therefore the most important among them, was La Liberté, a tall fellow with a squarish head set on a squarer neck, thick-shouldered and lean-thighed; he had something the look of a chrysanthemum. His good wide jaw with its set of small even teeth he got from his Potawatomi mother. The short aquiline nose and flaring eyebrows were probably the gift, long since, of a French lord to the children of a daughter of the soil. He was dressed in a capot, or heavy woolen cape, cloth trousers, a striped cotton shirt, moccasins, and wore about his waist a belt of knitted worsted with ends fringed in scarlet. From his belt were hung his knife, a small ax, and a tobacco pouch. His hair was short, grizzled and curly, the straggling ends projecting from under a red silk neckerchief with which his head was bound, and lying against the weather-beaten, seamed dark leather of his neck like the edges of a bear's pelt.

The other men were much like him in general appearance. Some of them wore fur caps, one wore a green handkerchief; one had trousers of buckskin instead of cloth; their woolen belts differed slightly in color and pattern, the calico of their shirts differed slightly. They all wore moccasins. The interpreter, although he was the youngest of the group, being hardly more than seventeen years of age, also counted himself an hivernant, for he had been in the service since he was fourteen. His mother had been an Ottawa, and it was this language he spoke, the difference between Ottawa and Ojibway being so slight as to make either language seem to a man of the opposite nation his own language spoken with a villainous accent. He was a short, upstanding youth with a big frame and a pleasant face; he had, in comparison with the other men, a look of greenness and sappiness, like that of a tree whose newly shot twigs are not yet hardened into wood. He was called Florentin.

While the men were busy with the canoe, their bourgeois had left them, going a short distance into the woods in search of a place for a permanent camp. Pushing through a dense wall of tag alder, he entered a wood of small poplars, and, continuing through that, came out of the trees into a narrow glade full of goldenrod and tall grass. It was very quiet. The farther wall of the opening seemed to be of birches, new growth, encroaching upon what once had been a meadow. In a few years, perhaps even next year, the

11

advancing ranks of seedling balsams, the poplars, the white birches, would fill the space entirely; this glade was the last vision of the meadow, perhaps of a cornfield. About the knees of the birches the yellowing bracken was thick; he heard, far away beyond the rampart of trees and the rising bulk of the island, the roar of the wind on the lake and nearer, but not loud, the voices of his men. Meanwhile he stood in silence as palpable as the deep sunshine that lay unruffled all about him. As he walked forward the long grass and flowering autumn weeds brushed against his thighs, almost up to his waist, and he crossed something that must have been a deer run, a narrow line where the grass was bowed. The tranquillity of the place, after his month and a half of stormy travel, touched him as a premonition of good fortune and of charm. Being alone, he ceased to see things as through the eyes of the voyageurs, and a number of pleasant perceptions lifted themselves slowly in his mind, like grass straightening after the passage of steps.

Son and grandson and great-grandson of Scotch-Irish merchants, army officers, and semipublic officials, nephew of the Bishop of Belfast, in the Anglican communion, and of the Rector of Coleraine, also Anglican, with a background of English Latin Schools and Dublin drawing-rooms, he carried an entire continent of culture about with him, separating him definitely, however subtly, from his men, these having all been born here and there, like conies, in the woods they habitually traveled. He was then in his thirtieth year, having privately celebrated his twenty-ninth birthday on the twenty-fifth of August somewhere on the St. Mary's River, possibly at the foot of Sugar Island. In person he was tall, being just under six feet in height, and well set up. He had a small dark eye, deeply set, but very bright and penetrating; a forehead high, clear, and sloping, the hair already receding a little at the temples; a humorous mouth with sensitive, mobile lips and deep corners; a nose well formed, with the same humorous expression lurking at the nostrils; the whole face was rather broad, fair, and amiable—an open and friendly countenance. The hair which fell upon the shoulders of his capot from under a small fur cap was straight and yellow. He wore the soft moccasins common to all those who traveled by canoe, and, instead of the knee breeches and silk stockings to which he had all his life been accustomed, long cloth trousers like those of his men. He had not, however, managed to conform entirely to the wood-runner's costume; he wore beneath his capot a coat of light blue with buff facings and brass buttons, and beneath his blue coat a fine white shirt, of which the collar band resolved itself into a stock with ruffled ends.

He was John Johnston, the son of William Johnston, retired naval officer and surveyor of Port Rush. His mother was Elizabeth McNeil of Coulreshkan.

His last recollection of his father was that of a rider, his clothes heavy with sea water, galloping into the courtyard at dusk on a horse coated with brine. He had been on a visit to a friend on the other side of the River Brush and, finding the tide in on his return, he had swum his horse across the river rather than go two miles out of his way to a bridge. He dismounted and called for a boy to take his horse, and went inside in search of a fire and a hot rum toddy. An acquaintance, however, a Doctor Stephenson who had been treating him for dyspepsia, had that day, without explaining it, given him a dose of mercury, the which, combined with the ducking, conspired to give him a fever which carried him off. Young John, then seven years old, was sent off to school in Coleraine, near by, while his father yet lay delirious, and he never saw him again.

Next came a long series of recollections more or less monotonous, and somewhat vague also, of the benches of the Latin School where his ingenuity enabled him to learn very little, of the snuff-speckled frock of the Anglican curate who presided over them, and of holidays at his mother's house near Coleraine. When he was ten his uncle the rector, who had been placed in charge of his mother's financial interests together with those of his Aunt Nancy Johnston, had so mismanaged matters that the business which should have been a source of comparative wealth had become a constant expense, and entailed a system of close economy. This brought young John home from school, when his Aunt Nancy discovered with horror that he could hardly write his name, and that his knowledge of grammar, either English or Latin, was nil. Thereupon this gentlewoman, her modestly powdered curls hidden under a great pleated cap of white holland, her lustrous taffeta skirt beneath a white holland apron, became his tutor in those subjects, and a young man was called in from the village to instruct him in mathematics.

At tea time they gathered in the drawing-room—his sisters, Eliza and Jane and little Charlotte, and his younger brother William, his mother, freed from her household duties, and his dear Aunt Nancy—and when the tray had been set aside and the candles brought in, one or the other of the women read aloud from the works of Dryden or Pope or Shakespeare, while the older girls cut patterns for bobbin lace and Charlotte, gentle creature, sat curled on a tuffet at the side of her brother John. Long, happy evenings! In winter with the pointed candle flames, in summer with the slow, equable light from the garden and the lawn. The huge illuminated vellum with its blobs of green sealing wax spread over Jane's knees, and from which she was clipping her pattern, had been presented to his father and to his Uncle Mussinden by the City of Edinburgh. It was unsurpassable for patterns, Jane considered; she was already at the signatures.

When he was fifteen John took to riding, hunting, and coursing greyhounds, spending long hours on the rainy roads and meadows and at the country fairs; and when he was seventeen he was sent to Belfast to take charge of his grandfather's business, the management of the city's waterworks. These had been constructed by his grandfather William on a forty-one-year lease from the Earl of Donegal. Had the then Earl not been insane, a purchase of the property might have been effected, but under the circumstances the tutors of the Earl had not the power to grant anything more than a lease; however, when the works had been built and were in operation the grateful city had given a dinner in honor of the designer, and at that dinner the Earl's heir, full of good feeling and wine, had publicly pledged himself to grant the lease in perpetuity to William Johnston and his heirs, all present drinking to his resolution and applauding it. At his grandfather's death the management of the works had gone to his uncle the rector, who, either through dishonesty or through great financial incapacity, had brought the business into such a tangle that it meant nothing but loss to the shareholders. This tangle young Johnston was called upon to straighten out, and he did so well that before long the waterworks were yielding an income and power equaled only by those of the lord of the soil, and this success in turn increased his difficulties. The city of Belfast applied to the Earl; the Earl, the son of the young heir who had so gallantly promised a grant in perpetuity, felt no responsibility for his ancestor's fine gesture, and it was agreed that the waterworks, as soon as the latest renewal of the lease should be expired, were to be turned over to the city. In vain did young Johnston wait on the Earl and remind him of his father's promises. The Earl urbanely felt that the city should control a business so eminently involved in its welfare, and the young man was forced to consider the complete ruin of his fortunes.

While there were still some years remaining before the expiration of the lease he sent off his brother William to New York to be indentured to a merchant of that city, and he himself set about raising four hundred pounds on the remainder of the lease with which to try his fortune in other parts. He thought first of India, and called upon Lord Macartney with a request for letters to friends in Calcutta, but being discouraged by that nobleman as to the ease with which fortunes might be made in India, he decided to set sail instead for Canada. Lord Macartney, approving of this latter choice, very kindly procured him letters to Lord Dorchester, then Governor General of Canada, and in June, 1790, he set sail for New York.

14

The years in Belfast had been spent more gayly than wisely, perhaps, but they had at least given him an ease of manner and an insight into the follies of his age not to be obtained in any other way. He had read widely, if not altogether profitably, during those years; his Aunt Nancy's schooling yet remained with him. His political faith was simple, being that the first duty of a gentleman was always to the king, and his realization of the state of his country was vague. Had he known more about it, he might have joined the volunteers. However, the habit of his rank, of which he was not a little proud, and of his training kept him from any political affiliations, and 1790 found him in the new continent. Undisturbed by the affairs in France, and yet drawn outward toward the unknown country by something of the same emotion which the next year drew young Chateaubriand to the harbor at Baltimore, he went with a frankly romantic heart, a good head for business, and the most reasonable reason in the world, that of providing the necessities of life for those dependent on him. However romantic or fantastic his actions in the years to come, his life as a whole maintained the standards of the years that bred him; his personal habits, his manners, his dress, his ultimate individual attitude, remained always those of the eighteenth century gentleman.

So he arrived in New York, and, having spent some time with his brother William, then an independent merchant because of certain losses and kindnesses of his former master, he traveled by boat and coach to Montreal, and thence to Quebec to present his letters to Lord Dorchester. At Montreal his plans for the next year were materially altered by chance encounter with his old friend Andrew Tod, the nephew and subsequent heir of the great Isaac Tod, old baron of the Northwest fur trade. Andrew hailed him in a coffee house, his familiar face and snuff-colored coat looming suddenly above a littered table. Andrew was become a partner of the firm of Tod, Magill and Company. He promptly discouraged his friend in his hopes that Dorchester might be able to do anything for him and advised him, instead of trusting to the great, to enter a real and profitable business, namely, the fur trade, laying before him reports of sales, profits, bargains, opportunities, and adventures, and talking so well that before the evening was over Johnston was quite won to his way of thinking. However, he had the packet of letters to Lord Dorchester, which he felt more or less obliged to deliver; he was curious about the town of Quebec, and the season was already advanced for setting out for the Indian country. Accordingly he went to Quebec, presented his letters, suffered the expected disappointment, returned to Montreal, and, hunting up Andrew, made arrangements to go with him the following spring to Michilimackinac, the entrance to the wilderness.

15

Perhaps it was something more than chance, something social in the man's temperament, that led him to so many encounters with old friends and acquaintances. From New York to Montreal they did not fail him, and even at Mackinac he discovered in charge of the fort a one-time guest of his mother's house. This was Lieutenant Edward Charleton, in command of the Fifth Infantry. Although the accident was pleasant, it saddened the Irishman momentarily, bringing so freshly to mind the days of his own better fortunes.

They had come overland from Montreal, taking the Ottawa River route, avoiding the longer journey and the great falls at Niagara, but making many more portages and being almost constantly in the mosquito infested woods. The men who carried the packs on these portages, their hands being occupied, had no way of protecting themselves from the pest, and they went, their faces streaming with blood and sweat, green boughs rebounding from the shoulders of the man before striking their cheeks and foreheads, nevertheless laughing at their own sanguinary countenances and making sport of the younger voyageurs who were making their first trip. Johnston and Tod suffered extremely, their faces being so badly swollen as to be almost deformed, and it was in this condition, with misshapen features and travel-stained garments, that they reached Mackinac. Charleton received them at the fort in a cool, orderly room in a house of whitewashed stone. About them the parade grounds were grassy and almost as velvety as an English lawn; the cedars, masses of horizontally shattered emerald; daisies on the steep hillside. From the ramparts they looked down upon the crescent of the bay, the Indian wigwams, the few scattered houses—whitewashed logs and picket stockades—of the permanent Canadian village. Beyond, the water of the Straits, blue in the sunshine, ruffling and sparkling under a strong wind, and on cloudy days running into green, indigo, and purple. Charleton made them his guests. There was plenty of good liquor, roast game, and even a few fresh vegetables from the garden of the fort, and they stayed there from the date of their arrival, May 16, until Johnston's departure in August, when Andrew outfitted him with all things proper for a wintering, and he started forth, for the first time since his coming to America, entirely among strangers. September brought him to Ile St. Michel.

He went on through the glade and, reconnoitering farther up the western shore, pitched upon a place nearer the growth of old timber which seemed to be good for a permanent camp. When he returned he found the men throwing up a rude shelter of boughs, the canoe unpacked, and a fire going. Florentin had been busy with the nets and had taken four large whitefish, which were now in a kettle swung high above the fire, cooking slowly. Johnston undid the pack of tobacco and gave each man the usual portion for a regale, together with a ration of shrub. The whitefish improved the boiled corn enormously. Their meal was eaten before sundown, and when it was over the men took off their wet moccasins and hung them near the fire, filled their pipes, and settled themselves to rest.

That night a stranger presented himself at their fire, a man dressed in the moccasins and capot of a voyageur, but having a distinguished bearing, more nervous, more withdrawn than the easy grace of the canoe men. They had not supposed there was another white man on the island. He advanced from the shadow of the trees into their firelight and announced himself as the Count Andriani, adding, after a brief pause, with a slight humorous twist of the lips, of Milan. Johnston rose and introduced himself, John Johnston, of Craige, County Antrim, Ireland. They made a place for the stranger in the shelter of the canoe, and sitting there, cross-legged, leaning slightly forward toward the fire, he explained slowly in French his business in the country. He had come with the permission of the government to make certain scientific observations on the nature of the shape of the earth, which he had every reason to believe, he said, was flattened at the poles. He had been at La Pointe two weeks, taking measurements and making astronomical observations. They were, he informed them, six hundred and ninety feet above sea level, and nearly two thousand miles from the sea. He said that he hoped to settle, upon his return to the continent, this violently debated question once and for all. It was his firm belief that the earth at both the poles was covered by the ocean, nay, by a waste of frozen ocean so desolate that it would never be explored. But mathematics o'erleaped the poles, he said, and made him as certain of his facts as if he had gone over the whole territory a step at a time. He spoke slowly and carefully, with almost no trace of an accent save his meticulous care of the language. The Canadians listened respectfully, Johnston with enthusiasm. The white wilderness of the pole grew before their eyes like the approaching winter, and they were easily convinced of the power of mathematics. When he had finished they talked of the fur trade, of the treachery of Indians and the increasing scarcity of beaver. Andriani had a theory that the Northwest Company kept all its voyageurs in debt to itself, a means of assuring a sort of slavery. He even went so far as to say that most of the men were in debt to the extent of ten years' salary. The company did this in part by the ingenious device of shifting the standard of currency at the border of the Indian territory, a livre becoming in value double a Montreal livre. Since the men purchased in the territory and were paid at Montreal, or according to Montreal standards, they were easily confused; what seemed cheap in the territory was dear at Montreal, a year later, and they ran easily into debt. He said also that the village at La Pointe was one of the most profitable stations in the Northwest, giving yearly to the trade no fewer than twenty bundles of furs.

La Liberté, warmed by the rum and the unexpected conversation, began to tell stories of La Pointe, of the ground under the scrub oaks full of the bones of slaughtered Iroquois, of the old Ojibway warrior swimming the channel from St. Michel to La Pointe with his weapons in his teeth in order to strike one blow before all the Iroquois should have fled or been killed, of the Indian jugglers who could roll naked on live coals, who could escape from the most cleverly tied ropes, who could make a distant empty lodge tremble as with the ague, and lastly, lowering his voice and twisting in his fingers the braided morsel of tobacco, he began to tell stories of cannibalism on Ile St. Michel.

"It went on and went on," he said. "The people were frightened but the jugglers wouldn't let them go away. They wouldn't let them stop, non plus. When they put a spell on a person he died, or he was killed, and after he was buried the juggler dug him up, and ate part of him, and part he made to eat the wife or brother or relative of him who was killed, until many people in the village were cannibal. So then, one night a wife whose husband had been enchanted and killed watched at the grave and fought with the juggler when he came to dig. Then, soon after, there were ghosts. There were everywhere ghosts, and suddenly the people ran away. They went over to the mainland and they never came back for many years. They do not like to come now. They will come, yes, in the daytime, but they do not like to stay. That is why there are no wigwams on St. Michel." He paused, staring at the fire, bewitched by his own tale. Then: "In the old days all the wigwams were on St. Michel. It was very safe from the Iroquois. But now, nobody. It only lasted a little while, part of one generation, that was all. Before that nobody of the Ojibways ate human flesh. And now, personne."

It was late. Florentin rose to lay another stick on the fire. He stood a moment, scraping the coals together, and then went back to his place. The voice of La Liberté, although silent, repeated slowly, "And now, personne." Andriani left them. His encampment lay a little to the north along the west shore. He had with him half a dozen men. He would see them in the morning.

La Liberté wrapped himself in his blanket, drawing his capot over his head and shoulders. Florentin laid one more log on the fire and, lying

18

down on the ground upon his blanket, rolled over three times and lay still, a mummy. Johnston, a little apart from the men, folded his cap under his head for a pillow and went to sleep. The moon came up behind the trees, laying a color of ashes across the glow of the coals. The Irishman slept without dreaming, drugged with the cold air and with fatigue, but once he heard through his sleep a light hoof stamp imperatively on the ground near his head. He woke and lay still. The stamp was repeated, followed by a low, full whistle. Then the deer swung about and bounded into the brush, followed by another more distant.

III

In the morning they began to construct two cabins, one for the men and one for the bourgeois. Florentin was to bunk in the kitchen of Johnston's two-room house; the men's cabin had only one room. The site which Johnston had selected was level and they had to carry the felled trees only a short distance. The cabins were built of round logs, unpeeled, the ends hewed flat on two sides, leaving the core of the wood unexposed, and fitted together. The interstices were chinked with moss and mud, and a fireplace and chimney were constructed for each, of small logs and sticks thickly plastered with mud. The floors were the trodden earth. They hung a blanket over the door of the men's cabin, and fitted a door with peg hinges for Johnston's. For fastening, this door had a strong bar fitted to sockets on the inside. After the walls were fairly well up Florentin was detailed to the nets, and they began to lay in a plentiful supply of whitefish and sturgeon. A fire, with a smoking-rack above it of green saplings, was kindled near the beach, and at evening Florentin superintended the process of curing the fresh meat. Andriani's men offered to help with the building, and the Count himself came every evening to sit beside the fire and exchange opinions with the Irishman. They talked of the meaning of the aurora borealis, then wavering in brilliance overhead, of the cause of shooting stars, of whether the Irish had the right to rebel against an English monarch, of the reason for the seven-year tides observed, or supposed to have been observed, in Lakes Michigan and Huron, of the vogue for beaver hats in England, of the horse races in Belfast, of Johnston's uncle, the Bishop Saurin.

The houses once up, the winter's woodpile became the next pressing need; and the fishing went forward steadily. The Indians had learned of the coming of the new trader. On the third day after his arrival three canoes beached themselves softly, and the entire family of Le Ciel Vert came hesitatingly and shyly to the spot where Johnston sat on a newly felled log, writing in his journal. The place was fragrant with scattered chips and crushed herbs. Le Ciel Vert seated himself, his haunches on his heels, and taking a little tobacco and a little kinnikinnik from the pouch at his belt, began to crush and mingle them in the palm of his hand. His people gathered around him. He tamped the powdered leaves into the bowl of a long-stemmed pipe, struck a spark from his flint, and proceeded to surround himself with smoke like the haze of an autumn hillside. Johnston, who had greeted him, brought out a few of his wares, and the wife of Le Ciel Vert, at his order, unrolled a pack of otter and muskrat skins. Johnston, having inspected the skins, laid out a fathom of strouds, that inexpensive but durable and almost waterproof woolen, two pounds of powder, one pound of bullets, and a foot of braided tobacco. The trading proceeded by signs, Florentin being away on the water. Le Ciel Vert accepted this value for his furs and asked for a credit. He wanted two large traps, two little ones, a piece of red cloth and a keg of rum. Johnston refused him the keg, but gave him a drink because he was his first customer. The Indian promised to return the next spring with furs to the full value of his credit. He rose and shook hands solemnly with the new trader, and departed, his people casting lingering glances over their shoulders at the strange proceedings of the Saugaunosh.

La Liberté, who during this interview had been shaping and setting in place a pine log, now paused, ax in hand, and said to Johnston, "If you do not give them rum they will go to the other traders."

"What traders?" asked Johnston, somewhat surprised.

"The others at La Pointe," answered the Frenchman. "Florentin saw them. They are Canadians who speak the Indian language very well. They are independents, like yourself; they belong to no company. They do what they like, and they give plenty of rum."

Johnston said nothing to this; La Liberté shrugged his shoulders and went back to his work.

It was the usual plan for a trader to distribute as many of his goods before snowfall as he could. It saved him the responsibility of carrying them through the winter, and bound the Indians to bring him their furs in the spring. If he waited to trade with them until they had the furs actually in hand, they were just as likely not to come at all. They might travel off to Mackinac or to the Grand Portage in hopes of much liquor and a good time, or they might trade them to the men sent out to the very trapping grounds, to faire la drouine, as it was called. All through the month of October and well into November Indians were coming, bargaining, smoking, asking for rum, and investigating with childlike thoroughness and frankness the affairs, habits, and clothing of the new bourgeois.

After many conversations, many amicable disputes, Andriani loaded his canoe and departed, having embraced his heaven-sent friend upon both cheeks. Johnston detailed Tremblay and Paul Joseph with a small equipment to the Riviere Mauvaise. They were to winter there, and return in the spring with such furs as they might harvest. La Liberté and the other man, Leon, took them down and returned with the canoe. They said that an Indian had given them temporary shelter and that they should have a very good season. In the intervals of trading and fishing the woodcutting went on. The leaves had now all fallen from the trees, leaving only the ever-greens crisp and definite in shape. Beneath the haze of impoverished boughs the earth lay rustling with ashes of roses, primrose, champagne, and russet, colors of flowers, wine, and fruit. The sunsets, beginning early and going forward slowly until late evening, were a cold orange fading into a colder yellow, tinged with green. The color lay low in the sky, as if it were a heavier liquid in another liquid, showing just above the black serrated silhouette of the woods. A chillness breathed upwards from the earth in which the withered asters, the small twiggy bushes, seemed to bristle like fur in the cold. "A spirit passed before my face and the hair of my flesh stood up," said Johnston to himself.

The ice in the bay now began to freeze definitely. A canoe could progress only slowly, breaking the film of glass with each stroke of the paddle and with danger, for the ice tore and cut the birchbark. Then an unexpected thaw loosened it for three days. On the evening of the sixteenth of November La Liberté begged the privilege of smoking a pipe at the fire of his bourgeois. Johnston, who missed the talkative Count, was glad to have him. La Liberté remembered a childhood among the Ottawa wigwams on Lake Huron, below Manitouline, but could speak very little of the language.

"My father took me away when I was very little to bring me up French. I am French now, pas sauvage. Yes, I am raised French." He said: "It is true that the Indians still will eat a little of the flesh of a brave man, but it is his braveness they eat, it is not as in the old days. For myself," he said, "I would rather be a mangeur de lard."* He laughed. A soup of maize and deer meat, boiling for tomorrow's victuals in a pot set on a tripod of three rocks, rose slowly in a yellowish foam, and Florentin, leaning forward, dropped gently across the surface of it a small branch of balsam. The bubbling subsided

---

* Tenderfoot.

slowly and continued at a safe distance below the rim of the vessel. La Liberté said:

"Before I ever came here I heard of Le Pecan Blanc. Last year I saw him. He is a very great warrior and a good trapper. I will be telling my children some day that I saw Le Pecan Blanc." Again he laughed. "I, who am not sauvage, to brag at having seen a sauvage!"

"What is it," said Johnston, "a pecan?"

"A fisher. Like an otter, but smaller and more fierce. A White Fisher."

Upon leaving he saluted Johnston with a lift of the hand. The white teeth of his smile, the little black mustache, the ruddy cheeks and heavy shoulders, disappeared into the night, and Johnston told the boy to bank the fire and go to bed.

Morning of the seventeenth dawned upon a world of frost and mist. A pool of water near the door was frozen, and splintered underfoot, leaving an empty space between the ice and earth. The leaves were hoary, and through the mist the colors of all other things showed whitely. The Irishman went down to the lake and broke a hole in the skim ice for water with which to bathe his face. He noticed then that the ice had already been broken. He returned toward the cabin and saw that the canoe was gone from its place. He went back again to the shore, and cupping his hands about his mouth shouted into the mist, "Leon! Leon! La Liberté!" The shore of La Pointe responded vaguely through the mist, "Li-ber-té!"

Somewhat alarmed, he ran back to the cabin where Florentin was getting breakfast. "Why did the men go out so early?" he asked. The boy looked up at him a moment and mutely shook his head. The men's cabin, when he came to search it, showed plainly enough the loss. The nets were gone, the axes were gone, most of the supply of smoked fish was gone, and the men's private duffle, together with a good share of the pork and corn. He ran wildly back to his own cabin and shouted to Florentin, "They've left us!"

"Yes," said Florentin, bending above the bowl of maize and venison.

Johnston returned to the shore, where he sat down on a rock, and having stared desolately into the mist, sank his head in his hands and gave way to despair. No canoe, no nets, no axes, hardly enough supplies for the winter, no help and no neighbors. Unless the Canadians? As this thought came into his head, Florentin called from the door, "The men at La Pointe they tell them they better go. They don' like to make so much enemies, and they go. Me, I don' mind. You better come eat." Having thus bestowed his best consolation, the boy returned to his meal, and waited for the return of his bourgeois. When after half an hour the latter, with utterly dejected countenance, reentered the cabin, he found Florentin whittling an ax helve. He then remembered that he had ax heads among his bundles, and that the wood-cutting had not progressed far enough. He took the ax, when the boy had finished and wedged it, and went off into the woods feeling like Robinson Crusoe, and, having invoked this hero of his childhood, spat on his hands and fell to. The hands blistered shortly, and after that the blisters broke and the new ax handle was stained with blood. Florentin, who had been carrying wood, now chopped, and Johnston carried, and turn and turn about they added to the woodpile and staved off despair.

The week after, the bay froze finally and the snow in a few days merged the outlines of land and water. Ile St. Michel became one with La Pointe and the mainland. The visits of the Indians ceased for a time. As long as the depth of snow permitted, Johnston and his man chopped and carried home firewood, rolling the logs that were too large to carry, and constructing a massive barricade between their doorway and the bitter weather, but soon a blizzard put a stop to such activities. There was no window in the cabin, but by the light of the fire Johnston got out his books and went carefully over his accounts, trying to calculate his profits for the spring. Every man employed by the Northwest Company was obliged to keep a journal which was to be presented at the winter's end to the partners at Grand Portage. Johnston also kept a journal, but it was for no one's pleasure save his own, and he filled it with reveries, moral observations, and verses of his own composition.

He had ample leisure now to remember Ireland, and between the entries in his account book and the neat pages of his journal he envisioned the parlor at Craige, his sisters cutting patterns for bobbin lace, his mother reading aloud from Dryden or Shakespeare, or himself, had he been there, riding to the county fair through the mild drizzle of an Irish winter. The happiest sight of all, to his mind, was the post rumbling into Coleraine at the hour when the windows were lighted. He would have given half the continent of America for a sack of letters.

To Le Tems Couvert credit for sixteen plus

To Le Genou credit for four plus

To Le Gros Pied credit for six plus Note, Le Gros Pied is the father of the chief.

A blob of snow fell from the chimney and hissed in the fire.

The plus was the value of one good beaver skin, the monetary unit of the Northwest Fur Company. All other values were reckoned from it, thus: a good bearskin was worth two plus, a deerskin one-half plus, ten muskrats were worth one plus, a carrot of tobacco (two or three pounds) was worth two plus, a brasse (fathom) of cloth, two plus, a pair of scarlet legging, two plus, a keg of unwatered rum, forty plus.

Malhiot twelve years later at this same station gave an Indian for the meat of a bear credit for four plus. Before they parted at Mackinac, Andrew Tod had instructed Johnston in the values of the trade, giving him a written memorandum to which Johnston now referred by the unsteady firelight.

His mind deserted Coleraine for the winter before at Montreal. Montreal was O'Sullivan's Coffee House; was the Beaver Club, the social organization of the Northwest Company at which he had occasionally been a guest, not being then eligible as a member, since he had not yet spent a winter in the Indian country; was the house of Sir John and Lady Johnson, where he had known such lavish and repeated hospitality. A gentleman with a long Scotch countenance and a shrewd bright eye appeared sometimes at the coffee house, was to be passed on the street or met with at the door of the Assembly, a gentleman whose upper lip was long and clean-shaven, whose hair was clipped close to his long narrow head, whose broadcloth, whose linen, were faultless, whose whole bearing bespoke a canny elegance imposed upon a certain hardiness of flesh and spirit—Simon McTavish of the Northwest Company. And there was also Alexander Henry, with his long nose and high forehead, the hair growing down in a peak on the forehead, with the arrogant carriage of the head and the mettlesome profile, to be found most often at the carousals of the Beaver Club, and already grown a little heavy and reminiscent. This was the man who lay hidden under the pile of bark sugar buckets in the attic of M. Langlade at Old Mackinac while the bloodiest of massacres went on below, lay in hiding because he had waited in vain to hear the trumpet blow to a rally. This same man with the Scotch accent still thick about his tongue had also been adopted blood brother by an Ojibway chief. And there was also the sleek and easy countenance—easy when not stubborn—of the son of Sir William Johnson, Sir John Johnson, well liked in Canada and cordially hated in the valley of his birth, the Mohawk; and the vivacious features of his wife, the charming New York woman. He remembered the balls given for Lady Johnson and her daughter. He remembered the evenings at Varennes, across the river from Montreal, where he had taken lodgings in order to save expense, and amiable M. Vienne, his landlord, who had so patiently instructed him in French. Then he would sigh, and turn to Florentin with any question that offered, just for the sake of hearing him speak, and Florentin, sometimes puzzled at the interruption, would lift his straight thick eyebrows a little and answer slowly.

The cold deepened. The continual inexorable approach of it, in its silence, its weightlessness and invisibility, were strangely ominous to one unused to it. It increased after it seemed to have reached its maximum, and then again it increased. And the snow fell dry and powdery. When Johnston opened the cabin door at night to fetch in another log, the glow from the house penetrated the darkness a little way and showed it full of whirling whiteness; these flakes defined the space in which they moved so that the house was not surrounded by a flat curtain of darkness but by a hollowed and receding gulf of black, filled with a restless white air, and breathing cold. He shut the door against it as against a living presence and steadied the new log across the embers of the old, bracing it with the forelog until the flames curled in a broad fluid sheet across the shaggy surface. Florentin was making a net, the only indication in the world, it seemed, that there would ever be a spring. He held a small tapering stick in his hands, the mesh marker, and tied his loops around it one after the other as patiently as a woman knitting. His hands were brown, and clever in spite of their great size. The ball of net twine on the floor beside him twitched now and again, and rolled over a little, twitched and lay still, as if an invisible kitten were playing with it. On the black throat of the chimney little clusters of sparks appeared, burning sharply for a moment, then disappearing, golden constellations. When they appeared so in autumn it meant that the wild geese were flying overhead, but tonight there were no geese. The woods had seemed deserted.

They were seated like this one evening, Florentin with his net, Johnston with his recollections of the vice-regal ball and the governor's lady, when the door opened slowly, although no one had knocked, and an Indian entered the room. The storm flew in after him. He shut the door, and lifting his blanket from his head and shoulders, shook the dry snow upon the ground. His hair was white, his face wrinkled, and the upper part of his body, which was bare, was wrinkled at the armpits and across the abdomen. He stooped a little. He wore moccasins and leggins of dark blue cloth, and at his belt he carried his knife, his hatchet, and two small bags. He seemed very tired. He smiled a little at the two men, lifting his hand in sign of greeting. Johnston recognized him as an Indian to whom he had given a small credit earlier in the fall. The Indian said, "My father, pity me. I am very hungry and I ask you for food." Florentin translated. The Indian went on:

"In the early fall I went up the Mauvaise with my family and gathered plenty of wild rice. We came back to Chegoimegon Bay and I put my rice in a cache. Then I left my family and went with my traps to the beaver

25

grounds above the Mauvaise. I took seven good beavers and some muskrats. I am an old man. I cannot hunt now as I used to. When the cold weather came I returned to Chegoimegon. I said, 'I will take these beavers to the Yellow Haired to pay for the credit which he gave me, and he will give me pork and blankets for the winter. I shall have the wild rice, also. My family is small and we shall not need so much to eat.' The water was freezing. I came with my family along the shore by La Pointe and as I passed the house of the Canadians they called to me. My father, I remembered that you gave me a credit. I did not answer them. Then they ran into the water and seized the prow of my canoe. I am an old man, I could not fight with them. They took from my canoe my beavers and my pack of small skins, and they made me come ashore with them. They took me to their house and gave me whiskey to drink. I do not know what happened. They gave me more whiskey. By and by I looked at the water and I saw that the ice was thick and that I could not go away in my canoe. I said to them, 'Give me my furs and I will go on foot and pay my credit to the Yellow Haired.' They said, 'Fool, you have traded all your furs.' Then I said, 'Give me the goods for which I traded them.' They said, 'You drank the goods.' Then they put me out of doors, with my women. It was very cold. My wife made a wigwam for us, and she had hidden a little fish and dried corn for us. We lived so for two, three weeks. Now for five days we have eaten nothing. The snow is very deep. We set snares for rabbits but they are all hidden, they will not come to the snares. If I had snowshoes I would go to my cache of wild rice, but I am old, I cannot walk in the deep snow without snowshoes. My father, give us something to eat."

He knelt then, and unfastening from his belt one of the small pouches, drew from it a bundle wrapped in printed calico. The pouch seemed to be made of a dark, strong fiber, closely woven. It was pliable, yet stiff. From the bundle the dark trembling fingers drew a roll of blue and white beads, which, unrolled, became a wampum belt of blue with figures in white. Beside it he laid a silver gorges. Blue sky, white clouds. He said:

"These were given to me, to Ma-mongazid, twenty-seven years ago. Sir William Johnson, Warraghlyagey, the white chief of the Mohawks, gave them to me. I have kept them without stain twenty-seven years. When I die, my son, Waub-ojeeg, will keep them without stain. There will never be any stain on them. I will pay you back the credit. If I die, my son will pay it back. My father, we are starving. Give us food."

Johnston was strongly moved by this appeal, but he had been told many tales of begging Indians. He preached a little homily about paying one's debts and keeping away from strong drink. He reminded himself somewhat of his uncle the Bishop, talking to an Irish cottager. The image disturbed him, and he hastened to add that the friend of Sir William Johnson was his honored guest. Florentin brought food and a bearskin rug for the old man. Before the fire Ma-mongazid recovered a little of the manner of his youth, and Johnston sorted out a bundle of provisions for him.

"Look," he said, "I am giving you what I can. I too have very little food for the winter, but while I have food, you shall share it."

He told the story of the desertion of his men. The Indian did not seem surprised. He listened gravely, nodding now and then. Johnston brought tobacco, and they smoked to the new friendship. He also offered a drink of rum, but the Indian motioned it away. Florentin, meanwhile, was full of good ideas. He suggested that Ma-mongazid ask his women to prepare a deerskin for a window, and that Ma-mongazid himself make two pairs of snowshoes. The following day Ma-mongazid brought his two wives and his daughter-in-law to the cabin and work on the snowshoes was begun while the women selected a deerskin for the window. The snow had ceased to fall, and the air, filled with sunshine, was pure and rare. Johnston, stepping out of doors, experienced once more the joy of living. Ma-mongazid, following him, insisted on smearing his cheeks below the eyes with grease and charcoal. He said, "It will keep the snow blindness from you." He went with Johnston into the woods and showed him how to set a rabbit snare.

The snowshoe frames were of ash wood, steamed and bent into the shape of two half moons placed together. The tips curved up a little. The wife of Ma-mongazid laced them with narrow strips of deerskin and wove a socket for the toe of each foot. The heel was not fastened down, but lifted with each step, the tail of the shoe dragging on the snow. Three pairs were made, one each for Johnston and Florentin, and one for Ma-mongazid in part payment for his labor. He received also a deer-skin and a sack of corn.

A window, two feet long and one foot high, was cut in the cabin wall near the door, and the deerskin stretched across it. The wife of Ma-mongazid had taken the pelt, stiff, hairy, unclean with withered flesh, and brought it back supple, smooth, translucent, and almost as thin as parchment. It let into the room a rectangle of mellow light by which it was possible to work even when the fire was low. For this Johnston gave the woman a brasse, that is to say, a fathom, of blue strouds, of which she made a shirt for her husband.

The weather for some time continued clear and bright and the dryness of the air was deceiving. One morning while he was chopping wood

Johnston was astonished to see the steel ax head break in two and fall from the helve; and the struck wood rang musically, as if it had been metal. Ma-mongazid came to tell them that he was going to La Riviere Mauvaise with his family. He shook hands with the bourgeois and his man, and told them that in case they were in want, to let him know. Johnston did not even smile at this offer, with such dignity and simplicity was it made.

IV

Waub-Ojeeg and his people had ascended the Wisakoda and, leaving it, had moved from lake to small lake through the beaver country toward the southwest, it being the intention of the White Fisher to make the circuit of his hunting grounds and return to the great lake by way of the Montreal River. In December they were encamped on the shore of a small lake high in the Kaug Mountains, a lake blue and changeable in summer, but now white and distinguishable only as a long glade between the crowded evergreens. Here a visitor came to them in the person of an Ojibway hunter seeking justice. He, Little Thunder, had found the traps of Cloud Approaching set within his own trapping territory. Being very angry at this intrusion, he had taken from the traps six muskrats and a beaver and left a bark message to the intruder to remove his traps and be gone. Cloud Approaching not only had not gone, he had come to the shelter of Little Thunder and reproached him with the theft of one beaver and six muskrats. Therefore Little Thunder had broken camp and come to his chief for advice. He laid this story before Waub-ojeeg with many justifications for his actions, and explanations of why he had not immediately attacked Cloud Approaching. Cloud Approaching was a relative of his wife's mother. He did not wish to murder his wife's mother's relative, and moreover Waub-ojeeg had forbidden his people to fight over traps. He drew a map on the ground, indicating the disputed territory. Wayishkee, seated near him, corroborated his statements. Wayishkee knew the territory of Cloud Approaching, and said that he was truly the transgressor. This dispensing of justice was as much a part of Waub-ojeeg's duty as leading his people to war, for he was both war and civil chief, an instance rare in Ojibway history. He deliberated the case with a pipeful of tobacco, and finally told Little Thunder that he had best return the pelts. The meat, which he had partly consumed, he might keep. He asked him to return the pelts because Cloud Approaching was a relative and it was not wise to quarrel within one's own family. Moreover the traps and the labor were Cloud Approaching's, and Little Thunder had been late in his hunting. He would

28

give a message to Little Thunder to present to Cloud Approaching, warning him to stay in his own territory, and he would send one small mokkuk of sugar to the wife of Little Thunder as a gift from Waub-ojeeg. He, their chief, would make this small present to the family of Little Thunder to compensate him for the wrong done him by Cloud Approaching, and to keep peace in his tribe. They smoked another pipe on the decision, and Wayishkee made ready the message for Cloud Approaching, which consisted principally of a piece of birchbark incised with the figure of a fisher touched with white—but not on the mouth, which would have signified starvation—surrounded by figures which declared the totem of the fisher, the deer, and the names and totems of the quarrelers arranged in such a way as to make plain the White Fisher's intention toward the other two. The plaintiff was satisfied with this justice, the more so since in winter sugar was scarce in his wigwam. He told Waub-ojeeg that he had stayed long at Chegoimegon to fish and had smoked a great quantity of sturgeon and whitefish. He had not left until late in October, and before his departure a new trader had arrived at Ile St. Michel. The trader had yellow hair, like corn tassels, he said, and laughed easily. He had taken a great many things on credit from the trader and promised him all his pack; therefore he felt it important to take as many beavers as he could that winter. Truly, the trader had let him have a very large credit. Waub-ojeeg replied that before his departure there had been two traders at La Pointe, and that they were more than enough. He preferred to have his traders remain at the Sault or at Mackinac, but what could you do? The Northwest now sent traders to the very trapping ground to take the furs before they had been scraped or dried.

The winter went on. Waub-ojeeg had taken enough furs for three packs. He talked a little of stopping, and returning to Chegoimegon before spring. Then, suddenly, he became very sick. He coughed a great deal, and said that he was burning up, but in the early morning he woke his wife and asked her to bring him more covers. She laid a bearskin over him, but he still complained of being cold. Toward noon the next day he began to burn again. She was frightened and sent Wayishkee for a Jossakeed. The Woman of the Glade made a mixture of parched corn and maple sugar and put it in a bag for her brother, together with a small package of neebish, black tea. She brought out his snowshoes, and gave him four extra pairs of moccasins, and he started at once, traveling down the unbroken white surface of the lake, lost to sight finally behind a projecting point of evergreens. Waub-ojeeg was restless. He felt better now, and talked of going to his traps. He called for his moccasins and mittens and snowshoes, and when his daughter had brought them, was tired again, and laid them beside him on his bed. He ate very little for supper. After the dishes had been cleared away, and while his wife was putting the little children to bed, wrapping them in furs and blankets in the far end of the lodge, and drawing a fold of blanket over each little face, he called to Ozhah-gusco-day-wayquay to bring him his drum, and began to sing the lament of the Battle of the St. Croix. He sang the first words of it to the slow beating of the drum, and then, laying down his stick, said, "It is here that it hurts me." He put his hand on his breast, above the old scar. He said, "It is a Sioux devil, after all these years. It hurts very much." Then he picked up the stick with its head of deerskin padding and went on with the song. It seemed to tire him to sing, and his wife begged him to stop. He shook his head and went on, and soon he was weeping. The tears ran down his cheeks, and now and again he laid his hand on his breast, and said, "It is here that it hurts. It hurts in my heart and in my breast."

When he had finished the lament, he sang his war song, and then a song for a dance, and then, laying aside the drum, he began to tell again the story of the Battle of the St. Croix. The girl had heard it many times before, but never before had her father wept as he told it. He tired himself, but he would not stop. Again the warriors gathered at Chegoimegon, three hundred Ojibways in full regalia of paint and feathers. The novices, who had never been to battle before, were painted black upon their breasts and faces. They left Chegoimegon in small canoes, easy to carry and easy to turn quickly, and ascended the Mauvaise. It was summer. They made the portages with great caution, going so quietly and slowly that it was seven days before they reached the St. Croix portage, seven days of drinking from the going-away side of their bowls, seven nights of sleeping with their faces turned toward the country to which they wished to return when the battle was over. They encamped at last on the upper end of the portage, only to discover to their great surprise a large war party of Sioux and Foxes encamped on the lower end. The two war parties discovered each other almost simultaneously. The novices leapt into the water and began to wash the black from their faces. Waub-ojeeg extended his arms and made his exhortation to his warriors. The air was full of war cries. In the Sioux camp, within plain view of the Ojibways, similar preparations were going forward. Then the battle began. The Sioux, full of vainglory and seeing themselves twice the number of their enemies, divided in two, one half to fight, the other half to sit on the rocks above the portage and cheer. The battle ground was a "mere neck of rugged rock," from which there was but one way of escape, save the desperate one of the rapids. This way of escape was occupied by the Ojibways. The fight went forward with fury. When the first contingent of Sioux had been defeated, the second, unfatigued, swept down upon the tired Ojibways, and would have annihilated them had not a party of sixty men from a northern village arrived at the critical instant. These sixty had received the wampum of Waub-ojeeg and had started for Chegoimegon, arriving there too late to join the main body, and had come on by themselves. To the confused Sioux and Foxes the air was suddenly full of multiplied Ojibways, fresh as the morning and merciless as winter. Many of them fled, leaping into the rapids, and many of them were drowned. When the last living Sioux had disappeared, Waub-ojeeg turned to count his losses. His brother was dead. He himself was wounded in three places, on the breast, on the left shoulder, and on the thigh, and all around him lay his friends, wounded or dead. He finished his story. He forgot to say that the Sioux had never once returned in twenty years to the rice lakes of the St. Croix. He drew his blanket over his head and wept as his people had never seen him weep.

His wife brought him furs and laid them beside him, covered the fire with ashes, and motioned to the others to go to sleep. The Woman of the Glade drew her blanket over her head, and saw in the darkness the rapid waters of the St. Croix running bloody between the jagged rocks.

Wayishkee returned on the evening of the second day with a Jossakeed who was also a Mide of the third degree, and a small lodge for the sick man was speedily constructed at a little distance from the others. They swept away the snow, covered the earth with balsam boughs, and the boughs with skins. They brought the sick man and laid him on the floor. His wife and Ozhahguscoday-wayquay were there because he had asked for them, and Wayishkee in order to assist the Jossakeed. The Jossakeed beat his drum and threw tobacco on the fire. After long singing he knelt beside the sick man with a narrow tube in his fingers, the leg bone of a heron, hollow and polished. He pressed one end of this upon the old bullet wound and, leaning forward, sucked vigorously. After a while he rose, and spitting into his hand a small shell, said, "It was the Sioux manido. Here it is. I have sucked it forth." He then showed it to every one and dropped it into the fire. Then he covered his patient and gave instructions for his care. Wayishkee took the Jossakeed to the lodge and entertained him, and the Woman of the Glade brought her father a bowl of soup. He smiled at her. He said that he felt better but very tired. For nearly two weeks he remained in the small lodge, sleeping a great part of the time, and being fed soup and boiled rice, and finally, on a day when the sun was shining and the air mild, he came from the lodge into the open and declared himself cured. He was

31

not, however, very strong. He did not wish to continue his trapping and hunting, and soon after this illness they broke camp and returned, all of them, to La Pointe, coming down the long portage of the Montreal with their possessions on dog trains or in bundles carried on their shoulders with the tumpline about the forehead. They had taken furs enough for that season, and at La Pointe Wayishkee would be able to spear fish.

V

With Johnston, on Ile St. Michel, the visits of Indians had become few and far between. Occasionally they brought him fish, and more rarely were willing to trade him the flesh of a bear or a moose. In January his supply of goods was much depleted and he had accumulated peltries to the amount of eight packs. He counted on the credits given in the autumn to bring the final total up to seventeen packs, and matters on that score looked well enough, but the food situation began to be serious. He had depended upon the continued visits of the Indians, but these presently ceased altogether and he found that he had on hand only very short rations of corn and no pork whatever. He knew that there were a few families at the Red Cliff Point as well as at the village on the Mauvaise, and remembering that Tremblay and Leon might still be at the Mauvaise, possibly with the two other deserters, he decided not to venture in that direction, but sent off Florentin the last week in February to the Red Cliff village, with instructions to bring back whatever he could find to eat. He waited for the boy ten days. At that time there were in his larder corn enough for three days, tea enough for three months, and plenty of rum, but one cannot sustain health on a diet of tea and rum. Accordingly, on the morning of the eleventh day he built a smudge fire in the fireplace to give the house a look of habitation, barricaded the door, and set off on snowshoes for the mainland.

Although he had never been to the Red Cliff village, he knew the general direction in which it lay and that the distance from his cabin should not exceed fifteen miles. He set out cheerfully, expecting to be at the village before noon. Once out of the lee of the island, he felt the cold more sharply, and an intermittent wind which lifted the dry snow in whirlwinds confused him as to his direction. He made as straightly as he could for the wooded shore, but was long in reaching it, and knew that his uncertain course had more than doubled the distance. In the shelter of the trees he went forward more steadily, and at noon, being still far from any habitation, made camp and ate a little dry corn. He tried to make a fire, but the wind carried the spark away from his flint. After a half hour's rest he got up and went on. His fatigue was great, and he began to experience a profound personal humility in the face of the snow and wind and the silences which followed the wind. He heard, now and again, from the depths of the forest a muffled sharp report, resembling a pistol shot, which he knew to be a tree cracking in the intense cold. There were no human noises. In the morning his feet had stung painfully. Now they no longer pained him, and once he seemed to wake from a sleep to find himself still traveling between the monotonous dark woods and the more monotonous lake. Late in the afternoon he saw, a short distance ahead of him and about a half a mile out on the ice, something that might have been a log or the prostrate body of a man with a very large pack on his shoulders. It was lost to view and reappeared as the dunelike drifts of snow shifted their attitudes with his approach, but at last he made it out to be a man lying flat on the ice, his head and shoulders hidden under one of those small lodges of cedar boughs which the Indians, when they were spearing fish, erected to darken the water as a man hoods a camera; and even as Johnston looked, the shaft of a fishing spear rose through the opening designed for the purpose, and abruptly fell.

He gave a halloo, and at once pitched forward into the snow. He felt, rather than heard, the fisherman approach; he knew, as drowsiness overcame him, that he was being lifted to some one's shoulders, and believed that his rescuer was young and an Indian. After a time he was slid to his feet, and a word was said to him in Ojibway which seemed to mean "Enter." He opened his eyes and saw a long wigwam of birchbark, silvery gray in the purity of the snow. The boy who had brought him there was holding aside a tawny deerskin which hung at the entrance. Beyond this curtain he saw an interior which trembled slightly in a ruddy glow. Some one from within said "Bindigay, Bindigay." The young Indian pushed him gently forward and he entered the lodge of Waub-ojeeg.

The warmth of the place made Johnston a little dizzy, and from this dizziness presently emerged a low cry and the pressure of hands on his shoulders; he looked up from the bench where they had seated him and saw floating before him the delighted face of the old Mamongazid. He dropped his eyes to the bent head and busy hands of Wayishkee, who was rubbing his feet with snow, and beyond Wayishkee he saw the curious, wondering face of a very young girl. Gradually the lodge steadied itself, the face of the girl disappeared, his feet began to come to life again, and another figure joined the figure of Ma-mongazid in front of him, that of a man perhaps forty-four years old, tall, astonishingly tall, slender, erect, and well made.

33

The upper part of his body was bare save for a red blanket thrown loosely about the shoulders; he wore a red sash about his middle, and long leggins of white buckskin elaborately fringed. His moccasins were worked with colored quills. Ma-mongazid began to speak, and Johnston realized that he was meeting Le Pecan Blanc of La Liberté's admiration.

Florentin, he made out, had never appeared. He managed to explain that he had sent Florentin to them eleven days ago, and when they understood this, Waubojeeg dispatched a man to look for him. The man who went was the younger brother of the chief, a handsome man, but not as handsome as his brother. It took him barely five minutes to make his preparations and be gone. By luck, he met Florentin that night, returning to the cabin at St. Michel, and the two of them spent the night there, arriving the next morning at the Red Cliff. The Canadian had not gone to the Red Cliff at all but, frankly disobedient, had hoped to find his old comrades at the Mauvaise. He had thought it more likely that the Canadians would have food than that the Indians would, and he had not intended to desert, but the Canadians were not there. An Indian told him that the Frenchmen had left in the fall. Two men came to get them, he said, and they all went off together. This Indian had been kind to him, had given him food and shelter and advised him to return to the Red Cliff village. He had stayed at the Mauvaise longer than was necessary because he was very fatigued and they were very kind to him. They had given him enough corn to make the journey home.

Waub-ojeeg received Florentin as he had received Johnston. He gave him a place on the bed next to Johnston at the men's side of the lodge. Wayishkee insisted on keeping the Irishman away from the fire for three weeks. At the end of that time the frozen flesh began to slough away from his feet, and the new skin appeared, healthy and well. The fourth week he was quite restored, and ready to return to the cabin had the weather permitted, but the spring thaws had now set in and the ice was not safe for crossing. Neither was it possible yet to use the canoes. So it happened that Johnston stayed with Waub-ojeeg and his people until May.

With the first thaw, the second week in March, the sap started running in the maple trees, and the women of the lodge were gone all day, working in the sugar bush. They returned at evening, carrying in their clothes and about their persons the scent of wood smoke and syrup. Johnston followed them to the bush one day, walking painfully, and sat upon a bearskin spread on the ground at the foot of one of the trees. The snow was yet everywhere, but softened. The bitterness of winter had melted from the air, and as he sat there, leaning against the trunk of the tree, he heard far and near about him the light, regular ping, ping of the sap drop-ping into the birchbark buckets. The thin liquid was collected into vats made of deerskins, and from these dipped into the boiling-kettles. Some of these kettles were copper, such as he had brought among his goods, but some were made of bark, and he was astonished that they should hang above a fire hot enough to boil the syrup and not burn. When the sugar began to form, the thick syrup was poured into other bark containers, set in the snow, and stirred until it assumed the consistency of brown sugar. He watched the women coming and going at a distance, their arms bare, their long black braids bound up at the back of the head in clubs. There were no birds except the winter-staying chickadees, but the voices, the crackling of the fire, and the continual musical dropping of the sap gave to the woods a stir and a feeling of life which had long been absent, and were as beautiful to him as the actual songs of birds.

They ate a great deal of fresh sugar in those days. Ma-mongazid told the trader that once when he was quite little and there had not been enough corn in the wigwam he had lived for nearly three months on nothing but maple sugar. "I became very fat, too," he said, "and shone like a puppy." It seemed to take the place for these people of the chicory and mustard greens of Ireland, of the mustard and molasses of the New England settlements.

The children of the lodge soon became quite free with the visitor. They leaned against him, fingered his clothing, and were never tired of wrap-ping a lock of strange yellow hair about one of their small bronzy fingers. The warmth and pressure of their bodies pleased him. He liked to watch the coming and going of the women about their work; the easy domestic affection and confusion of the lodge surrounded him and warmed him. The figures of the lacemakers at Coleraine and the woman seated near the window reading from a tall, red book became delicately united with these figures around the fire. Wayishkee had cut a quantity of bark from the cedars and given it to his mother for mats. The inner bark, now full of sap, was pliable and strong. The woman tore it into strips half an inch wide and six feet long, biting it first to start it, and then ripping it the length of the fiber. The girl laid the strips before her on the ground, and began to weave them into a mat, an appukwa. There were other such mats on his bed, made in other springs. They were brown and glossy, and very light and strong.

The girl, he noticed, resembled her father very much save that her youth and growing womanliness softened the severer features of the warrior. There were, however the same hawk nose, the same strong brows and nar-row lips, the same carriage of the body. She was tall, also taller than her mother, almost as tall as Wayishkee, and serious and quiet. With her mother she waited on the men, moving behind them softly; she had almost full charge of the littlest children. Almost never did she speak to the Irishman, although she sometimes came and stood behind the little boy as he leaned against the trader's knee, waiting a little, and smiling over the child's head before she led him away.

Wayishkee was teaching him Ojibway. He laughingly corrected the Ottawa accent which Johnston had acquired from Florentin, and drilled him patiently in the smallest phrases, making him repeat them over and over, insisting on curious aspirations and muted vowels. It was neither a *d* nor a *t* he would say, but both, neither a *k* nor a *g,* but something in between. "You do not want to speak like an Ottawa," he would say when Florentin was beyond earshot. "An Ottawa is not of importance." One day Johnston asked him the meaning of his sister's name. The Indian spread out his hands. He said, "When you are going through thick woods you sometimes come to a place where there are no trees. Do you know? A green place, nothing but grass, and with trees all around." "Yes," said Johnston, "a glade." "Well, then, that is it. The Woman of that place in the woods."

As Johnston lay that night on the bed of boughs and skins the memory of his first afternoon at St. Michel returned to him. He saw again the sunlight on the bracken in the long glade between the birches, the ferns unruffled, yellow leaves dropping quietly through the still air, and heard far off the wind behind the rampart of the forest. The meaning of the name came to him with a symbolical force, and he saw the daughter of Waub-ojeeg, for a moment, as the glade itself. Perhaps he had already begun to fall in love. He knew that he wanted that tranquillity and seclusion, wanted it for his own, to hold in his arms, to fall asleep in.

With May, spring began. He walked in woods that were bare and pure as if the snow and ice had minutely scoured each twig and tree trunk. The leaves of last autumn lay underfoot, beaten together and bleached to the color of the rush mats made by the Woman of the Glade. It was a tissue like wasp nest, breaking crisply. The sunlight was brilliant upon it, and above it the poplar trunks assumed a pale velvety green like the wings of the luna moth, the willow withes a new red bark, which from a distance was a haze like wine. The snow had not disappeared, it had merely given way on the higher ground and the less shaded places. It lay in drifts two and three feet deep under the cedars, and a foot away from it, in the hot sunlight, began the uncurling of the silky yarrow, the furred heads of brake. In the maple bush where the sugar had been made, dogtooth violets were appearing, together with the watery, thick-stemmed, fragile-

36

headed spring beauties. Wayishkee brought from a distance a handful of woody-stemmed arbutus with a fragrance that made the heart stand still for an instant, so eerie was it, so sweet and chill. Then overhead the Indian plum—pembina—and wild cherry broke into bloom. Pussy willows and poplars were covered with polleny catkins. All the small beasts were changing their fur, and there was no talk of hunting. The deer came close to the village; he often saw the two-petaled tracks in the sand. The clearings were full of white rabbits with a dusting of brown across their backs which seemed like the pollen of spring.

The season was incredibly rapid. Nothing in Ireland could have prepared him for so sudden a transformation. Overnight a tree broke into bloom, into leaf; the young green seemed to whirl upward from the earth, and meanwhile the nights were so cold that an aerial ice descended in imponderable cataracts over flowering shrub and sleeping wigwam. The very water of the lake seemed more fluid and more swift. Through this fragile turmoil, day after day, quiet and deft, moved the figure of the Woman of the Glade. Johnston felt then the full exhilaration of his adventure. He had no wish to return to Ireland or even, for that matter, to Montreal; he had fully made up his mind to ask the war chief of the Ojibways for the hand of his daughter. It was 1792. The ferment which in Europe was to produce the *Lyrical Ballads* and the romance of *Atala* was working in the uncharted portion of America in the spring. He walked among the poplars and a hunting song of Wayishkee's came into his head—"By the power of flowering plants I lay him low." He knew that "he" was the quarry, and the "laying low" all other than that which was working upon himself; nevertheless he repeated it to himself many times, transforming it to his own uses.

As soon as the water was clear enough for a canoe he sent Florentin in a borrowed craft to the cabin to receive such furs as might be turned in, and to prepare things for their departure. Waub-ojeeg offered to find him four Indian voyageurs, and arrangements were made with an Indian of the village for the construction of a transport canoe. Word had been sent out that the Yellow Haired was at the Red Cliff, and many of the hunters came to him there with their winter's taking. From the Mauvaise the furs for the credits placed by Leon and Tremblay began to come in, and he found that he was going to lose very little by the delinquency of his men. He watched the construction of his canoe where the stakes were driven on the shore and the bark covering, sewed together with wattap, a thread made from cedar roots, hung loosely between them. The ribs were fitted into it, and shaped by hot stones laid upon the wet wood

37

until it dried. The bark mantle was drawn up about the skeleton thereafter, and bound firmly to the rim, and all the seams were carefully pitched with melted balsam gum. He paid for this craft from his stores, giving the canoe-maker a letter of credit, birchbark, to Florentin. He was very happy. The morning of his departure he begged to see Waub-ojeeg in private and asked him with suitable formality for the Woman of the Glade in marriage. The Indian pondered this request for a long time without taking his lips from his pipe, and said at last, after a deliberate exhalation of pale smoke:

"Englishman, your color is deceitful. I have watched your people now for many years. You come among us and marry our daughters, and when you are tired of them you say you are not married, and go away. I cannot let you marry my daughter and desert her. But I have watched you and your conduct has been right. I think you are better than the others. I say to you now, go back to Montreal, to your own people, and look among them for a wife. If you do not find a woman who pleases you, and if when the summer is gone you still wish my daughter, return to this place, and I will give her to you. If you take her you must keep her forever, as you would a woman of your own race. I have said." He rose, opposing his six foot six to Johnston's five foot ten.

In vain did the Irishman protest. The interview was over and Waub-ojeeg was laying aside his pipe. He escorted his guest to the shore with every courtesy, saw that he was well supplied with food for the voyage, and bade him farewell. He did not linger to see the canoe afloat.

VI

The last of May found Johnston at Ontonagon. He had stopped at St. Michel for Florentin, and had found there packs bringing his total up to nineteen, all good furs, each pack weighing a full ninety pounds. This gave him, with his men, personal baggage, and provisions, a moderate load of two tons. The transport canoes of that time were built to carry four, an apparent miracle for so frail a vessel. His canoemen were followers of Waub-ojeeg, more skillful with the paddle than the Canadians. They came into the mouth of the Ontonagon, a clear stream with red clay banks, at evening, and were somewhat surprised to find there a large camp of Canadians belonging to a M. Jean Baptiste Perreault, who had that day come down the Ontonagon from the interior, where he had wintered. He had been only forty leagues inland, but the way was so obstructed that it had taken him twenty days, the previous fall, to reach the station. He had come out in much less time, ingenious soul, for having made round canoes covered with mooseskin, in which he loaded his packs, and which had come down the rapids with no injury, rebounding from rock to rock like so many stuffed leather balls. These curious bowl-like craft were lying bottom up around the fire, for, as he explained, they had to be thoroughly dried every few days or the skins became water-logged and the canoes impracticable. He reported having heard, before he left the interior, a terrific explosion, like thunder but more loud, and seeming to come from within the earth, which reverberated among the mountains in a terrifying fashion. For some days before the occurrence, he said, the weather had been uncommonly still and sultry, and he believed the explosion to have been an earthquake.

The encounter was pleasant for Johnston, and he was sorry the next morning to leave the Frenchman, who had still before embarking to repair the birch canoes left en cache at the mouth of the river.

With June the mosquitoes began and the nights were spent in misery. The Indians seemed fairly immune to them, Florentin was resigned to them, but Johnston suffered. As in the spring when he was approaching Mackinac, his face and hands became swollen, and he was slightly feverish. During the day, being far out on the water, they escaped the pest, and at night they did the best they could with a smudge.

Beyond the humming maze of insects the spring progressed, constantly swift. Flowers bloomed and fell, a darker green infused the leaves, and by the time they reached Mackinac, late in June, the meadows were rich with daisies, wild roses were in bloom everywhere, and the tremor and fragility of spring had sunk into the security and strength of summer. The first week in July saw the last of the mosquitoes, which breed but once a year in that brief season.

Mackinac, with its rocks and cedars, Mackinac was filled with voyageurs, Indians, and traders, the entire shore of the bay beneath the fort being occupied by their canoes and wigwams, the latter in rows three deep. French, also, from the neighboring settlements, the Sault, St. Ignace, Old Mackinac, had come to visit the priest; and marriages and baptisms, all the ceremonies demanded of life through the winter but postponed till the spring, were celebrated with festivity. John Johnston, Lieutenant Edward Charleton of the Fifth Infantry, and Captain William Doyle stood leaning over the whitewashed stone breastworks at the top of the hill. Between the French village, with its whitewashed log cabins, and the bark wigwams, some conical, some oval, a few fires burning here and there among them, a constant coming and going was taking place. The Canadians, tricked out in shirts of brilliant colors, and with new sashes, the Frenchwomen in bright fullskirted dresses that reached to the ground, were tiny, distinct, and noisy, their gesticulations and their cries floating up from the sunny green purified of meaning. The Indians, quite as brilliantly dressed, though with less uniformity, were more quiet, joined the French, left them. Every one was moving about, and no one seemed to be working. Beyond them Lake Huron, under a light breeze, shifted through all the colors of a peacock's tail to the hue of the serenest summer sky, and back again. On Bois Blanc the leaves of the poplars reversed into silver, and turned over again. Edward Charleton said, "We had a fight here yesterday, oh, quite a brawl." Doyle, behind him, a long white clay pipe in his hand, leaned forward against the wall, a smile of recognition in his eyes, waiting to hear how Charleton would recount the anecdote. Johnston, a little tipsy from the air, a glass of excellent sherry, and the unaccustomed experience of so much good company, leaned forward also with an expression of interest.

"Oh, it was really a serious affair," said Charleton cheerfully. "I shall have to write a letter about it. An Indian attempted to stab a trader. A Chippeway from up in your direction. No doubt he was drunk. Mr. Michel came up in time fortunately, and prevented much damage being done, but got a nasty cut himself in taking the knife away from the savage. Then they tied the poor fellow's hands behind his back, and Michel—I've no doubt he was drunk too—and four or five others pitched upon the poor beast and kicked and stabbed and beat him most unmercifully. I don't know who all—there was an engagé named Lambert, and Etienne Campion, Stork, and Campbell—"

"And Georgie Young and Blondeau," put in Doyle.

"Will and myself came up just in time to see the end of it. We pulled them off and had them locked up. Shall have to hold them, I think, until we hear from the Colonel."

"And the Indian?" suggested Johnston.

"Oh, the Indian was done for. Something like it happens every year. It's a pity they give them so much rum."

A cry came up from below, as two Canadians engaged in a mock scuffle. Somehow yesterday's fight did not seem very real, purged of its meaning before the delightful scene much as the voices from below were freed of their intention by the distance. In his pocket Johnston had a letter from Andrew Tod, inviting him to join him in a fur-trading project in the Spanish Territory of New Orleans. It did not tempt him much, but it reminded him of something which he had to ask of Doyle, and presently they went back to the stone barracks, the three of them, where, at the long rough table,

Doyle wrote out what Johnston requested of him, a grant of land dated July 1, 1792, for three hundred feet on the south side of the river bank at St. Mary's, running back forty acres in depth, bounded on the northeast by a lot of land belonging to Antoine Landry, and on the southwest by the old Jesuit burying ground. Captain William Doyle, Commander of the Twenty-fourth British Regiment, in his trim uniform with the narrow scarlet front, standing, and leaning with his left hand on the table, wrote it out, sanded it, and gave it to Johnston, and when he had finished Charleton took the quill and laboriously wrote his report to Colonel England of yesterday's fracas . . . "on which the Savage was overpowered and secured from doing eney injury by tying his hands behind his back . . . who kicked Beat stabed and Tomahawked him untill they perceived me accompanied by Capt. Doyle.... Michilimakina, dated July 1, 1792 . . . signed Edw. Charlton, Capt, 5th Reg't Com'g."

An Indian girl came in as he was writing and built a fire, and when he had finished they brought out another bottle of sherry. It did not trouble any of the three that Doyle had bestowed a grant in the King's name for territory ceded almost ten years before in the Treaty of Paris to the United States.

The letters which had waited for Johnston at the offices of Tod, Magill and Company, accumulating month by month all winter, from New York and from Ireland, consumed a long afternoon. He sat in O'Sullivan's Coffee House, where the previous fall he had encountered his old friend Andrew Tod, and slowly broke the seals and slowly read them. By and by he called for pen and ink and began a joint letter to his mother and his Aunt Nancy, a letter which called for all his epistolary skill and all his natural tact. He set forth in glowing terms his plans for the next winter; he spoke of the beauty and richness of the country; he mentioned lightly the hardships it was necessary to endure; and he finally announced that he was about to wed the daughter of an Indian chief. He made it quite plain that he was no squaw man, that this was to be an alliance between two noble houses; he praised the beauty of his lady, and her virtue, and he promised to bring her to Ireland one day. He wrote also to his brother Will. He sent his letters off, but could not hope to wait for an answer. The answer he looked forward to perusing the following spring.

On the Champ de Mars that summer there was much talk of the possibility of a war between France and England or, as the royalists preferred to phrase it, between England and the Republic, a war of liberation for a king who lay in prison. The French ladies made it a point of loyalty to powder their hair, although English gentlemen were forsaking the custom. There had been riots in the Vendee, he learned, and France had that spring declared war upon Austria. The stiff brocades and high heels urged on the war; the McTavishes, the McGillivrays, the Tods and Magills, in their neat, bottlegreen smallclothes, their high-lapeled coats, their snowy stocks and short, unpowdered hair, with an eye to the hazards of shipping and the profits of the beaver trade, offered the opinion that a nation should be allowed to go as crazy as it liked, provided it did so at home, and prayed that the ministers of England might feel the same way about it. Johnston called upon his friends, accepted invitations to dine, drew up new contracts for new engages, made the purchases necessary for another Indian winter. The wedding gifts to Waub-ojeeg for his daughter were among the most important of these; there were also gifts for the bride herself, among them one purely quixotic, and which was to cause him no little trouble on the journey north, a stove—not a large one, it is true, but still of iron, and inexpressibly awkward in all those loadings and unloadings of the Ottawa River route. The men who carried the pieces threatened to leave him at every second portage.

Pleasant as it would have been to linger, he was off again before the summer was well advanced. The journey was much less trying at that time of year than in late May or June. There were no mosquitoes. At the Sault he added one more man to his outfit, young Michel Cadotte, a half-breed born at the Sault and friendly with the Ojibways, who proved to be remarkably dependable.

VII

At Chegoimegon the canoes gathered, the light tepees sprang up once more for the Mide ceremonials. Waub-ojeeg was not well. He performed his part as usual in the sacred rites, but he returned at evening from the long day of dancing and singing very tired. The Woman of the Glade knew about the Irishman's offer. At first it had amused her, but later it worried her; she was afraid that her father would give his consent. She told her mother of her fears, and her grandmother, overhearing, said: "It is time the child made an apowa. She is already old never to have made one. This is a sacred time when the manidos are here because of the Mide, and she would surely have the right sort of dream." So it happened that Ozhah-gus-coday-wayquay began her fasting.

On a hill at a little distance from the village but quite out of sight she built herself a small lodge of cedar boughs, covering the ground inside with cedar boughs also. Then she painted her face black, and having curtained the doorway with green boughs, she lay down and tried to sleep.

The first day it was very difficult. She lay staring up at the layered green roof through which the sunlight filtered minutely and thought of the perils of marrying a white man. Pale green cedar berries clung to the under side of the twigs, smooth and shaped like little shells the two valves of which would open when they were brown and dry. She became very hungry, and even more restless than she was hungry. The day was long, although at nightfall her grandmother brought her a bowl of water and went away without speaking. The second day the hunger seemed to have left her, and she was not so restless. She was very lonely, however, and not a little awed at the idea of awaiting the visit of a spirit. She heard, far away, the sound of the village, the drum, beginning and ceasing, beginning again. She fell asleep in the afternoon and did not waken until after dark. An owl came and hooted in a cedar near by, and when he went away she was glad. On the seventh day, she dreamed that a white man came to her, carrying a cup of water. He said, "Poor thing, why are you tormenting yourself? Take this and drink." He was accompanied by a dog who laid his head on her knee and looked up into her face as if he knew her. The dream repeated itself three times. Then she dreamed that she was seated on a hill overlooking water and she saw upon the water many canoes filled with Indians coming to her to pay her honor. The dream changed, and she was looking down upon a country filled with flame, like a great forest fire. She cried out, "My people! My people will all be destroyed!" Then a voice spoke to her, saying, "They will not be destroyed, they will all be saved." She knew the voice for that of a spirit, for the accents were not human. Then she woke and saw the pale light of early morning filling her shelter. She wanted to rise and go home, but she was very weak, and she fell asleep once more.

In the middle of the morning she was wakened by her grandmother, who had come to bring her water, and when she had told her dream the old woman was very pleased and went back to the long lodge to prepare them for the girl's return. Meanwhile the Woman of the Glade filled her arms with cedar branches from her lodge, and throwing them on the ground before her as she went, trod on them, and came to her father's lodge. She entered the lodge, still casting the cedar boughs before her and walking on them, and having spread a few of them in her old place beside her mother, seated herself upon them.

Her grandmother had gathered bitter herbs, laying, when she had drawn them from the earth, a small pinch of tobacco in each hole as an offering to that other, older Grandmother. These herbs were boiled with corn and given to the girl to break her fast. For ten days she ate nothing else; for another ten days she ate nothing but smoked meat. After that she washed the black from her face, and came and went about the lodge as usual, partaking of the food of her family, and performing her usual tasks.

Soon after the return of the Irishman the wedding took place which united John Johnston, Esquire, to the Woman of the Glade, daughter of the White Fisher, and granddaughter of Ma-mongazid, the Big Foot. The ceremony began with the exchange of presents: calico, ammunition, and blankets from Johnston, furs from Waub-ojeeg. Then Johnston went to the lodge erected for him for this occasion, and seated himself behind the fire. Waub-ojeeg took his daughter by the hand, and in the presence of witnesses led her around the fire and bade her sit down beside her husband. He then made a long and dignified oration in which he instructed the girl in her duties as a wife, Johnston in his duties as a husband. In order that the Irishman might realize the intervention of a sacred will in his behalf, the story of the dream was repeated. He made Johnston swear to take the girl forever, in the manner of the white men, and to have no other wives, and ended by saying:

"I feel that I am soon going away to join my fathers, my mother, and my elder brother in that country where Chibiabos is ruler, and I am happy to leave my daughter in the wigwam of an upright man."

Simple as this ceremony was, Johnston found it very touching. He grasped the Indian firmly by the hand and thanked him heartily for the honor done him. The next day the wedding feast began, according to the time-honored custom introduced by Manabazho, and the whole village played at boggatiway, which the French call lacrosse, the women playing together according to one set of rules, the men according to another. On the second day there were races and dancing, and on the third day dancing again.

Wayishkee beat his drum and sang:

In heaven the walker,
In heaven the walker,
The bright sun walking around.

Do you hear the noise he is making?
The red bird is making a noise.

In heaven the walker,
In heaven the walker,

In heaven the walker
Is looking this way.

They went to Ile St. Michel, to the cabin built the winter before. Florentin had been there and had made all straight according to his notions. The new stove was set up in front of the fireplace, the bed was filled with fresh balsam and spread with the gayest blankets. There was even a wedding present for them, a bag of wild rice with a nosegay on top. Johnston called her attention to it, smiling with pleasure; it was as if he were again among the beguiling peasants of Antrim. The Woman of the Glade looked at Florentin's offering. She looked at the stove and the bed, and then, drawing her blanket over her head, she went into the farthest corner of the cabin and lay down on the floor. Johnston did not disturb her. Since the afternoon was growing late and the air chilly, he built a fire in the stove and put a kettle on to boil. He unwrapped the presents he had bought for her in Montreal and laid them on the bed, setting the little ivory comb on a piece of scarlet cloth so that its delicate shape was clear to see. Then he called to her to come and look at them. She gave no answer. For a while he waited, hovering over his gifts and glancing at the quiet figure in the corner, and then, taking the comb, went softly over and knelt beside her. "Look, sweetheart," he said, in Ojibway, having learned the word especially for this occasion, "look!" But his wife turned her head, laying her face close against the floor, and answered not a syllable.

He busied himself in preparing supper, setting the food when it was ready on the table against the wall, and still the child in the corner made no motion. In some perplexity he removed everything from the table and set it on the floor in the center of the room, and then, remembering that the Ojibway women never touched their food until the men had finished, he ate his wedding supper. After supper he went for water to the lake, and when he returned observed that a little of the food was gone, although in her corner Ozhah-guscodaywayquay lay rolled in her blanket as before. He cleared away the dishes, and as he was doing so his men appeared, led by Florentin. They had come to wish him well, and to share in any festivities that might be going forward. He met them at the door, his finger on his lips, and, indicating the figure in the corner, welcomed them, shaking each one by the hand. They tiptoed into the room and were given each a noggin of rum and a half a carrot of tobacco. When they had finished their drinks, and wiped their mouths on the backs of their hands, they again saluted their host, clapped him on the shoulder, and departed as softly as they could. Johnston sat down before the stove and waited. At bedtime he collected the presents, laid them in a little pile near his wife, spread an additional blanket over her shoulders, and laid himself down on the fresh balsam, under the new blankets, alone.

The next day the same performance was repeated. Half distressed, half amused, Johnston went about his usual business, left the house for an hour or more whenever he had prepared a meal, received his usual visitors, went over his accounts. He gave his men orders, which they took with perfect good nature, not to go near the house. For ten days she neither spoke to him nor showed him her face. He had been in love when he married her, and each succeeding day his pity and tenderness increased, until, on the tenth day, he was nearly out of his wits. He sat on the doorstep with his head in his hands, repeating to himself, "An Indian would beat her. Perhaps she is waiting to be beaten." At last, remembering that she was indeed his wife, and according to her own tradition owed him certain duties even as he owed her sustenance and protection, he resolved to be firm, and approaching her commanded her gravely to rise and tend the fire. She stood up obediently, the blanket falling back from her head to her young shoulders. "Look," he said, "this is where you will put the wood."

The fire did not in the least need mending, in actual fact. He had forgotten that; and as he lifted the black iron lid from the stove a flame shot upward like the tongue of a serpent. She had stood quietly until he opened the stove, but at that dreadful apparition she brushed suddenly past him and was gone through the door. He followed, and saw her running down the shore to the south. Even in his dismay he thought, "She runs like a deer. No woman in Montreal or Dublin could match her." He spent that evening in sorting out the furs given him by Waub-ojeeg. He had no heart to pursue her, and he did not think that she would ever return.

Therefore, one morning a week after her flight, great was his surprise to behold a canoe approaching the shore in which were Waub-ojeeg, Ma-mongazid, and the Woman of the Glade. They disembarked and came up the path to the cabin, the two men heavily laden with choice peltries and mokkuks of corn. The girl said not a word but went into the house. Waub-ojeeg laid his furs at Johnston's feet, Ma-mongazid did likewise, and folding his arms across his breast, Waub-ojeeg said:

"My son, I am full of humility. Never did I dream I should own so disobedient a daughter. Accept these furs as token of my sorrow, and take back my disobedient daughter. She will never disgrace me again. If she leaves you again I will cut off her ears. I have told her so. Already I have beaten her. I will beat her again. It makes me very sad to talk of such things, but I have given her to you, and what I give I do not take back again.

"My son, I was away hunting, but I dreamed a dream. I saw my daughter in the wigwam of my father. She had been many days in the woods, she was tired and hungry, she had brought unhappiness upon herself. I knew then that she had run away from you.

"My son, I left my traps. I came two days' journey down the Montreal to the wigwam of my father. When I entered it I saw her sitting there beside the fire even as in my dream. Then I beat her with a stick, and now I give her back to you."

He turned and without a word of farewell went down to the canoe. The old man lingered for a moment, tapped Johnston lightly on the arm as if to say, "It will be all right, she will come around," and followed his son to the shore.

It was true; she never tried to run away again. After a few days she twisted her braids into a knot at the back of her head and pinned them with the ivory comb. She laid the three-cornered red shawl about her shoulders, crossing the ends over her bosom, and tucked them in her belt. She went about the ordinary tasks of an Indian woman, and gradually her fear of the Yellow Haired became affection and then love. They were very happy. Upon one thing only she insisted: she wanted the stove removed, and after a little arguing Johnston took it down and set it out of doors, where it gradually became red with rust. The Woman of the Glade did her cooking at the fireplace.

He noticed that she never crossed before him or sat in the place in which he was accustomed to sit. For any noise she made he would hardly have known she was there, but he delighted to watch her. She was very beautiful, like the austere country in which she lived, her youth clouding her features with gentleness as the spring twilights made delicate and dreaming the shapes of rocks and gaunt pines. The voyageurs noticed her beauty and told her children of it years afterward.

Her husband wished to treat her as he would have treated an Irishwoman of his own rank, but she did not always permit him to do so. She refused consistently to eat anything until he should have finished his meal, waiting on him as she had done at the Red Cliff, and in all the years they were married he never persuaded her to relinquish this custom. She assumed many small labors which he would never have thought of delegating to her, and took full charge of all things pertaining to their comfort in the house. She gathered wood, she carried water, she skinned and prepared game, she scraped another deerskin and made a second window, she set snares for rabbits, she kept the cabin neat. After the fantastic behavior of the first few weeks there was no one more practical than she.

Fall passed, the winter deepened, and the Indians, who had been fairly constant in their visits through the autumn, came less often and when they did, came as guests, to smoke and tell stories and stay a night or two or a week. They brought gifts of fish or game and received gifts of tobacco, cloth, or any little trinket that might please them. They came without invitation, they entered without knocking, they stayed as long as they pleased, but they were quiet, courteous, and even thoughtful. Sometimes they slept on the floor in the Johnstons' kitchen, sometimes in the men's house. Waubojeeg himself was among these visitors. Johnston felt that the attitude of the Indians had changed toward him, and realized in himself also a changed attitude. A corner of the blanket of Waub-ojeeg had descended upon his shoulders, involving, besides the greater favor of the Indians, greater responsibilities. He took pains to pay them in good measure for their pelts, and there was no talk this year of their going to another trader. When, in the spring, he left for Montreal, he took with him twenty-four packs of prime furs.

He had made his plans for the summer knowing that in the fall the Woman of the Glade would be delivered of a child. He left her in her father's lodge, hoping, if all went well with his journey, to return for her and take her in October to a new house at the Falls of St. Mary's.

The night of the sixteenth of October, 1793, was cold; frost lay on the leaves, and toward Chegoimegon long points of white mist floated on the surface of the bay where the waters had given forth their day's meager warmth. In the sky the stars were like suspended snow. Johnston walked slowly back and forth on the beach of St. Michel, between the liquid chillness of the waves and the uneven shadow of the woods. The pines, plumed and unwithering, rose above the empty twiggy branches of birch and hazel, and under their shadow he could make out the conical shapes of the wigwams. One was used as a storehouse and kitchen. At this hour there was no light above it, but above the large one, and above the small one set at a distance, inverted cones of firelight were reflected, and occasional flights of sparks, all golden in the blackness, whirled and disappeared. He heard at last the cry "N'yah, N'yah," the traditional woman's exclamation of pain, astonishment, or joy, saw at last the curtain blanket of the smaller lodge flung aside from within, and as the figure of a little girl darted out and across the clearing toward the central wigwam, he knew that he was sent for.

The interior of the women's lodge held a curious compounded odor. He was aware, in the unsteady golden light, of the texture of appukwa and bark sloping down to shelter a circle of ground spread with balsam branches and furs; a litter of mokkuks, blankets, and woven fiber bags, near the edges, near the fire a basswood bowl full of warm water, and a small birch mokkuk half full of bear's tallow. Beyond the fire the Woman of the Glade lay with half-open eyes, staring into the fire, her face relaxed and happy. At her feet sat the old woman, Waub-ojeeg's first wife, who now and again patted the girl gently on the ankles, or, rising on her knees, adjusted the blankets closer to the long body that was now flat and slender as it had been nine months ago.

The baby was naked on a pile of furs almost directly at its father's feet, kicking feebly as its grandmother rubbed it with tallow. It was neither white nor brown as yet, but the universal sullen red worn by all babies, yellow, brown, or white, when they enter this world. It opened its slaty-blue eyes and looked at its father angrily. The grandmother, who was not many years older than thirty, said proudly, "It is a son." Later, having been thoroughly greased, wrapped in rabbit fur, and packed with dry moss into a cradle of bark and linden wood, of which the flat back, prolonged beyond the head and surmounted with an arch, surrounded the baby's face with a stiff archaic halo, the namesake of the Bishop of Belfast was brought to his father and grandfather in the wigwam of Waub-ojeeg, displayed, and taken back to his mother.

The village at Chegoimegon had been deserted for some weeks, and Waub-ojeeg was delaying his departure for the Wisakoda only until Johnston and his wife should set off for St. Mary's. At the trader's return, a week ago, the long lodge at Chegoimegon had been dismantled, and Waub-ojeeg's people, crossing to St. Michel, had set up the cluster of smaller wigwams, devoting one of them to Ozhah-guscoday-wayquay and her mother. Now that the child was born, they began to count the days before it might be possible for her to travel. In late September and early October the weather had been changeable and violent, and even now, Johnston, hearing the lake roaring behind the pines of St. Michel, seeing the early snow, dry and thin, eddying between the denuded hazel branches, wondered if they would be able to make the journey that season.

During the day Waub-ojeeg sat at the door of his lodge, his red-bowled pipe with its long stem of reed resting on his knee, smoking and watching the women as they threshed and cured in smoke the wild rice gathered the month before. They poured the grain into shallow holes lined with deerskin, treading it or beating it with paddles, and winnowed it afterward in the gale blowing in from the lake. The Woman of the Glade, lying in her wigwam, with the child hung near her in his cradle, could see and hear them; they chattered like squirrels. In the evening Waub-ojeeg from his place behind the fire on the low platform smoked and told stories or questioned the Irishman.

"My grandfather," said Waub-ojeeg, "was Nokay, also a chief. In one day's hunting at Crow-wing River he killed"—Waub-ojeeg held up his hand with the fingers spread—"sixteen elk"—he closed his hand finger by finger, enumerating the items—"four buffalo, five deer, three bears, one lynx, one porcupine. He was a hunter." Or he said: "Four days' journey on the other side of the Riviere Brule, to the west and to the south, in the mountains there are very fine maple woods. We were there two years ago in March to make our sugar.

My daughter"—he used the single word which signifies eldest daughter—"was then fourteen years old. She was with her cousin who was a woman seventeen years old. They were in the woods by themselves, they were climbing the mountain, they came to a cliff, straight"—he motioned with his hand—"and very high and standing so that the sun at morning shone on it clear. Here they sat down to pick wintergreen leaves and here they found what I am going to tell you about, a piece of yellow metal very smooth and flat, and as large as this." He shaped in the air a brick or slab about four inches thick, a foot broad, and a foot and a half long. "They tried to lift it, and the two of them together could raise it only a little. They were very puzzled. Then my niece said to my daughter, 'It belongs to Gitche Manido,' and they were frightened and ran away." He paused, lifting his pipestem level with his forehead. "My friend, what was it? You are a wise man. Tell me what is was."

"It may have been a block of hammered copper," said Johnston. "The copper of this country is often very yellow."

"Cannot two strong women lift a piece of copper of that size?" returned the Indian scornfully. "I say that they could not lift it."

"Could it have been gold, then?"

"I do not say. I have not traveled. I have not seen much gold in my life," said the White Fisher. "I ask you, who are wise. I see that you do not believe me. Very well, my friend, in the spring I will make my sugar at that place, and in May I will bring you that piece of yellow metal."

Johnston slept that night to a vision of Peruvians worshiping the sun at an altar of gold on a cliff side in the Porcupine Mountains. He had heard instances of trade carried on among the tribes of the interior from the borders of Mexico to Hudson's Bay, and stories of Ottawa women found on the plains of Tartary, having been captured and sold from tribe to tribe across the Bering Straits, and it seemed not impossible to him, as the lodge poles vibrated slightly in the wind, and leaves and small branches were swept against the side of the lodge, and Waub-ojeeg and his people slept in the dying firelight, that a band of the Inca Indians should have traveled so far and carried with them so great a quantity of the pure heavy metal of their kingdom, in order to worship under a strange cliff in sight of glacial waters.

On another evening they talked of the Christian mystery. "I understand you," said the Indian, "when you say that your god becomes bread and that you eat of the bread, not to eat your god but his godliness. We too when we eat of the heart of a brave man eat not the heart but the courage. There is no Ojibway who would taste of the blood of a coward." And again: "We are like you. First there is Gitche Manido, the Great Spirit, the Master of Life. Then there is Gheezhay Manido, the Merciful One. Then there is Manabozho who interceded for the red man and brought him the Mide ritual so that he might live again after dying here; then there are all the other manidos, the eight winds, the sun, the moon, the bear, the earth, many manidos. There are also the manidos underground which Manabozho made before he knew any better. They are bad—they are the mudji manidos. But we have no hell. If the Master of Life made a hereafter of fire he made it for the white man, not for us." He smiled, the long lips tightening slowly, slowly relaxing. He went on: "Do you know what Gitche Manido said when he had finished making the white man? He said, 'Now you shall buy land and sell land, always buying and selling.' For my people the land used to be free, always growing, michigan, the growing land that Manabozho made. When he put more animals on the land, they ran around and it grew. Now I think the land has stopped growing."

With great regularity the child, Lewis Saurin Johnston, was brought to see his father and grandfather, since Waub-ojeeg never entered the lodge where his daughter lay, although he took great pleasure in his grandson. The face of the child was a soft brown, and silky as the inside of a milkweed pod, the eyes dark, though still blurred curiously with blue, the iris indistinct, the little pupils inky black, widening and contracting as they were turned towards or away from the fire. One evening as the grandmother was taking the child back to his mother, his grandfather said, softly, affectionately, "Very soon he will be doing the only thing that Manabozho could never do. You will be proud of him then."

"And what was that?" asked Johnston innocently.

"Manabozho could not put his toe in his mouth."

On the morning of the tenth day the Woman of the Glade announced herself strong enough to travel. For some time all had been prepared, the mokkuks of smoked rice and of fish and of bear tallow made ready, and Waub-ojeeg, having delayed long, was anxious to be gone to the Mauvaise. In less than an hour the lodges were dismantled, the poles, first, laid in the

51

canoes, on them the furs and blankets, the rolls of mats, and the various bundles. For a little while the canoes floated together on the lake, and then Johnston and his voyageurs turned to the south, Waub-ojeeg and his people to the north, and the Woman of the Glade was with Johnston.

It was the beginning of November as they moved down toward Kewenaw. The storms which Johnston had encountered on his trip up the lake and which he had dreaded for this journey with the young mother, all had disappeared. The violent winds had stripped the trees, had startled the wild fowl and sent the wild geese honking overhead, had swept and scoured the sky and water, and now they were fallen; and in a quiet more dreaming than that of summer, day after sunny day they moved along, the lake rocking so gently that the paddles of the men hardly splashed. The Woman of the Glade half lay and half sat on the floor of the canoe, furs beneath her and a roll of blankets at her back, the cradle of her son lean-ing against the cedar thwart. She felt the motion of the water, the motion of the canoe balancing itself against and moving over the motion of the retarded waves, a movement as familiar to her as that of her own body walking. The lake never changed; the shore, though changing, was always her own country, and at night and at early morning she saw the familiar pattern of the Fisher stars swinging in their wide circle around the fixed polestar. Every night her lodge was built and carpeted; she slept under the appukwas she had woven as a girl. The men sometimes sang, always in French; she could speak with them in French if she chose, or to her hus-band in Ojibway, which he now understood very well. The small face of her child was a constant delight, and the joy with which, having unfas-tened the wrappings of his cradle, she laid him to her breast was almost as sharp as the pain she had felt in bearing him. If they had wind it was the northwest wind, the Keewaydin, blowing against the men's shoulders, and she remembered that it was called the Wind Going Home. They were going in the direction of the wind.

Their journey lasted three weeks. One afternoon, in a haze as if the smoke of all the councils of the century had hung undispelled above the trees and water, they rounded Cape Iroquois, where the bones of her ancestors' enemies lay whitening and uninterred upon the sand, and she heard for the first time in her life, far away, the sound of the rapids.

VIII

They were there in a landscape so unmarred that it seems, from this dis-tance, a time of early morning. There were the rapids, entire and fresh, the

whole half mile of glancing water, set here and there with islands, unfet-
tered, unobliterated, and harboring in the still, swift water at their foot
thousands of whitefish, of a size, and their flesh of a delicacy, no longer to
be met with. The place was called by the Ojibways, Bawating, the Place of
Water Tumbling over Stones; the French had called it a Sault, and the
inhabitants, Saulteurs. Since La Honton has designated them as "a sprightly
and active people," perhaps Leapers would be a more accurate term for
them than Men of the Leap. Men of the Rapids they truly were, however,
to be seen any day in the summer or early fall, gliding down the watery
toboggan, or waiting, the canoe poised momentarily against the deep current at the foot, one man at the paddle, another with a foot on each gunwale of the canoe, a long-handled net in his hand, peering into the
unruffled green translucency for the long white body and silver fins of the
fish they called the reindeer of the water. For the distance of a mile the
rumble of the rapids could be heard, a sound not so deadening and terrifying as the roar of Niagara, which has kept people from sleeping and
sometimes unsettled their reason, but a refreshing, vigorous splashing and
rushing, not too loud to spoil the sound of wind in the grass or of voices
or bird calls, and over which the sound of a gale in the upper lake might
come in undiminished force. Many people have wondered, from the days
of the first Frenchmen to the present, at the shallowness of the rapids,
considering that behind them is all the vast body of Superior's icy water,
and the conclusion has been, by Indians as well as white men, that the
great lake seeps away through subterranean channels. Indians will show
you this day springs on rocky islands farther down in the St. Mary's River,
which, they say, because of their coldness, surpassing even the coldness
of the river, are fed by rifts in the foundations of the earth directly from
the bottom of Superior. At any rate, there below the steady blueness of the
lake was this beautiful, dangerous, shallow spillway, refreshing all the air
with its breeze, as it were, providing to any one who had a net and a
steady arm quantities of the most delicious food imaginable, and blocking
the free passage of the voyageur with his heavily laden canoe, so that the
meadows on the southern shore became a natural meeting place for
traders, trappers, and fishermen.

A narrow footpath for towing and portaging led along the southern
edge of the Sault, picking its way carefully on a slight rocky elevation. East
of this was the site of the Old French Fort, which burned at Christmas
time, 1762, and at the eastern edge of this again was the log house of Jean
Baptiste Cadotte, spared by the fire, and in which Cadotte then lived. Still
moving eastward, one came to the Jesuit cemetery, a garden planted by

Father Marquette, Father Allouez, and Father Dablon, of dark-leaved plants with vermilion petals, sweet with the odor of sanctity, the garden plots themselves low under daisies in June, under mallow in August, in October under goldenrod and pale blue asters. This garden-graveyard was the southwestern boundary of Johnston's land. Before it lay the river, wide and tranquil after its swift descent, moving away to embrace the numberless islands of its downward channel; behind it lay the Indian green; behind the green, the woods. Three hundred feet on the river, running back forty acres in depth, bounded on the northeast by a lot of land belonging to Antoine Landry, "to be held during the pleasure of His Majesty and of the governor or commander-in-chief of Upper Canada." Landry who was he? His name comes down to us on a piece of paper held as the first recorded deed of land in Chippewa Township. He probably looked like La Liberté, and wore a red worsted belt about his middle, worsted from an habitant wheel. They were there among the dustless, sharp-needled pines, the unlittered, ripplemarked beaches, the flowering meadows, and their nearest neighbor was Jean Baptiste Cadotte, the old steward of the Chevalier de Repentigny, loyal servant of King Louis the Fifteenth of France, God rest his bones.

This same Cadotte was a son of a Cadieu, or Cadot, whose father came to the Sault from France with the Sieur de St. Lusson. His mother was an Ojibway, and in due time he married an Ojibway woman by whom he had two sons, Jean Baptiste the younger, and Michel, Johnston's Michel. When the Chevalier arrived to take possession of his grant, in 1751, there was Cadotte. The animals brought from Michilimackinac, "a bull, two bullocks, three cows, two heifers, one horse and a mare," were put in the charge of Cadotte, and so also were the acres cleared and planted with corn, of which they expected to harvest that first year "from thirty to thirty-five bushels." And when the Chevalier departed in 1759 to go to the aid of the French garrison besieged at Niagara by Sir William Johnson of the Mohawks, Cadotte remained in charge. News came to the Sault some months later that de Repentigny had been taken prisoner by Sir William, and later still, that the King of England had offered him rewards if he would become a British subject, but that the Chevalier had refused. Then no more was heard, and a young English trader by the name of Alexander Henry, arriving at the Sault in May, 1762, became Cadotte's partner in the fur trade. Since the English troops, who came in the summer of that year to establish a British garrison at the Sault, found Cadotte to be a friend of Henry's, they did not disturb him in his log house and garden, but took possession of the fort and began to lay in a winter's supply of fish. Three days before Christmas the fort burned, store houses, stockade, and all—all but Cadotte's cabin—and, provisionless and shelterless, the men saw no other course open to them save flight to Mackinac. By some miracle the river was open for canoes, and they left at once, all save the Lieutenant, who was too badly burned to travel. So it happened that Henry and Lieutenant Jemette wintered with Cadotte.

Johnston had not been two years in the Indian country without hearing the remarkable story of Alexander Henry, and he had seen Henry himself at Montreal, a white-haired man whose digestion was not all that it had once been. Nevertheless it was strange to have this shrunken little Frenchman, as they went among the cattle to select a milch cow for Johnston, or as they stood on the meadow near the shore, discussing timber and foundations, suddenly refer, as to events of a year ago, to that disastrous winter and the even more difficult winter which followed. He was confused as to sequences of events, occasionally; he sometimes even transferred the adventures of one man to another. But what he lacked in coherence he made up for in the accuracy of his separate recollections, and his very obliqueness ended by adding to the final vividness. In February of that winter, Jemette being considered sufficiently recovered to travel, Henry had set out with him for Mackinac, the old Mackinac on the mainland. That was a terrible journey.

"My friend," said Cadotte, "they were seven days in reaching the Grand Detour, seven days, one whole Christian week. And after that, to wait there in the snow with no food but a little pork until the men come back to me, all the way back to me, here at the Sault, for more food, and then to go across on the ice, across those straits—My friend, in February those straits are very terrible—all the while suffering from burns, here and here, almost over all his body, for what? To be scalped in June. Stabbed and scalped. But Henry, with his Indian friend . . . Ah, it is very strange, my friend, how some things happen to one man, some to another. That year we see Monsieur Henry here at the Sault once more, and we make sugar together. Sixteen or seventeen hundred weight of sugar, certainly. Then Henry goes back to Michilimackinac, and he is there when Monsieur Jemette is killed. You know all that. We did not see him again for a year, we are sure he is dead, and all the time he is with that Indian brother of his. It was my wife who found him and who brought him back here." Another time he would say: "My friend, when you suffer from le mal de raquette you must do the right thing. There is only one thing to do and it is difficult. You must light a piece of touchwood and lay it upon the tendons of the leg. There you must leave it until the flesh is well burnt, bien brule. This Henry did not do, and that March in coming back from Michilimackinac his snowshoes made him much pain. He was afraid to cure himself and he suffered."

To such an accompaniment Johnston built his house, sent out his commis to their various stations along the southern shore, and established a small fur press between his house and the river front. He had brought books from Montreal on his last trip, together with many other luxuries—dishes, mirrors, and a few small panes of glass for a window. And to such neighbors, such a scene, he brought his young wife and her son. It was not Athanasie, however, the mother of Jean and Michel and the rescuer of Alexander Henry, who came in that far-away November with a cup of milk for the Woman of the Glade, but Marie Mouet, Cadotte's second wife, a woman slightly over forty, experienced and kind. The Woman of the Glade held the wooden cup in her dark fingers and, smiling at the smooth warm surface of the liquid, said to Marie Mouet in French, "It is the first milk I drink since I leave the breast of my mother."

At the end of the month the last Montreal Express, on its way from Grand Portage, stayed with them overnight and told them of the assassination of Marat and of the progress of the war with France, and went on in the morning with its packets of sealed letters, leaving them to their winter silences.

IX

Word having passed from village to village, from one band of hunters to the next, through the deep snow, the message finally reached the Sault where the Woman of the Glade heard it, seated before the fire, on the floor, her son in her arms. Waub-ojeeg-e-bun. The White Fisher *was*. The Indian who brought it from the village sat on his heels, his hands dropped loosely before him between his knees, his eyes on the face of the young woman who stared quietly into the fire, motionless. After a time he said, "You will call it Wayishkee?"

"It has already a name," she answered, and to Johnston, who waited behind them, "Tell him."

"Lewis," said Johnston. The Indian looked blank. "En français, Louis," said Johnston.

"Oh," came the slow response, "like the French king, Louis."

Johnston nodded, and beckoning to the Indian, led him into the kitchen, where he made him a gift of sugar, flour, and a small glass of wine, and let him out of the house by the kitchen door. Waub-ojeeg had died in the late autumn. The Woman of the Glade sat by the fire and did not weep. She had known many deaths since her girlhood, going with her mother and step-mother to help prepare the dead, but this was the first death of great personal importance. She did not need to see her father to know how he looked. His long frame, stretched on the bed of skins, would be clothed in the fringed white buckskin suit of the Mide ceremonials, and his face would be painted, green and white and black, according to the ancient ritual imposed by Manibush. He would not be buried, not because of the hardness of the winter earth, but because it was not a custom of his people, although many had become converted to earth burial since the coming of the French priests. His body would be incased in those mats of reed, of cedar, which his women had woven in happier hours, in the frail days of spring, and thus stiffly enshrouded would be set on high above the beaches of Chegoimegon on a scaffold in the trees. Years later the bones would be interred on the north shore of Lake Superior in the great burying pit, the walls of which would be lined with valuable furs and presents of wampum and copper. Meanwhile, the Mide ritual would not be neglected, nor the four nights' fire, nor the gifts of food and implements. Wayishkee would become the head of the family, deferring always to his mother in matters of importance, in the spring the reeds would be green about the mouths of the small rivers and creeks, and her mother and the old woman would go among them in the small canoe. A wish as profound as life rose in her body to see her people and the sand beaches of Chegoimegon in the spring.

Johnston had come back into the room. He sat down behind her in the armchair that was reserved for his special use, and said nothing. The Woman of the Glade continued to search the fire with her eyes as if this universal element, ever the same, here, at La Pointe, ever fresh in spite of its own recurrent deaths, contained the images which rose almost in commemorative sequence in her mind. She was remembering the stories which had surrounded her father in his lifetime, and which became solidified into legend, as it were, upon his death. He had gone, when he was a little boy, with his father to hunt in that middle ground between the accepted Sioux territory and that accepted as Ojibway. It was autumn. Her grandfather Ma-mongazid was a young man, confident and straight, and he had brought all his family with him. His lodge, covered with cedar bark, and gray and shaggy in appearance, stood in a hazel thicket; the leaves were yellow, spotted with brown, and falling from the branches. Squirrels stripped the fuzzy husks from the small nuts and ran away with their cheeks bulging. The boughs shook under them, and in the lodge, separated from their light racket by the narrow thickness of the cedar bark, were all the customary morning sounds of a family. Suddenly a shot was fired, then another. In the still frosty air they sounded like the cracking of two branches, magnified. A dog screamed, and a young man came running into the lodge, where he dropped, holding the upper part of his body from the ground with his elbows, but dragging the lower part as he tried to crawl forward, for he had been shot in the thigh. The dog had been killed. A woman, her grandmother, who had been cutting meat into strips for smoking, sprang to her feet and ran to Ma-mongazid, and Ma-mongazid, putting her aside, went to the door, left the lodge, and standing in plain view, called to his hidden enemies in the Sioux tongue. He asked if Wabasha or his brother were among the attackers, and while the terrified Ojibways waited, the bushes rustled and parted, and a Sioux warrior, some years older than Ma-mongazid, and very tall, appeared and crossed the intervening glade. It was Wabasha, the half brother of Ma-mongazid by an Ojibway mother. He was clad in full war regalia, his head crowned with feathers and his face painted, while Ma-mongazid wore only his hunting shirt, and carried no weapon but the knife at his belt.

The Sioux and the Ojibway embraced, the Sioux was invited to enter the lodge. He bent his head, did Wabasha, to pass under the looped-back curtain of deerskin; his feathers brushed the curtain, and before he could lift his head he was struck a violent blow with a war club, yet not so violent that it caused him to fall. He straightened, turning abruptly upon his assailant, not seeing at first in the shaded light who this might be, and encountered a boy of five, who still grasped the club and glowered at the intruder. Wabasha laughed. To those in the lodge the sound was like the first decided rush of rain after a sultry day. Wabasha laughed, and lifting the boy in his arms, began to prophesy. He prophesied a war chief for the Ojibways who should bring terror to the Sioux and whose name should be powerful beyond the Namakagun River until the last day of his life. Then he embraced the young Waubojeeg and set him on the ground.

Johnston had left his place behind her in the armchair and was lighting a candle, which he carried to the table, and there seated himself. Presently a light scratching noise told her that he was writing, an occupation which she understood, but which interested her little.

Again it was autumn, either late autumn or early winter. There was snow on the ground and the streams were frozen, but the winds had not yet stripped every dry leaf from the thickets. Waub-ojeeg was setting marten traps. The Battle of the St. Croix was some years over; the rocky gorge was quiet, the waters had purified themselves, and the Sioux no longer molested Ojibways gathering rice in the still autumn days. In his lodge were two women—his first wife and her son, Wayishkee, the First

58

Born, and her own young mother. In a cradle made of bark and interwoven strips of rabbit skin lay, or leant, according to the position in which her mother chose to set her, a baby girl, herself, all the crevices about her tiny body carefully packed with moss in order to hold the little feet, the little back, in the posture which should be habitual before she learned to walk. Waub-ojeeg, clad in his hunting shirt and leggins, a short knife at his belt and a small hatchet in his hand, cutting spruce boughs and twisting them to his uses, set forty marten traps, establishing a line for the season, and, having set the last, turned towards home. He had traveled perhaps half the distance between the last trap and the place where his lodge was, when, rounding a small ice-shagged evergreen, he came suddenly upon a moose, which confronted him with its head lowered, and barred his way. A great beast, gray and sulphurous, with curious long lips and intelligent eyes, it stood there, taller than the man, balancing the broad palmate horns before him, and regarded him with a determination and hostility rare to its species, a if it had set itself up challenger and defender for its race. Waub-ojeeg retreated slowly one step, and the moose attacked, lunging heavily in a straight line. The man dodged, circling the evergreen, and found the moose again confronting him. Having no suitable weapon and not being in any great need of meat at the time, he would have been glad to go his way without molesting the beast, but the moose would not permit it. For half an hour the pursuit continued, the moose lunging, the man dodging, until, as he ran, the Indian picked up a long stick, undid the fastenings of one of his moccasins, and with the moccasin string bound his knife to the end of the stick. He then stationed himself behind the trunk of a tree, his lance in his hand, and the moose flung itself upon the knife-head. The blood streamed from its throat, smoking, but the moose, undismayed, reared and plunged again. Again the Indian met him with the lance, and again the blood gushed from the gray shagged body. The sky clouded, as if to snow, and cleared again, and a wind rose, shaking the withered leaves and lifting the loose snow in feathers, and still the moose, though staggering, pursued the Indian and met the lance, and still Waub-ojeeg, bespattered with blood, his breath tasting bitter upon his tongue, his forehead damp with sweat in spite of the cold air, dodged from tree trunk to tree trunk, avoided the skillful colossal horns, and held steady his lance. Finally the moose dropped. Waub-ojeeg approached it, and kneeling before the solemn head, cut out the tongue. He unbound the knife from the stick, put it back in his belt, fastened his moccasin again, and taking the tongue only, set off for home. The women, following his directions, found the place of the fight easily, for the snow was trampled down in a

59

great circle, and trees and snow and bushes were besprinkled with blood as if thirty men had been fighting there. The moose, they said, was the largest ever killed within the memory of any living Ojibway.

Now that the moose was dead the woods were quiet. The room was quiet, also. Johnston had finished his writing, but the Woman of the Glade still looked into the fire. She presently felt his hand on her shoulder. "Come," he said, "it is very late."

What he had written he hesitated to show her then, but left it folded in his portfolio.

Death Lament of the White Fisher,
by John Johnston, Esq.

My friends, when my spirit is fled—is fled,
My friends, when my spirit is fled,
Ah, put me not bound in the dark and cold ground,
Where light shall no longer be shed—be shed,
Where daylight no more shall be shed.
But lay me up scaffolded high—all high,
Chiefs, lay me up scaffolded high,
Where my tribe shall still say, as they point to my clay,
He ne'er from the foe sought to fly—to fly,
He ne'er from the foe sought to fly.
And children who play on the shore—the shore,
And children who play on the shore,
As the war dance they beat, my name shall repeat,
And the fate of their chieftain deplore—deplore,
And the fate of their chieftain deplore.

In the spring Michel Cadotte was going to La Pointe, and Johnston, having purchased a small schooner from the Northwest Company, equipped it with goods for the winter's trade, presents for the Woman of the Glade to give her family, and every small device he could imagine to make the journey easy for her and the child, intrusted her to the care of Michel, and sent her to Chegoimegon to visit her people.

X

The Northwest Company was at a disadvantage with the Hudson's Bay Company chiefly in that it had no charter, although the partners had applied for one, but was a common-law company. It had been organized and reorganized tentatively through a number of years from the day in 1779 when Simon McTavish had first bound together as one, for the duration of one year, nine small fiercely competing companies. In the fur trade, competition meant ruin to the competitors, a fact which held the Northwest together through varying fortunes until 1821. A smaller company, younger by more than a century, and unchartered, the Northwest nevertheless became a most formidable rival to the Hudson's Bay, the "Great Company," partly because of its personnel. Whereas the Hudson's Bay servitors, clerks and voyageurs both, were Orkney men, stubborn and slow, a stiff-necked generation, the Northwest Company had taken over from the French regime the French half-breeds who knew the forest and its inhabitants, men of an extraordinary character and as if created expressly for the fur trade, gay, dogged, cajoling, loyal. They were the nimble tentacles by which, octopus-like, the tough business authority of the Scotch-Irish traders, the McTavishes, McGillivrays, and Mackenzies, penetrated and controlled the wilderness. These were the voyageurs. But any man in the Northwest who indentured himself and served his full five years as commis, or clerk, was very likely to be one day a partner, so that every man enrolled in the company felt himself a part of it; his own fortunes and those of the company were inseparable, and the whole outfit, from Jean Baptiste, mangeur de lard, to the "Marquis," Simon McTavish himself, hung together with a sort of feudal strength.

Johnston never took advantage of the occasions which offered to become a part of the company. The recollection of his family's experience with the Belfast waterworks left him with a disinclination to involve his fortunes in affairs so far beyond his personal control, nor could he very well countenance the idea of signing away his liberty for the term of five years. He remained an independent, as during his first winter, with all the hazards and privileges thereunto appertaining.

The Northwest Company flourished. Alexander Mackenzie discovered the river which now bears his name and traveled down it, or up it, as you like, to tidewater, where, although in doubt as to whether he had approached the Pacific or the Arctic Ocean, he found it necessary to turn back. He returned to the Grand Portage, the primary rendezvous of the Northwest, and told his partners about his trip, but they were too concerned with the reorganization of the company then pending to be much impressed. A few years later he went overland to the Pactfic, and inscribed his name and the date on a rock there, on the Pacific shore, in bear grease and vermilion. This also left his partners unimpressed, but Mackenzie him-

61

self began to envision a fur company comparable to the great East India Company, a company composed principally of the Hudson's Bay and the Northwest, trading from coast to coast and from the Arctic to the forty-fifth parallel, an empire company. Simon McTavish, concerned with the more immediate problem of keeping nine squabbling companies at peace, began to be irritated with Mackenzie.

The Northwest had been deliberately trading for some years from posts in the United States territory, giving as justification some convenient theory that the United States had not fulfilled completely conditions of the treaty of 1783, and the post at St. Mary's was one of these. Year after year the Northwest canoes landed at the southern shore, were partly unloaded, and taken up through the rapids on the cod line; year after year the Montreal partners bound for Grand Portage broke their journey at the Sault, and not without revelry; and year after year John Johnston continued to hold his acres by the grace of God and the King of England. Even the rendezvous of the Grand Portage was in territory belonging to the States. However, in 1798 the Americans had begun to be meticulous about their boundary lines. They threatened to collect customs on all Northwest Company goods, and the Northwest, making the best of a bad business, moved across the rapids to the stony northern shore, where they built docks and warehouses and constructed a small canal, and a lock having a wooden gate and a lift of nine feet. The southern gate was single and operated by a windlass; the northern gate, carrying the weight of Lake Superior against its hand-cut timbers, was double. The whole canal was hardly more than half a mile long, the lock itself thirty-eight feet long by eight feet nine inches wide, just large enough for the great transport canoes, thirty-six feet long and from six to seven feet wide. Nine feet subtracted from the twenty-one-foot drop of the rapids was not a great deal, it is true, but it eliminated the most difficult part of the course and allowed canoes to go up fully loaded, towed by oxen along the corduroy road from the head of the locks to the canal. The company also built a sawmill to be operated by water power from a short canal parallel to the lock. These were improvements, but the men continued to complain that the lower part of the Northwest's property was as likely as not to be under water half the time, and they regretted the move.

Johnston had not the heart to move. He continued to consider himself British, but for his purposes the northern shore was out of the question. And what of his house and barns, his gardens and plowed fields, his fruit trees and his seven years' labor? Moreover, at this distance from Washington, from London, in a land so intrinsically wild, the reality of the affixed boundaries was not great. Why, he felt, should not some day some other treaty, no more remote than that of Paris, return to the crown, and as easily, what the Treaty of Paris had taken away?

The Northwest continued to flourish, and McTavish and Mackenzie continued to bicker. Rum and high wines, powder and shot and vermilion, were unloaded at the company's wharves at St. Mary's and at the Grand Portage, and the Montreal canoes returned loaded to the gunwales with pelts—smooth beaver, tawny moosehides, marten and mink and muskrat and an occasional fisher, buffalo skins from the Red River and the Pembina. A gun, if sold to an Indian, cost as many beaver skins as might be laid flat one on top of the other and pounded down till the pile equaled the height of the gun. The guns in those days had not short barrels. The company was employing, in '98, fifty clerks, seventy-one interpreters, one thousand one hundred and twenty voyageurs, and thirty-five guides, and its capital had increased to at least eleven times that of the original coalition. In '99, at the Grand Portage rendezvous, Alexander Mackenzie announced his intention of withdrawing from the company. In November, having returned to Montreal, he carried out his threat, and sailed for England.

The Woman of the Glade had a new name. She was no longer called Ozhah-guscoday-wayquay, but Neen-gay, My Mother, and she was content. Even Johnston had adopted the name. A little more round in body, but still young, still beautiful, she moved between the Johnston house and the Indian village, increasingly important in both.

In 1800 Jane was born, a little creature with dark eyes and a haze of black silk over her little round skull. Lewis, who was seven, and George, who was four, both looking far more like their mother than like their father, stood about her, watching her with the careful gentleness of extreme curiosity, the romantic tenderness which very little children often show for children smaller still. She was born in January. In spring, in the garden behind the house, lilacs were in bloom on the low bushes; marigold and sweet william and mint in square beds and round ones; daisies in the long grass at the garden's edge; currant bushes in a row; sweetbriar, transplanted from the woods. Johnston's voyageurs had brought Neengay the seeds, the roots, the cuttings for her garden, from old gardens at Mackinac and from Detroit. Before the house, sheep were cropping the grass down to the water's edge, leaving clumps of wild iris and buttercups untouched. The beach was sandy, and a narrow dock ran out toward the deeper water in order that the larger bateaux might have less difficulty in unloading. The warehouses were larger now, there was a fur press, a wine cellar, a windmill, a root house. Neengay had learned to make butter, beating it in an upright churn, and pressing it into stone crocks to be placed in the spring house, but she had not learned to eat it. She did not dislike it; she simply forgot to use it except in preparing food for her husband. A carpenter's shop had been added to the blacksmith shop built when Lewis was two years old, and bunk houses had been erected for the men who were constantly arriving and leaving, so that the Johnston property alone had the air of a little village, or more rightly, that of a feudal estate. Mr. Cadotte still lived to the west of them, but he was old and went about very little. Michel left that year to establish a permanent trading post at Chegoimegon, and although he was to be in every way an independent trader, his friendship for Johnston assured them of the Chegoimegon furs. Indeed, by this time Johnston exercised what amounted to a monopoly of trade along the southern shore of Superior, and in spite of the smallness of his army of voyageurs and commis, found himself much in the position of a Scottish border chief. During the next fourteen or fifteen years he handled annual capital amounting to forty thousand dollars, and being of an extravagant disposition, he enjoyed spending somewhat lavishly on his house and furnishings. He brought in books and pictures, fine china, fine wines, some beautiful old silver plate which he had engraved with a crest of his own devising—a crane, totem of the home band of St. Mary's, several elk heads, and the motto *Vive ut Postea Vivas*. He had his portrait painted, and in a broad gold frame it hung above the wooden mantel of the fireplace, shedding the luster of the red coat, the white ruffled shirt, the gold frame, upon the large, low-ceilinged room. More and more the interior of the house took on the aspect of an affluent country house in Ireland, a great fascination to French and Indian alike, and more and more Neengay found herself involved in the duties of a lady of the manor. For the gentlemen of the Northwest, and for other distinguished visitors, there was the lavish hospitality of the living-room, and for the Indians and the men whom Johnston called mes gens, the broad hearth in the kitchen and Neengay, ready in case of illness with homely remedies—opodeldoc, friar's balsam, salts, opium, castor oil, bitter herb stews, mallow for the kidneys, bonewort for a fever, juniper berries for calculus, balsam twigs for a rheum, poultice of red willow or of chokecherry bark to stanch the flow of blood.

· In 1800 also a United States Customs official visited Grand Portage, informing the Northwest that he meant to collect duty on every bale of goods and on every bale of furs unloaded there, and the Northwest began to make its arrangements to remove to the mouth of the Kamanistiquia, afterward called Fort William, in honor of William McGillivray.

In 1802 Sir Alexander Mackenzie returned from London, where he had got the account of his discoveries published and himself knighted, to take more active charge of the New Northwest Company, and trouble began to be felt at once through all the fur-trading country. The New Northwest Company, sometimes known as the Alexander Mackenzie Company, but more commonly as the XY Company, was small, and composed of those few men who had seceded from the old Northwest with Mackenzie. It gave the Northwest a rival which knew all the ins and outs of the trade, and which seemed imbued to a man with the furious tenacity and energy of Sir Alexander himself. Prices of goods to the Indians dropped in both companies in desperate efforts to undersell each other; salaries of commis and voyageurs went up. More than twice as much liquor was sold as in ordinary times, and fights among Indians, and between traders and Indians, and between trader and trader, increased proportionately. Some of the Northwest traders, having made their bargains and dispensed their rum, made a point of suddenly moving on a day's journey in order to avoid the effects of their gift. One trader, having given an Indian an over allowance of high wine, attempted to quiet him with a dose of laudanum. The dose proved to be an overdose; the Indian died, and there was trouble with his band, who held that he had been murdered. At Lac du Flambeau a commis by the name of Francois Victor Malhiot conferred with his Indian customers as to the prices paid for furs by his XY rival, "old Chorette," and exclaimed in despair, "One would think that the goods cost him nothing or that Lucifer brought them to him through the air." And Alexander Henry the Younger, the nephew of Alexander Henry of Mackinac, stationed on the plains of the Pembina, did not hesitate to waylay and use force upon a band of Indians, mostly women, who were taking their furs to pay a credit to the XY trader for that district.

Johnston, whose popularity with the Indians had never depended upon a lavish use of rum, thanked heaven he was an independent, and his trade went on much as usual.

Then, in 1804, the Marquis, the elegant McTavish, suddenly departed this life; the Northwest Company immediately sought a reconciliation with Mackenzie, and, as the news went north and west from post to post, a gradual sigh of relief rose from the harassed commis and wintering partners.

So went the opening years of the nineteenth century. In spite of a mysterious plague which had attacked the beavers in 1804, the animal wealth of the country was still fabulous. Alexander Henry, riding over the plains of the Pembina, saw great herds of buffalo and killed two for sport, taking from the carcasses only the tongues. In a small wood the trees were

65

rubbed bare of bark and the ground was thick with dung as in a cattle yard. In the early spring, the ice in the Pembina River breaking suddenly overnight, vast numbers of buffalo which had been sleeping on the ice— the ice and the plain indistinguishable under the snow—fell into the river and were drowned. Day after day their bodies floated down past Henry's camp, or were lodged on the shore in ranks four and five deep, and as the weather increased in warmth they rotted, the stench making the shores of the river uninhabitable. The wilderness was rich also in berries, in wild grapes, little sweet apples, and the Pembina was named for the "summer berry," the small round Indian plum. It was a treasure house laid open to looting.

Alexander Henry the Elder to John Askin:

Montreal 8th May 1799

. . .I have symptoms of old age advancing rappid, so much that unless I see you this summer I am affraid I never will. but I have no reason to complain since on calculation since my time there has been Two Thousand Million buryed a few years can make no difference, if we can only approve of our conduct while here we need fear nothing hereafter Hope and Rliance on Providence is all we can do. there is no fear of being worse treated than others. . . it is supposed the french will not stop till they have taken all the continent of Europe. the Idea of Liberty and equallity, is still gaining ground. England is intending to make a Union with Ireland which will I expect be a bad business before it is settled, as the Irish is much against it, and even our friend Isaac [Todd] disapproves of the English cramming the Irish with what they don't like. I am sorry I have nothing to ammuse you further my family is all well and joins in best wishes for yours . . . and remain while there is a spark remaining your sincere friend

Alexander Henry

John Askin Esquire at Detroit.

Montreal, Jan 18, 1800

. . .I have been laid up since last Oct with a complication of disorders. . . Mr. Todd is going with me. He is always complaining when his intestines are empty, but after Dinner recovers wonderfully. . . boys [Boise] asked me seven and eight hundred livres and would engage for only one year. the Old N. West Company is all in the Hands of

McTavish, Frobisher and McKensey is out, the latter went off in a pet, the cause as far as I can learn was who should be first—McTavish or McK. and as there could not be two Ceasars in Rome one must remove. . . Muskratts is the only article which may keep at twenty four, good—and this is owing to Astore and me being in opposition . . . . Robinson is well. General Washington Dead. My family all join in praying for the Happiness of yours and remain your affectionately

Alexander Henry

Rum is selling five ski. Spirits high, proof Mr. Sharp died yesterday of an inflammation of the Bowells, which shall be a great loss to Leath.

XI

Eighteen Eight, early September. The rain was falling, a mild autumnal rain, dotting the water with circles that spread and interlaced. A few leaves, yellowed and speckled with brown or bright green, showed among the hazel thickets, and in the balsam woods the fine branches held the water like so many brushes, to be released at the slightest jar. Jane sat on the bed beside the visitor, regarding the blond young girl with dark eyes full of wonder and solicitude, a Jane eight years old in a little calico frock with long skirt and very high waist, with leggins and moccasins, and about her shoulders a sort of knitted spencer with long sleeves and a high collar. Her right hand, lying in her lap, was closed upon some treasure; the room was full of shadow from the rainy day, although it was mid-morning. The visitor, "the little Miss Campbell," who was only a few years older than Jane, had been unpacking her belongings. The older of the Johnston children, Lewis, George, and Jane, had been warned not to speak to her of her father, who had been killed only a few weeks before in a duel, and it was for this reason that Jane had been following her about with a silent childish compassion that would, for an older person, have been quite as distressing as floods of tears and protestations of sympathy.

John Campbell had been a trader on the upper Mississippi since 1792. He had been stationed at Prairie du Chien in the early part of the nineteenth century, where he had held the office of justice of the peace for that part of the Indian territory, and had performed marriages for the reasonable fee of one hundred pounds of flour per marriage. He was well known at Mackinac and at St. Joseph's, where he had sometimes stopped on his way to Montreal, and it was at Mackinac in a drinking bout that he became involved in the quarrel that was the cause of his death. Duels were common enough in those days, almost as common among gentlemen as brawls among half-breeds. Even Johnston, for all his peace-loving disposition, had fought his duel, standing, with a pistol that was as likely not to fire as to fire, before an equally uncertain pistol, had felt, before he had succeeded in firing his own weapon, his brow grazed by something hot and brief, and, upon realizing what had occurred, had fired into the air. He had lost a lock of hair from his temple and although he searched the grass for it, wishing to carry it home as a scalp lock to Neengay, he did not see it again. Poor Campbell's affair had no such fortunate ending. He and his challenger, Red Crawford, met first at Mackinac, but, their friends having informed the justice of the peace of their intentions, the proceeding had been interrupted. No longer drunk, still obstinate in their quarrel, Campbell and Crawford had arranged to meet later near Point Detour, and it was there that Campbell received his mortal wound. A dying man was ferried across the river to Point Fort St. Joseph, and two days later a downward-bound bateau conveyed his body to Mackinac. He had been well liked in the territory where he was best known, so much so that John Askin, writing to his father of the affair, ended his letter: "As its probable that Mr. Crawford and Dickson [the second] will return to the country where this man's family resides, I'm apprehensive that they will meet with a great deal of difficulty & its the general Oppinion they will lose what property they may take in that country." He continued, "You'll receive one Mocouts Sugar, a Bundle of Mats & a Mocout of dried Huckleberrys which you'll please accept of." So John Campbell was buried and his little traveling companion became a visitor in John Johnston's house.

"Look!" said Jane, unfolding her hand. "It's my father's watch." The other child bent her head above it and smiled with pleasure, for Jane had opened the gold hunting-case to a design cut fancifully from white tissue paper, already pale ivory with age, a design of cupids and hearts and flowers. "It's from Ireland," said Jane, "he brought it in his pocket when he came. And do you know, every time he crosses the bay at L'Anse Kewenaw it runs down all at once! So he never takes it in his pocket any more when he is going there. Some day I am going to Ireland, and I shall learn to cut tissue paper like that. I'll make one for you, then."

The dark head and the fair leaned close together, and the rain beat softly on the window panes.

XII

The curiosity of Andriani regarding the shape of the earth was but one of the many curiosities of the time regarding the physical universe. As if the cosmos were a delightful and ingenious arrangement, waiting there to be investigated by the mind of man, and all unsuspecting that such investigation might lead them, for a time at least, into terror and confusion, secure in an established background of Divinity, Johnston, along with Andriani and Kalm and Linnaeus, began to poke and pry and wonder about tangible things. Priestley had come, the year after the building of the Johnston house at St. Mary's, to America, a refugee from British intolerance. News that the air was one fifth oxygen trickled northward to the Sault, and took its place in the imagination beside the idea that the earth is flattened at the poles. Indians came to the house with bits of native copper. Johnston listened to long stories about manidos in copper, of an island in Lake Superior littered with pieces of pure copper, an island forbidden to campers. Indians who had camped there but one night and come away the following morning were seized with illness before their canoe touched the mainland, and died, all but one. He heard also of a boulder of pure copper lying in the River Ontonagon, and deeply revered. Because he placed the specimens brought him in a special cabinet with the cured wings of strange birds, dried flowers, seeds of strange plants, as if in a shrine, and because he listened seriously to their stories, the Indians brought him other pieces of the spiritual metal, and also reddish-brown lumps of iron ore, heavy, cold gray lumps of hematite, chunks of snowy quartz veined finely with gold, like a pattern of lightning. He conferred with Jean Baptiste about the story of the forbidden island, and Jean Baptiste had also a legend, an inherited Jesuit explanation. The Indians, said the old Canadian, seated in his greasy hunting shirt and Ojibway ornaments, his face colored by Ojibway blood and Ojibway habits of living, yet speaking from his paternal culture, the Indians, he said, when they are preparing food, frequently heat stones which they drop into the kettles containing the food. Especially in the old days did they do so before kettles of iron or copper were much used, and when most of the cooking was done in birchbark vessels. Camping upon the forbidden island, he said, they had doubtless picked up lumps of copper sulphide, which, being boiled with their food, had poisoned them. Why the Indians considered copper more manido than iron is hard to say, unless the color had something to do with it, but the fact remains that they were right, for although iron has perhaps been the more powerful of the two in its influence over human life, copper, the electrical affinity, is certainly the more magical substance.

On business expeditions along the southern shore and into the wooded mountains by river routes, and from his daily visitors, Johnston gradually filled his cabinets and his notebooks. He stuffed owls; he took reckonings with the sun compass, labeled and numbered minerals, and sent for books on the new philosophies. There were also a few fossils, gray stone worms, and shells from Garden River, and the petrified skull found at St. Joseph's Island, of which he wrote, "This last was almost perfect; the eyes, ears and part of the nose and mouth were quite discernible, the interior of the mouth and cavity of the skull seemed a perfect crystal; the last could easily be distinguished through the sockets of the eyes." O man, to crystal grown! For one whose temperament combined so deep a moral strain with such a love of the fantastic and extraordinary, what a memento mori! In that crystalline air beside that lively water, all the air about him fragrant and nimble and balsamic, he held this curious object, which may have been no more than a remarkable geode, in his hands, and read its message, perhaps so far beyond its first intentions but none the less powerful and true. There was the report, also, brought by an Indian, of the footprint of Manabozho in the solid rock on the north side of St. Joseph's Island. And there was always in the back of his mind the story told by Waub-ojeeg that last autumn of his life about the god ingot in the Porcupine Mountains.

In 1809, September 21, at the request of Roderick McKenzie, who, in Montreal, was beginning to collect documents relative to the early days of the Northwest Company, he wrote *An Account of Lake Superior.* He got out the journals which he had carefully kept those first years, and, in the serenity of the big, empty living room, his women busy in the kitchen, his storehouses, his fur press, his wine cellar, his blacksmith shop all prosperous and sturdy, ranged to the right and left of his dwelling, his garden flourishing, his men busy about his errands, he gave his first conscious look backward to those windy days along the southern shore, to the distant silhouette of Ile St. Michel, now shortened to Ile Michel for Michel Cadotte, to Andriani, to the stained ax handle.

Of the Sault he wrote in a fine legible hand: "The situation of the village is pleasing and romantic. The ground rises gently from the edge of the river." He wrote that the houses were scattered over a slight ridge, four hundred yards from the river; that there was a great deal of sweet clover; that the soil was a light mold mixed with sand, twelve to eighteen inches deep over a bed of cold clay, that the whitefish season was from May to November; that the largest fish caught in the past season weighed fifteen pounds. He wrote that the rapids were one mile wide and half a mile long, descending over a bed of red freestone interspersed with white rocks, and that the Northwest Company had a fine sawmill on the north side. He wrote, "The southwest channel of the rapids takes its course S.W. for five leagues to the rapid called Nibith, the whole extent of the shore covered with maple and is the one continued meadow of the richest soil I ever saw." He mentioned the Northwest Company's shipyard at Point aux Pins, reported the finding of pure silver ore at Point Iroquois, of cinnabar at Vermilion Point, compared Gros Cap and Point Iroquois to the Pillars of Hercules, and called for a poet to immortalize them. He then proceeded, with many moral and geological reflections, to a minute description of the southern shore, cove by cove, indentation by rocky indentation, exactly as it was revealed to him in all its beauty and danger on that slow, shore-tracing journey. It was a record for a voyageur, with warnings about winds, currents, reefs, good and bad camping places. He had a theory that the water of Lake Superior was exceedingly pure and light, giving for its support the fact that it ruffles very easily. He said, "At the Falls I have often seen the water rise from two to three feet in as many minutes, the rising followed shortly by a Northwest breeze."

Of the rivers which enter Superior from the south he said only one, the Ontonagon, was not black, "as if their source were turf bogs," and ascribed this color to the presence of iron ore. He was charmed with his subject. As he wrote, the landscape grew before him brightly; the fatigue, the mosquitoes, the muscles cramped from long hours in the canoe, melted, faded, became as nothing, and his pen grew agile. Having passed Les Grands Sables, he came to the Portails, white freestone harbors, "placed by Providence for safety on a hazardous coast. I once passed here in the month of May, immediately after a gale of wind which continued for four days, with severe frost and snow from the north. The effect on the fall was beautiful. It was frozen up entirely except a little gutter in the middle, not more than a foot wide. The sides resembled pillars variously fluted; the shrubs at the mouth of the rivulet were perfect figures in ice, which appeared like Corinthian capitals. A young pine about thirty feet high which grew in the middle of its bed, and sparkling like a conical pillar of crystal sculptured in fretwork, crowned the brilliant perspective." He came next to the Pictured Rocks, of which he wrote: "The several strata from which exude different mineral waters, tainting the smooth white freestone with innumerable grotesque figures in a variety of drapery, are easily distinguished . . . the summit of the precipices crowned with lofty maples, every shelf and vein filled with shrubs and evergreens, sometimes in festoons, and at others spreading like hanging gardens." At Miner's Bay, where in 1772 the Duke of Richmond had established a small camp to look for silver and copper, he found excellent grindstones ready made on the beaches, and at Grand Island, beholding the great bay with its green even slopes, he thought of Milton's "shade above shade, a woody theatre." The Indians came there on calm nights to spear whitefish by torchlight. At Dead River, Riviere des Morts, he explored for copper, and noted that the mineral-bearing rocks never had anything growing on them, while others, not so high and equally devoid of soil, were thickly covered with stunted pines. But on those metallic rocks he found one spring a quantity of seagulls' eggs, "which when fried in the pan with some pork, made an excellent supper with a dish of aromatic tea."

Still traveling west, he found in Potter's Bay a part of an Indian bowl made of clay and very old, and off Potter's Head he observed a little island, "apparently round and pretty high," on which he never set foot, but which, however, charmed him infinitely. "When I made my first voyage in the Lake . . ." he wrote, "I tarried opposite Contemplation Island, as I called it, for four days, and I recollect having filled ten or twelve pages of my journal with reflections, remarks, and some poetical effusions, the result of so much spare time." And again he wrote of this little island, which had the privilege of filling his mind "with a pleasing melancholy and a desire for quiet sequestration, where every worldly care and every mean passion should be lulled to rest, and the heart left at full liberty to examine itself, develop each complicated fold, wash out each stain with a repentant tear, and, finally, become worthy of holding converse with nature, approach the Celestial Portals, and, though at an infinite distance, be permitted a glimpse of its Almighty Sovereign, but our Father and God."

He was still east of Keewaynan (Kewenaw), the "way made straight by means of a portage." But when he had described the bay, the portage, the Indian village on the cliffs above the portage lake, he remembered an evening in May some years later, an evening in 1803, and wrote: "The sun was nearly settled and just gilded the skirts of the Keewaynan Mountains with its horizontal rays, tipping the tops of the trees in the lower part of the ridge with burnished gold. I made my men rest for a few minutes on their oars. . . . As the rays of the sun became fainter, I saw the trees on the skirts of the mountains, even to the extremity of the point, all in apparent motion and manoeuvering like an army attempting to gain a position. Soon after, the mountains began to rise, each retaining its proper form, the valleys, though high in the air, still kept their humble distance from the hills; among the real trees a few scattered rays of the immerging sun were still perceptible. At length the majestic edifice gradually descended, and to the air-built fabric succeeded a general blush which tinged the whole horizon." This remembered radiance lingered in his mind as he went on conscientiously with his detailed report, on past the stiff red clay of the

Ontonagon, the sand hills and cherry shrubs of the Bay St. Charles, the beech and maple forest of Ile Michel. He told the story of the gold ingot, of Perreault and the earthquake, gave an account and criticism of the site of the new British fort on St. Joseph's Island, which seemed to him hardly well chosen from any point of view, a "desolate landscape, although the seat of honor, justice, politeness and the most liberal hospitality." Then to record the temperature of St. Mary's, in winter shifting from forty below to zero in a few hours, in summer varying from ninety to forty-five in the same day, but on the whole an excellent climate, a healthy place, "where nothing shortens life but intemperance." And so to sand his paper, and fold it, and after dinner to take it across the river, where he delivered it into the hands of the Montreal Express of the Northwest Company.

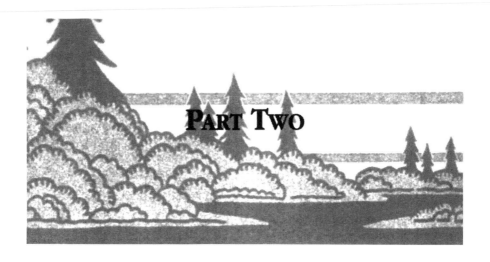

PART TWO

The winter of 1810 was long and very bitter. At the Sault the gayety of the French and the good liquor of the Northwest Company lightened the days and it seemed not unlike other winters. At Fort St. Joseph, "the seat of honor, justice and the most liberal hospitality," visitors were few and the sight that greeted the eyes of the Irish and English soldiers quartered there was always the same, the river, solid ice under drifted snow, spreading away into the beginning of Lake Huron, the dark tufted lines here and there in the whiteness that were the shapes of Point Detour, Harbor Island, Ile à la Crosse. In April, that sweet season, when English thickets were beginning to grow wick, the Commander of the garrison set himself down to compose a letter to his superior officer concerning a conspiracy to desert brought on among his men by the extreme cold and monotony of the place. Two of the men only had attempted an actual escape. One morning early in March, without proper provisions or equipment, in spite of the terrific cold, they had struck out across the ice for Mackinac. Their departure was observed but not reported until late that afternoon. The first party sent after them had to turn back at nightfall because of the weather. Two days later the body of one of the deserters was found, frozen and deep in snow, at Goose Island. A little farther on, that of his comrade, still living, was found and taken back to St. Joe, but the hands and feet were frozen and later it became necessary to amputate both legs and the fingers of both hands. These two examples, the one living, the other dead, were sufficient to check the conspiracy without further action on the part of the commander, and the garrison waited on, minute and isolated, for the spring.

II

It was July, 1812. In the garden behind the house the lilacs had ceased to bloom, but the sweet william and pinks were unfolding a warm sweetness upon the air. A little girl with a delicate brown skin, dark eyes, and black hair, Eliza, then ten years old, leaned over the sweet william to observe the velvety colors, maroon, purple, white and purple, and a dark-haired, dark-skinned woman with a hawk nose and gentle eyes, Neengay, stood near her, a large woman in a costume of blue cotton cloth, with a three-cornered red shawl folded over her bosom, but wearing quilled moccasins and scarlet legging, and in her ears loops of silver, each bearing two long silver bobs. The day was immensely fair, immensely tranquil. Between the leaves and grasses and in the woods beyond the Indian green were intervals of coolness and shadow, but the day itself, arching over the river and the meadows and the far hills, was transparently and vitally hot. The river was cold and unruffled. Sunlight, descending into the green water, illumined it, but never warmed it. And across the cold, still water a canoe came floating, darting, pausing, darting again, and beached its prow near the Johnston dock. Johnston was in the long living-room at a table full of papers. He glanced up casually to observe the messenger, but sprang to his feet when he had heard the news, called for a bottle of the best sherry, and drank the King's health on the spot. The news had come from Fort St. Joseph that England and the United States were at war, and the plan was to attack Mackinac at once and regain it for Britain. The Northwest Company was arming to a man, the Indians were glad of an opportunity to fight; would Johnston and his people be at Fort St. Joseph not later than the afternoon of the fifteenth, and would he observe lest news of the war and the attack reach the ears of some one who might convey it to Mackinac?

The early morning of the fifteenth found everything prepared and in motion. Since it was summer, most of Johnston's men were at St. Mary's, as was also the greater part of the Saulteur band. The traders in bateaux, the Indians in their long canoes, the whole little fleet, according to report comprising some two hundred men, moved out around the head of Sugar Island into Lake George, and so south.

The water was quiet, as on the day before. From the oars of the bateaumen drops fell on the still surface to form interlinking circles, and each boat and canoe was accompanied by its colored reflection. The mouth of Echo River lay hidden in its reed bed; they crossed the shallows in the upper part of the lake where the floating heads of pickerel weed broke the fine glaze of water, and passed, at the foot of the lake, a small island with a single beautiful young elm. The channel narrowed between Sugar and the rocky coast of the mainland on the east, the current becoming very powerful, and they made good time down into Bear Lake. They passed small islands of polished silica, each with a high hump or ridge of rock, breaking off suddenly into stony harbors with deep water or running down in sandy, verdure-covered points, each island the color of a walnut shell, the rock, at the water line, banded with vermilion where the iron had seeped through in rust. The ruddy band, the tawny rock, the little fantastic tufts of pine in the clefts of the rock, were reflected upside down in the green water with such precision that the perception was mocked with a multiplicity of islands. Blueberries, just beginning to sweeten, grew in the seams of the rock, and lady's slippers, now fading, in the swampy hollows of the points. On the right, Sugar Island was still and rich with maple leaves and sandy beaches. A slight wind, flawing the water in Bear Lake, indicated the division between Sugar and Big Neebish Island, as the covey of boats rounded the northern end of St. Joseph's and continued south between it and the Neebish. All wooded, all calm; the maples of Sugar giving way to conifers, particularly the plumed white pine. The steady line of Neebish and Little Neebish, or Encampment Island, ran out southward into reedy points, as if the river had drawn the green downstream with it, frayed out, like silk, from its proper substance. The river, known as St. Mary's, widened into Muddy Lake, of which the farther shore, the Michigan mainland, lay low and blue, distinct, yet cut from the surface of the lake by a band of silver, a band of atmosphere, an actual apparition, a looming. Past Hay Point they went, past Round Island and Lime, called then, after the game which the Indians played there, Ile à la Crosse. They went between Lime and St. Joe, whose low shores rose gradually through acre upon acre of hardwoods to the mountain which gave the island its Ojibway name. It stood, a symmetrical gentle form, covered with leaves and blue haze, not very high, but with an air of permanence befitting a member of the oldest range on earth. At noon, the sun beating down on them and upward from the glassy water, the voyageurs and Indians lifted their gaze to this form so blue, so cool.

About three in the afternoon they saw on their left the white limestone chimneys and walls of Fort St. Joseph, and dropping below the Point, came to haven on the eastern side of it in a weedy, sandy bay. This little cove or bay was already crowded with the bateaux of the Northwest, and with the usual vessels of the fort. The square dock was no longer accessible; the shore, beyond the ranks of the alders, was alive with men. Johnston climbed the hill through grass where the three bright leaves of the poison ivy, just beginning to root itself on that slope, looked freshly sinister, and found Askin and the Commander of the regulars consulting in one of the whitewashed houses of the fort. Every one was very hopeful, very gay. Although the American occupation of the Sault had been a purely nominal affair, with no troops and no garrison, and practically no American settlers, the matter of licenses and customs was something of a hindrance and an irritation, the Non-Importation Act and the Embargo had every one by the ears, and at Mackinac the high customs exacted was causing a good deal of embarrassment to the trade. Every one was anxious to return to the old regime. The Indians, tired of being handed from nation to nation, having spent some three generations—Indian—in transferring their affections from the French to the English, were unwilling to transfer them again to the Americans, and there is not much to indicate that the Americans had ever done anything to make this transfer easy. As for the British, they had built the fort at Mackinac, it was theirs, and although they hardly expected England to regain the colonies en masse, they had been suffering a nostalgia for the last sixteen years, and felt it would be pleasant to move back into their own possessions.

Therefore the toasts went round, and Mistress Madeleine Askin spread a holiday supper for the officers and unenlisted leaders. The chief business of the preparation was in distributing arms and ammunition to the Canadians and Indians. There were Ottawas and Ojibways from the lower part of the river and the Michigan side of the Straits of Mackinac, a company to the number of two hundred and eighty under John Askin. The two hundred and sixty Canadians were under Toussaint Pothiers, Le Beau Pothiers; the forty British regulars in their red-fronted uniforms under Captain Charles Roberts. All evening preparations went forward, musket rods rattling in guns, flintlocks being tested, powderhorns filled, the artillery of the occasion being mounted in the flat-bottomed bateaux; and below the fort the Indians by their fire were painting and attiring themselves for the ceremonial dance.

They left St. Joe at ten o'clock the morning of the sixteenth, and an hour before daybreak on the seventeenth they landed on the northern side of Mackinac Island, in a shallow bay now called British Landing. Their fleet, according to Askin, consisted of fifty canoes, each carrying ten warriors, and ten barges or bateaux; their artillery of two iron six-pounders, and they carried also scaling ladders. Johnston, in the center, was one of the first to land. The air was filled with the pure and vague luminance of very early day; the depths of the water were unusually visible. Standing in the

78

prow of his boat, well muffled in his capot against the chill fresh air, he looked down into the water and saw shoals of silver minnows and little bodiless pinheads scattering at their approach. They landed quietly, boat after boat sliding up with a soft crush of prow upon sand, and disembarked as quietly. Askin formed his Ojibways on the left, the Canadians and regulars held the center, and about one hundred western Indians, Sioux, Folles Avoines and Winnebagos, under red-headed Colonel Dixon, had the right. The artillery was "dragged with Velosity" through dry underbrush, cedar swamp, and thicket, and planted on the rising ground to the northeast of the unsuspecting fort. The Indians, no longer in ceremonial regalia, but stripped of everything but paint and weapons, were like hounds in leash. As the heterogeneous army advanced, interpreters, both Canadian and Indian, crept back and forth from wing to wing, repeating instructions to the Indians not to attack before ordered. The morning advanced with light and heat. At ten o'clock, such had been the "Velocity" of the artillery, all was ready for the attack, and a flag of truce was sent to the fort with orders to capitulate. Captain Hanks received the delegation with some surprise, since he had not heard there was a war afoot. When he learned of the disposition of the army in the surrounding woods, and heard the whooping, directly under the pickets, of a few uncontrollable Indians, he very reasonably surrendered. The white flag was hoisted in place of the flag with the red and white stripes and the wreath of white stars on blue, and this was followed shortly by the British cross. The Indians, British, and French Canadians trooped into the fort, shook hands with their defeated enemies, admired the beauty of the grounds, the spaciousness of the barracks, and in general made themselves at home. Some men were sent to take over two small schooners lying at anchor in the harbor, some to prepare breakfast, and Mackinac was again British. Not a gun had been fired, not even an old hen killed. Johnston, Askin, and the other traders found their chief employment for the rest of the day in seeing that the Indians, who were somewhat disappointed by such a peaceful victory, "committed no improper acts."

It had been twenty years since Johnston sat with Lieutenant Charleton in the officer's headquarters while Doyle made out the paper for his grant. Since then the grant had become worthless according to the American law, although no one had tried to dispossess him. Now, perhaps, it was to be made secure again under the Crown. He was too busy today for contemplation, and he had also been many times since to Mackinac, but the vision of that day of a beginning must have followed him, beyond the movement of the naked painted figures with feathers in their loose black hair, of the loungers in fringed buckskin shirts and knitted caps, of the women, appearing an instant in a doorway, and disappearing to scurry about some household readjustment, beyond the voices and the sound of feet. Some days after the victory, a party of Nor'westers arrived from Fort William. They had stopped at Fort St. Joe with the intention of joining the expedition against Mackinac, and finding the place more than half deserted, and hearing the good news, had come on to the island, partly to join in the jubilations and partly to verify the astonishing tale. They stayed only a few days, and then returned to Superior. Johnston went back to St. Mary's. The English fell into their old ways about the fort, and Astor and certain gentlemen formerly of the Northwest were left to straighten out their business as best they could.

The war went on, with little change for St. Mary's except that most people considered themselves British subjects once more and were pleased. Lewis Johnston, who was nineteen, insisted on joining the King's Navy. George would have liked to go with him, but his father persuaded the younger boy that he was needed at the Sault. Johnston's frequent and irregular absences on trading expeditions left the sixteen-year-old the head of the house, and the boy matured early in matters of responsibility. In 1813, September 10, at the Battle of Put-In Bay, Lewis was wounded, and came home that winter with great tales to tell. His ship had been the *Queen Charlotte,* which the Americans took. There had been fire and carnage and spectacular heroism, but what seemed to have impressed him most was the funeral on the south shore after the battle, when the British and American officers were interred side by side, to the same music, the same solemn words, with common mourning.

The Northwest Company and the independent British traders continued to convey supplies to the British troops whenever there was need. The schooner Nancy, which had plied the waters of Lake Superior for the XY Company, was requisitioned by the British and made into a transport, and in August, 1814, was sunk at Natua Sackie to prevent her falling into the hands of the Americans. She had wintered the preceding season at St. Mary's, locked in the ice, shrouded with snow, but still warm at the heart, where her custodians kept a fire in the galley stove. In August, lake water invaded stove and all. To the Americans, it seemed hardly fair that the Northwest merchants should give so much aid to the military. There seemed to be some vague idea among them that wars were between armies, not countries, and they cherished an irritation against the Northwesters out of all proportion to the situation.

Meanwhile for month on end everything was so quiet on the St. Mary's as to warrant Jane's traveling with her father on one of his mercantile visits to Mackinac. Ever her father's best companion, the little girl of thirteen who knew his jokes, his favorite quotations, and for all her dark skin had such pretty Irish manners, followed him shyly about the green lawns of the fort, and dined with him at the officers' mess. She heard there talk of the fur trading, and of skirmishes at Detroit and desultory Indian warfare along the border, and once she saw a strange visitor, an Ojibway woman whose husband had been killed in the war, and who had assumed her husband's ornaments and weapons and taken his place in the war party. Even her mother, when told of it, could not remember another instance of an Indian woman's going to war. This feminine warrior was small, not nearly so tall as Neengay, and delicate in build. She came into the room on the arm of one of the young lieutenants, smiling and shy, and was introduced to the commanding officer, to Johnston, and to Jane. Her face was not painted, there were no feathers in her smooth hair, she had retained the fringed skirt and leggins of the Ojibway woman, but she wore the silver armlets, the medals, the scalping knife, the medicine pouch, of her husband, all the insignia of war, even to the tomahawk. The officers led her to a large mirror, and their amusement was no greater than her evident pleasure as she turned herself around and around before the bright surface, laughing aloud in her delight. She was invited to dine with the officers, and although obviously unused to sitting at a table or eating with a fork, she conducted herself with great decorum. A presentation of gifts followed the meal, and the officers conducted her back to her lodge with due honor and respect. Jane and her father, leaning on the breastworks, watched the small procession wind down the steep hillside, the Ojibway woman alert and gay, smiling up at the young lieutenant who escorted her, an infantryman following, his arms piled high with cherry-red four-point woolen blankets.

The year 1813 turned slowly into the year 1814. Late in July the Americans decided to regain Mackinac, if possible, and a small fleet of seven vessels under Captain Arthur Sinclair and Colonel Croghan appeared in Lake Huron and stood to anchor opposite the island. They carried seven hundred men and should have been able to take the place, but their intentions seemed obscure and hesitant. The British, observing them from the whitewashed breastworks of the fort, and from the square projecting tower of the blockhouse, were able to proceed leisurely about preparations for a defense. A prize which interested the Americans quite as much, however, as the fort, was the annual flotilla of the Northwest Company, due to pass at any time now from Fort William, down the St. Mary's, and across the upper part of Lake Huron to the mouth of the French River, a caravan of canoes loaded to the limit with beaver and muskrat furs, skins of wild swans, bearskins, moosehides, every kind of peltry, and valued at no less than a million dollars. They wished to capture this flotilla far more than they did the fort, and in view of what they considered injuries from the Northwest Company, together with the liberties of war, they considered it legitimate prey. They dreaded being involved in an attack on the fort at the moment when this rich booty might be passing. So they manifested great indecision in their movements, and on the morning of the third the British were surprised to see the greater part of the fleet weigh anchor and disappear into the blue distance of the Grand Detour. The Americans proceeded under a fair wind past Drummond and, veering to the left, moved upstream past Harbor Island and all its unnamed, minute green comrades, to Fort St. Joe on its stony rounded point, like an inverted bowl. Here they landed, and finding the defenders few, since the British were holding two forts on Mackinac Island, took possession of the schooner *Mink,* the property of the Northwest Company, which was in harbor there laden with two hundred and thirty-nine barrels of flour for St. Mary's, and burned the fort and storehouses. The wind dropping a little, the flames went up from the top of the low green dome in a nearly perpendicular roar; the American vessels and the *Mink,* standing out in mid-channel for safety, felt the heat shake against their canvas. Then it was all over, except a black smoke and an occasional crashing timber. The great stone chimneys and fireplaces remained, blackened and gaunt and isolated.

News of this reached the Sault very promptly. Neengay saw the canoes of the Northwest moving off downstream shortly after noon. By early twilight Johnston was ready to leave. George was with him in the first canoe. He was taking with him practically every able-bodied man from his own employment, but the body of his troops was Indian. Tradition says there were a thousand warriors. He had waited for them to prepare according to their own customs. All afternoon the air and water had throbbed to the beat of their drums until the summer landscape had taken on a tremor of excitement, seeming to retain actually the accumulation of the single powerful beat. Now the heat of the day was gone, and the wind, which had ruffled the straits all day, had as usual fallen away to nothing. The leader's canoe floated on the still water, and by ones and twos and threes the Indian canoes pushed off from the sandy bank and joined it, forming in order to the rear. All the women of the Indian camp had followed the warriors to the beach. Neengay, with the two little children close beside her and the four-months-old baby in her arms, stood on the grassy slope in front of the house. A little way down the shore Eliza, who was twelve, and the little Miss Campbell were seated on the grass. As the last canoe floated free of the beach, Johnston lifted his arm, a signal followed by the lifting of the paddles of all the Canadians, who at once broke into a song. The paddles descended as one, broke the water, and the fleet moved off, skimming. They took the passage through Hay Lake and down the West Neebish Rapids, the more difficult route, but one which the Americans would be unlikely to be observing.

Neengay returned to the house and began to prepare supper for Will and Charlotte and Jane. The room was shadowy, being at the east end of the building, and large. An Indian woman who helped her with the work, for there was much to do around the place, was there on her knees arranging curls of birchbark and pieces of split cedar between the irons in the big fireplace. The children drew near to her, waiting for the flame to light the room, for their mother was economical with candles. Neengay came and went, setting out corucake and blueberries and a jug of milk. She moved in a feeling of security and content. She had grown used to living in a house. The walls about her seemed permanent, a part of the natural scene, like the slope of the ground outside, and the slow indentation of the shoreline. She could not easily remember when they had not been there, as she could not easily remember herself without the children whose soft breathing and little smothered laughter in the corner by the fire mingled with the noise of the fire, an indoor murmur opposed to the murmur of the evening outside. The earth and the forest seemed to be sighing deeply and gently as they relaxed for the night, turning to sleep. The cows and horses shifted in their stalls in the barn to the east of the garden. She put the children to sleep in the west bedroom, returning to the kitchen through the large living-room, all quiet, all deserted, but deserted so recently that it yet held the sense of the life which had been in it. Johnston's quill pen and his papers lay on the table and he himself looked amiably down upon them from the portrait in the heavy gold frame, the painting indistinct in the half light. She went out to the barns, followed by the Indian woman, to do the chores of the men who had gone down the river, and together they filled the mangers with hay and, in the darkness, milked the cows and brought the full pails into the kitchen. They strained the milk into stone crocks, and the Indian woman took them out one by one to the swinging shelves in the milk house while Neengay began to make bread. She opened the top of a sack of flour and, making a hollow in the flour, poured in a little water, mixing her loaf thus, letting the moisture take up what thickening it needed. She shaped the dough with her hands into a round flat cake, and set it on an iron skillet tipped upright, facing the fire. She was preparing the surface of the flour for a second loaf when she heard the Indian woman calling to her, and although she did not make out the words, a note of excitement in the old voice brought her to the door, from which she saw a small pinkish glow in the sky above the Canadian hills. The glow deepened, broadened, and presently its earthly source made itself seen in violent gold close to the shore.

"They are burning the stores of the Northwest people," said the woman.

The fire spread from building to building along the shore, and a clamor rose above the noise of the rapids. They could make out small black figures running in front of the flames, and finally, above the shouts of the men, the noise of the fire itself, crackling electrically and sending the heavy log rafters of the warehouses crashing inward upon their gutted centers. From the Indian encampment a small figure in a shawl ran up to Neengay—the wife of Ahdeek, her youngest brother, a girl hardly older than Jane. She caught Neengay by the hand.

"Is it the Americans?" said the Indian woman.

"Who else would it be but the Americans?" said the girl.

The crowd of soldiers seemed now to have left the buildings; they were busy at the mouth of the rapids and they were presently seen and heard to be dragging down into the rapids, with great shouting and exultation, a schooner which had been lying at anchor in Lake Superior near the dock of the Northwest Company. It was in the midst of this uproar that people began running from the Indian camp toward the Johnston home, crying, "They are coming!"

Neengay awoke then to the fact that this spectacle concerned herself, and she turned and ran into the house. A swarm of Indian women followed her. Some one had let the cattle from their stalls and, giving them a smart switching over the rumps, sent them off into the woods. The children were picked up out of their beds and carried off half asleep, half awake. The house was looted, deftly and swiftly, and before the Americans arrived the looters were safe in the Indian village, where all the fires were out, all the lodges closed, the dogs tethered and hushed, a village lying still and hardly breathing in the hope that it would not be noticed.

This night the Americans were not concerned with the Indians. Some one—who, it was never known—had informed raiders that a Mr. Johnston, whose warehouses lay unprotected on the American side of the rapids, had gone to the defense of Mackinac with a thousand men, and had offered to guide the marauders to his property. They burned the house. They burned most of the barns and all of the warehouses, and seized a great quantity of flour, spirits, and dry goods, which they transported to

84

their fleet. The schooner, which had lodged in a granite ledge halfway down the rapids, they fired as a parting act. By midnight they were gone.

Neengay was in the lodge of Wayishkee, which resembled that of her father point for point, save that it was not so large and the insignia of the Owl was not present. The children, wrapped in blankets from their own beds, were asleep on the long divan which ran about the wall. The children of Wayishkee were asleep beyond them. Nearest Neengay was the blond head of the little Miss Campbell, who held the baby, Anna Maria, in her arms. Against the farther portion of the couch, Wayishkee's place, leant the oil portrait of John Johnston, still smiling his faint, good-humored smile. Neengay had salvaged it herself under the impulsion of some half-recognized fear that its identity involved his own, and that he would perish if she let the Americans take it. Behind it, in a pile on the couch, were the various other things which they had managed to save, some silver, some glassware even. The Indians had tried to bring those things which seemed particularly to belong to the Johnston way of living as distinguished from their own. Some that they brought were valuable, some valueless, but it was a little to show him upon his return. After the Americans had left, Neengay lifted the deerskin curtain that hung across the door. She could see the embers of her house, but she did not go then to investigate. She drew over her shoulders a bearskin coverlet and fell asleep. In the night air the fur quivered and lifted as it had done upon its original owner. Through the resumed tranquillity the roar of the rapids came distinctly, unconfused once more.

III

Ahdeek, youngest brother of Neengay, then aged twenty-one, naked except for moccasins and loin cloth, stood astride a half-stripped log of white pine, loosening the bark from it in long fragrant strips. His ax made a slishing noise, gliding between the trunk and the slivers of bark, and with each motion his long black hair, parted in the center and braided in two braids, fell forward from his breast or, as he straightened, dropped back upon it. The bark, rough and gray on the outside, yellow and wet with sap on the inside, fell away from the denuded log, leaving it white and shining, showing but faintly the marks of the ax. He was between the river and the charred foundations of the Johnston home, and near him another Ojibway, an older man, was working in similar fashion at another log. Logs were being brought in from the forest, dragged by groups of men through the deep fern and the long meadow grass, and some, cut down river, having been towed upstream, were being landed at the sandy beach, rolled ashore dripping. The heavy morning dew had dried from the garden and from the flaked charcoal of the discarded timbers of the former dwelling, and Johnston's Canadians had already set in place the first tier of logs above the new floor. The logs had been squared and the ends notched a little on each side so as to leave the core of the wood intact. Some Indian women and some French Ojibways, the wives of the canoemen or descendants of the earliest settlers in the old French village, were mixing mud and moss and attending to the chinking of the walls. In the Indian village, fires were smoking under kettles, women were skinning small game and cleaning whitefish; all the lodges stood open to the morning, and dogs and children were thick underfoot. Neengay was in the village, superintending the making of a feast, for a house-raising was in progress; any one who could give a hand with a log was invited. At noon and at night they would be banqueted by Johnston and given a regale. It was hardly more than two weeks since the Americans had departed, an interval of eleven days elapsing between the burning of the house and the battle at Fort Mackinac, but destruction had been so complete that reconstruction had of necessity to be swift if autumn was not to find them unprepared. In the morning Johnston would leave for Montreal to arrange for a loan and to make purchases for the winter's trade. It was already time for many of his men, those bound for the further posts, to be leaving, and there was hardly more than time for him to reach and return from Montreal before the stormy weather would be upon them. He stood now, in his blue coat and white stock, his hands behind his back, his hair, still long, still yellow although mixed a little with gray, falling across his shoulders, in the garden—where the beds, disfigured but not obliterated, and the shrubs, broken but not killed, gave forth an Irish sweetness to the air—and directed the work. Three mornings ago, standing in the same place, he had experienced the most complete despair of his existence. Not a building remained untouched save the smithy; the house and the principal warehouses were completely destroyed. His children were in the wigwams of their mother's people, and everything that he had tried to establish, some little corner of Irish thought and custom in the Ojibway wilderness, seemed gone forever. This morning, however, after three days of taking stock, a certain arrogance had brought him to reflect that if his fortunes had been high before the disaster, they were still fair enough to enable him to rise above it, and the sight of his house appearing phoenix-like in the center of all this good-natured confusion gave him great pleasure. It was a restorative. The day was splendid. A little breeze made it pleasant to work in the hot sun, and great masses of white cumulus cloud traveling slowly overhead kept the colors of the hills, the water, and the meadow changing and rich. Shortly after noon, one of these clouds, passing low, discharged a brisk shower on the river, the woods, and meadow, as it traveled south and east. They heard it coming on the leaves before it struck them, and when it struck, there was a great scurrying for shelter, like that of a huge Sunday-school picnic. The Indian village received most of the refugees. In Wayishkee's lodge all of the Johnston family, all of Wayishkee's family, and Ahdeek and his wife were gathered, laughing, breathless, and wet. Ahdeek, near the door, shook the loosened hair back from his gentle face, lifting his chin and turning his face from side to side quickly, with a gesture so like that of Waub-ojeeg that Johnston, seeing him across the distance of the lodge, his imagination sensitive from the events of the last two weeks, thought for a moment it was Waub-ojeeg himself, Waub-ojeeg young, in a world unencumbered by the quarrels of the Northwest Company with the XY, or of the Americans with the British.

The rain sang on the bark walls of the lodge, the drops rapid and stinging. The little wife of Ahdeek darted out into the downpour to cover the kettle of sagamite which still swung from the tripod above the fire, and darted in again. The fire sizzled and leaped up more briskly under the rain for a few minutes, and then subsided altogether. Then those near the door saw George, who had not been with them, running out from behind a neighboring lodge, his head down, and something long, wrapped in a piece of blanket, tucked under his arm. He arrived in the doorway and, looking around quickly for his mother, went straight to her. He made her sit down—he had something in mind of which he wanted to make a ceremony—and made the others stand a little away. Then he laid the long bundle in her lap and waited with his arms folded while she unwrapped it. It was a sword, the sword of an American officer, the sword of Major Arthur Holmes, who had led the marauding expedition and who had been killed twelve days later at Mackinac—for the attack on Mackinac had been a defeat for the Americans. Today an Indian, learning for the first time the identity of the man who had pillaged his friends, had brought the sword to George Johnston. After all, Neengay was an Ojibway. She closed her hand over the scabbard and a light came into her face. It may have been as well for the Americans in later years that there was at this time some symbol of revenge, not against all Americans, but against the American who had so injured her. She closed her hand over the scabbard and, lifting her head, looked at George and nodded.

As soon as the rain slackened, the men went back to their work, the women to theirs, and they saw the edge of the storm as it traveled down the river, dotting the water with interrunning circles. By nightfall the framework of the house, including the roof, was completed. An entire house stood there, built of new wood, pale and odorous. The doors and windows were yet to be completed; the old fireplace had remained. Around the campfires the builders were making merry, and Johnston, on a crest of revived hope and accomplishment, doubled the measure of the regale he had planned to give.

Only the face of Eliza, the little girl whose features were more purely Indian than those of any of the children, retained, between the moments when she was actually laughing or speaking, an expression of pain and anger, which strained and drew the child face into a concentration of woe, of vindictive grief, too old for it. A few days later, the flotilla of the Northwest Company, heavily guarded, came down from Fort William and passed safely through the St. Mary's, and down behind Manitouline, to the entrance of French River. At the entrance to that river they encamped for the night, having built the packs of furs into a rampart, while men with loaded rifles kept watch until dawn. However, the Americans did not reappear.

IV

The years went by, 1815, 1816, 1817. The new house began to accumulate such objects as the old one had held, a flat silver fruit dish on a stem, a crystal bowl that, tapped, gave forth a musical note, books, the periodicals of the day, a small rosewood piano from New Haven. Another son was born, John McDougall, October 12, 1816. In 1817 Jane was home from Ireland, bringing with her the art of making paper squills, of clipping cupids for watch papers, even as she had planned, of making sponge cake, of doing her front hair in ringlets, of writing verses and setting them to music, of embroidering at a frame, of copying costumes from *Bell's Court* and *Fashionable Magazine* or from *La Belle Assemblée*. Eliza and Charlotte and the "little Miss Campbell," now grown to womanhood, but especially Charlotte, hovered about her and were quick to learn these new accomplishments. When their mother was in the room they all spoke Ojibway, and to please her and to please Jane they set Ojibway songs to simple harmonies, dropping the troublesome quarter tones from the melodies (but not always from their soft, instinctive voices), and sang them in a little group about the instrument. Dotted mull and lutestring and fine woolens began to have a place in Johnston's Montreal orders. There was no weaving and no spinning in this household, but much sewing, fitting, and embroidering. Women's shoes had not then passed from the province of the dressmaker to that of the cobbler, and although Jane occasionally held out for a pair of cloth slippers to match some special frock, moccasins were the order of the day, plain, or with flowers and figures worked in colored quills.

In 1815, before the new house was a year old, the first American visitors appeared, General Jacob Brown and his staff, spending the afternoon and evening at the Johnston house, and sitting up all night with rifles cocked, ready for a massacre which never came off. In the morning they went back down the river without having visited Lake Superior, the object of their journey. The next year it was General McComb, with the Commander of the revenue cutter from Mackinac, who spent a week with the Johnstons and, going for a picnic survey to Gros Cap, was fired on by a drunken Ojibway. He also retreated down river in the morning.

Meanwhile the Northwest and the Hudson's Bay, or rather, Lord Selkirk, who had bought up one third of the shares of that organization in order to be sure that it would grant him the favors he desired, were at war, a private war, but very bloody. Every one at the Sault knew about it, for Selkirk himself had passed through the village with a regiment of hired soldiers and the intention of taking over Fort William and arresting all available Northwesters. He had tried to persuade Ermantinger, of the British settlement, to go with him as justice of the peace and lend some color of legality to the proceedings, and Ermantinger refusing, whether because of sympathy for the Northwest or because he was really too busy, as he stated, Selkirk constituted himself a justice of the peace, and went on his way. The row had begun as early as 1814 when Miles Macdonell, in command of Selkirk's Scotch colony on the Red River, ordered that no food should be exported from the colony for a period of twelve months, and seized a quantity of grease and pemmican belonging to the Northwest Company from a fort on the Souris River. The partners of the Northwest, holding first of all the theory that the Hudson's Bay had no right whatever to grant Lord Selkirk complete military and civil jurisdiction of territory amounting to one hundred and sixteen thousand square miles, and some of that in the United States territory into the bargain, and secondly that Macdonell had no right to seize property belonging to the Northwest, held a council at Fort William, and decided that the colony must be discouraged, removed—in a word, destroyed. They went about it quietly. In 1815 Fort Gibraltar of the Northwest was stormed and taken by Colin Robertson of the Hudson's Bay, allegedly to regain some cannon belonging to the Hudson's Bay and stolen by the Northwesters. The year following, the same fort was again seized by the Hudson's Bay people, torn down, and its timbers employed to strengthen Fort Douglass, a Selkirk stronghold. The Pembina House of the Northwest also yielded to the enemy that year. In June, 1816, a brush between the two companies occurred of which the origins were still, in 1817, veiled in darkness, but in the course of which Governor Semple of the Hudson's Bay Company and twenty others were killed, the Northwesters losing only one man out of a party of sixty. This was the Battle of Seven Oaks, or Frog Plains, and was the principal reason for Selkirk's passing through St. Mary's with ten canoe loads of Swiss mercenaries, the De Meurons. He succeeded in taking Fort William, which was not expecting the attack of a regiment, and held the partners prisoner for a time, until a justice of the peace from Fort Drummond appeared with a warrant for the arrest of Lord Selkirk himself. He scoffed at the warrant, but lived to repent of having done so, and the De Meurons were disbanded at the far end of Lake Superior, and left to shift for themselves. At this point in the story the Prince Regent sent a message to his subjects in the Canadian wilderness to cease firing, and the message, being couched in formal terms and containing a severe reprimand for all persons concerned, was intrusted to a Montreal barrister to be delivered at Fort William in the summer of 1817.

This same summer the principal visitor of note at the Johnston house was Ross Cox, a Northwester, arriving not from the East, but from the farthest West, the Pacific Coast. A rotund little man with a John Bull countenance, a dark, cropped head, and an almost inexhaustible delight in the resources of rhetoric, he appeared at the Johnston door one August evening in company with the gentlemen of the Northwest House whose guest he was, and one Hector McNeill, his traveling companion. He had gone under the auspices of the Pacific Fur Company, when Astoria still belonged to John Jacob Astor, by way of the Horn to the mouth of the Columbia, and he had been there through the transfer of that far post to the enterprising Nor'westers, who first purchased it and second saw to it that it was captured by Britain in the War of 1812. After four years of the Nez Perces, the Klatsoops, the Klamaths, he had come overland, changing canoes only at that point where it became necessary to leave the headwaters of the Columbia for the long portage over the Rockies which eventually brought him to that network of streams and lakes—the Saskatchewan, Winnipic, Lac La Pluie—leading to Fort William, the Sault, and the beginning of civilization. He was not the first man, by any means, to follow that intricate trail, but neither had it yet become so well established a route— as it did later—that the Northwest Express, leaving Fort George on the Columbia the first of April regularly, was as regularly expected at Fort

William on the first of July. It was then still something of an adventure; Cox himself was a walking geography of the Northwest, a fund of curious and otherwise unobtainable anecdote, whom Johnston received with open arms.

A few hours later, Johnston, Cox, and the others left the house, proceeding through grass thick with dew and glowworms to the sandy shore and the canoe of the Northwest Company, and crossed the darkly glossy water, through the magnificent still darkness, to the Northwest House. Here they built up a fire, for the night was chill and the building near the water, brought out candles, tobacco, pipes, and Spanish wine, and seated themselves about the uncovered table.

There were seven of them—Cox himself and, beside him, to the right and left, his two traveling companions, Wentzel and McNeill; across the table from them, Johnston, Fletcher, and their two hosts of the Northwest. Wentzel had been twenty-six years in the Indian country and the service of the Northwest, twenty-six years of boreal winters, of sudden, insect-infested springs, of hazard, of treachery, of eating horse or dog or tripe de rockier, of sleeping on the ground whether marshy, dry, or stony, of solitude, in short, of the Indian trade—all of which would have meant very little to him if he could have felt himself justly rewarded. But year after year he heard of the promotion to the coveted partnership of favored youths who had passed their apprenticeship in easy posts, young men who had never gone hungry or cold, or smelt gunpowder fired in anger, sons and nephews of Montreal merchants and their friends. So Wentzel was leaving the country and the company, and not without a certain cheerful bitterness.

Hector McNeill, on the other hand, as Cox said, was leaving the country for lack of some one to fight with. McNeill was an old soldier, a fighting Irishman, had served in the peninsular campaign against Bonaparte, and against the Americans in 1812. The end of the war had found him out of work, and the Northwest, being in need of a few fighting characters in its difficulties with Lord Selkirk, had taken him over. But McNeill fought too often and too well, and the Montreal partners were inviting him to retire with their compliments and a year's advance pay. He had a singularly military countenance, ruddy, fiercely mustachioed, and bearing above the right eye the long, transverse scar of a saber wound. He was glad to be leaving. He had come to feel the Indian trade a nefarious business, and was frank in saying so, his small blue eyes twinkling sardonically the while, since all those present save one were prospering or had prospered by it.

91

This one was the barrister Fletcher, whom Cox had overtaken between Fort William and the Sault, Fletcher being then on his way back to Montreal. He had delivered the Prince Regent's epistle to the Nor'westers and their opponents, and had made as full and exact a report of events as was possible under the circumstances.

The talk began inevitably with Fort William, since Fletcher, Cox, McNeill, and Wentzel had left there but a few days before, Fletcher and Cox, at least, having seen it for the first time. From the behavior of the men whom he was sent to report of, Fletcher had anticipated something decidedly baronial, but it was one thing to expect, another to experience, the testy loyal temper of the crowd of French, half-breeds, Scotch, and Indians that thronged the wooden hall, filling it with pipe smoke, wood smoke, the smell of clothing heavy with sweat and grease. The hall was capable of seating two hundred and Fletcher had seen it filled. The tables were arranged in feudal fashion, one for the proprietors, Montreal partners, and clerks, and, farther down the hall, those for the canoemen, guides, interpreters. At the upper end of the hall was posted Thomson's map, six feet high by thirteen feet long, a panorama of the Northwest Territory, carrying the crosses for seventy-six—or was it seventy-eight?—posts of the Northwest Company, each with its name, every line set down on the authority of personal observation, every portage indicated, every little creek and lake on the route from Fort William to the Columbia drawn with minutest care. It was a valuable possession, the finest and most complete record of the Northwest then extant, and the Hudson's Bay Company had more than once regretted the short-sightedness which had informed Thomson, originally one of its own men, that it had no need of geographers and cartographers in the business. Through its charter the Hudson's Bay held claim to all lands draining into the bay of its name, but through Mackenzie, Frazer, and Thomson the Northwest held a complete and almost secret knowledge not only of the Hudson's Bay territory, but also of the vast wild country that surrounded it. Men coming in from the Northwest stood in front of the map, as Cox had done, and with a curious fascination retraced their painful journeys, and men going out for the first time tried to imagine, from its inked rivers, the eddies, morasses, rocks, décharges, carries, and stations of their tomorrow's labors.

There was also, for decoration, a portrait bust of the old Marquis, Simon McTavish himself, a full-length portrait of Nelson, and a large painting of the Battle of the Nile, these last two a gift from William McGillivray, in whose honor the fort was named. This was the hall. In the courtyard that year a number of Selkirk's disbanded De Meurons sauntered and smoked, mingling but not exactly mixing with the Nor'westers. Cox noted a Negro and one or two Sandwich Islanders. The De Meurons were Swiss, Flemish, German, Italian, Austrian, anything that Europe had chanced to contribute to a band of mercenaries. There was also the notorious Miles Macdonell, in charge of a sheriff. Outside the stockade the Indians had pitched a village, and many of the French had joined them. The rest of the voyageurs were in little camps here and there between the Indian village and the fort.

"What did they give you to eat?" asked Fletcher in a dry, pleasant, barrister's voice.

"Oh, everything," said Cox. "Venison, fowl, hot cakes, fish, eggs, potatoes, milk, and cheese. I hadn't had cheese in years. The best victuals in the world!"

Fletcher nodded. "I was never better wined in my life."

"Yes, it's fine at Fort William, if it's hard on the road," said Cox reminiscently. "Look here," he added abruptly to one of the Northwest gentlemen, "it's a bad business to keep a hundred and twenty women and children on starving rations all winter. It's bad, even for the fur trade."

"When did we do that?" inquired his host.

"At Fort Ile à la Crosse last winter. I had the news at the place. You can't deny it. And all this fort-taking and handy murdering. You ought really to check it—it's a war."

Fletcher listened in silence, his long fingers interlocked before him on the table, his head bent slightly. He had heard the whole account, colored in many different ways, many times now, but his business was to report upon events, and he listened to each new recital, waiting for some casually revealed new fact, his face still and his eye bright, like a sparrow ready to pounce upon a crumb. Johnston, beside him, put fresh tobacco in his pipe and leaned back, deliberately relaxing against the growing tension.

"Let them get out, then," said the Northwester, hotly. "Damn them, what right have they to block the Columbia route with a strip of farms? Stole our pemmican too. You know as well as I do, every man here knows, that the Columbia men have got to be provisioned from the Pembina. Selkirk plants his filthy Scotchmen there—they are filthy. One of them sold his shirt to an Indian and the whole village had the plague—to choke the life out of us. And the Hudson's Bay, on its antique charter, grants him half the Indian territory of the United States! They call that legal!" He ended with a snort.

Johnston blew a cloud of smoke above the candles, and Cox laughed. "But do you have to go to war about it?"

"We offered the whole Scots settlement a free ride to Montreal," said the Nor'wester, "and they wouldn't get out. The lummoxes!"

Fletcher said nothing.

"What about the murder of Governor Semple?" suggested Wentzel.

"They fired on us first," said the Nor'wester. He gave his glass a little push so that the sherry slopped over the top and wet his fingers. He leaned back, digging into the pocket of his smallclothes for a handkerchief, and Ross Cox picked up the conversation with his nimble tongue and conveyed it to the banks of the Columbia, to everyone's relief.

"The last cheese I had, barring this at Fort William, came on the *Isaac Todd*. Mr. Donald McTavish, God rest his soul, brought it all the way from England for us. All the way around the Horn and nothing to eat but hardtack, and he never broached our cheese. He was a nobleman. He was drowned in the Columbia. Did any of you know him?"

"Old Henry's nephew was drowned at the same time, I believe," said the gentleman of the Northwest, still wiping his fingers.

"There was another chap with him," agreed Cox, "whose name escapes me. I saw their grave. It's at the edge of the forest outside the stockade. A curious place. The ground is matted as thick as a rug with wild honeysuckle, and there's not the sound of a bird or an insect even. The silence is a curious fact I've noted about those forests."

"Alexander Henry the Younger," the Northwest man completed his information. "He used to be at the Pembina. Was there when the Sioux appeared one morning and scalped his father-in-law."

"Ah," said Cox, "a father-in-law. I think he had another at the Columbia. There's many a better man been ruined by too many Indian fathers-in-law. The Indians have their virtues, I admit them, but their morals are as scanty as their clothing, aye, and frequently as in great need of cleansing."

"On the contrary," said Johnston, leaning forward and resting the bowl of his white clay pipe on the bare wood of the table, the stem supported meanwhile on his fingers, spread spider-shaped, "on the contrary, their morals are excellent. Cleanliness is a part of their religion, and chastity, my dear fellow, that most rare element, more often to be found among them than among their white superiors."

"If you had seen a certain gentleman of the Northwest, who shall be nameless," said Cox, leaning back in his chair and smiling broadly, "if you had seen this gentleman, as I have, and not so long ago, stuffed naked into the steaming entrails of a slaughtered horse, and the edges of the orifice tucked in neatly about his neck, and all because of his too frequent amorous relations with the chaste Klatsoop ladies . . ." He finished with a wave of the hand.

Fletcher, greatly amused, said, "As a cure, how did it serve?"

94

"Oh, excellently," said Cox. "It needed only three horses to restore him to comfort. He swore it was capital. I assure you, it was very quaint to see this canny Scot's countenance projecting from the belly of a dead mare."

But Johnston, still leaning forward, his hand and his pipe still resting on the table, said: "Gentlemen, I protest. I do not speak of your outrageous Pacific tribes, which I do not know, but of a people at my very door, and with which I feel myself honored, gentlemen, honored to be allied. And now, gentlemen, I beg to be excused."

Cox, somewhat surprised, surveyed him as he stood up, in build rather portly, but erect, the flesh soft about the chin and mouth, the mouth itself at this moment very firm, the naturally ruddy face slightly pale, and the hazel eyes, in anger become black, small, and penetrating, all the more striking because of the gray and blond hair of the temples. He stood a moment with his hand on the back of his chair. Then, tossing his pipe on the table so that the long stem snapped, he bowed, and left the room. Cox followed him instantly. At the landing, while the boatmen brought the canoe around, he made his apology, unable to see in the darkness the face of the man he was attempting to conciliate. Presently Johnston said: "You apologize, sir, like a gentleman. You will dine with me tomorrow." And as a further sign of forgiveness, after the canoe had pushed off into the watery blackness, Johnston's voice returned, "I have some excellent Irish mountain dew in my locker which never saw the face of an exciseman."

The answer of the Hudson's Bay Company to the Prince Regent's reprimand, expressed by Governor Williams of the company, was as follows: "I do not care a curse for the Prince Regent's proclamation; Lord Bathurst and Sir John Sherbrooke by whom it was framed are damned rascals. I act upon the charter of the Hudson's Bay Company, and as governor and magistrate in these territories. I have sufficient authority and will do as I think proper." He concluded by stating his further intention to "drive out of the country every damned Nor'wester it contains, or perish in the attempt." The attempt included, in 1819, a second capture of Fort William, with all its goods and stores. It also included the tragic death of a partner of the Northwest, Benjamin Frobisher, who, being captured and confined at York House, made his escape in the deep of winter and perished, before he could reach a settlement, of hunger and cold. The following year the two companies, somewhat sobered by this last death, consolidated under the name of the Hudson's Bay Company, Alexander Mackenzie's dream coming true to that extent.

V

The mirror was long and narrow, perhaps twelve inches wide, and the fluted gold frame was also narrow. At the four corners were carved the smiling heads of young girls, and each head was crowned with grape leaves. A very aristocratic little mirror. It reflected in its depths a room full of ladies and gentlemen, lit by wax candles and by firelight, a room of which the walls were of logs, but of logs rubbed with beeswax to a fine luster, and hung with pictures in gold frames; it reflected from its shallower surface the slightly anxious face of a serious-minded young man who had a few moments before been made to remember, for the first time in many weeks, by the sight of a charming young woman, his personal appearance. He had made himself as neat as he could before leaving the quarters which he shared with certain young army officers, but at the moment he wished to be assured of something besides neatness. There was not much time, however, in which to ruminate about the matter.

Mrs. John Johnston was entertaining guests at dinner, that is, she was performing those duties which her mother would have performed in her father's lodge and which she would have considered it beneath her personal dignity to alter in any way. She stood at the door while the gentlemen were arriving, General Cass and his staff, Lieutenant John Pierce (brother of Franklin Pierce, later President of the United States) in charge of twenty-two soldiers from Mackinac, a guard of honor, or a precaution; Lieutenant Eneas Mackey, in charge of the ten soldiers of the expedition; Major Robert Forsyth, the General's private secretary; Captain Douglass, astronomer and topographer; Mr. Trowbridge, assistant topographer; Dr. Alexander Wolcot, physician; the young Mr. Henry Rowe Schoolcraft, geologist; Mr. James C. Doty, official secretary for the expedition; for this was the Expedition to the Sources of the Mississippi River, sent out in the year 1820 to explore the upper regions of the great river and to take note of very many other things by the way.

Mrs. Johnston welcomed the gentlemen, regretted that her husband, who was then traveling in England, could not welcome them also, introduced them to her daughter Jane, her daughter Eliza, her daughter Charlotte, three comely young women ranging in age from twenty years to fourteen. Behind her stood her son George, who, as head of the house in the absence of his father and of his brother, Lewis Saurin Johnston, had invited the Governor and the savants to take all their meals at the Johnston house, and who now served as interpreter for his mother, not to translate the English speeches of her guests, for she understood the language perfectly, but to translate for them the formal Ojibway greetings which she refused to give in English. She stayed with them until a certain ease of manner seemed to have fallen upon the lighted room, and then, at the moment when the guests were invited to be seated at the long table at the far end of the room, she disappeared into the kitchen, and Miss Jane Johnston occupied the place of hostess with the General at her right hand. The General was then approaching forty; his face, not yet as jowled and heavy as in his later portraits, was nevertheless, in spite of all its ruddy health, somewhat forbidding and severe. Jane thought she had never seen so cliff-like a countenance. The features seemed to retreat upward and backward, perpendicular and unassailable, from the determined cleft in his chin to the high forehead against which the hair, cut short and brushed forward in the Roman manner, gave something of a Roman character. He was in uniform. He was a general, and he was also the first permanent governor of the Michigan Territory. Jane's voice, with its cultivated Irish accent and its tremulous liquid quality, derived from her mother's ancestry, became very low, obliging the Governor of Michigan to bend in order to hear her. He bent from the waist, as if he had a ramrod down his neck.

The meal went forward in ceremonious, orderly fashion, Jane presiding and eating very little in her anxiety to see her guests well served. Jane's face, an oval, faintly ivory, a little high in the cheek bones, a little wide in the jaw, had the mobility of her father's. The line of her eyebrows wavered and flared off in a pretty arch; her eyes were as dark as her mother's. Her hair, parted in the middle and brought smoothly down to two silky clusters of ringlets in front of her ears, was tucked up behind with a comb, an ivory comb once her mother's, and her hair was dark. She wore a tight-bodiced taffeta dress with a round dimity collar through which a ribbon was threaded; her ankles, tucked away under the table, were incased in black taffeta leggins brought in tight at the ankle and ruffled at the bottom like the little white pantalettes then recently in fashion for children. This was a concession to her mother, an adaptation of the leggins of the Indian women, and a rather charming one, she thought. Halfway down the table her sister Charlotte, in a similar collar, a similar dress, her hair fixed in the same way, looked like another, younger Jane. Jane, sparing an eye from the General, could see that Charlotte was being amiable, her pretty teeth showing in a smile, her head nodding, but Eliza, across the table from her, Eliza with her darker features and her straighter back, was speaking only Ojibway and not a great deal of that.

The wax candles in the silver holders flickered brightly, ran off now and again into smoky points as a slight commotion in the air unsteadied their

97

flame. The narrow goblets, half filled with port or sherry, dropped little pools of ruddy or amber light on the fine Irish damask, and a young Indian girl, stationed behind Jane's shoulder, waited to remove or pass any dishes that might be required. But for all the order and elaborate courtesy of the meal, a slight uneasiness overhung the room. George constantly lifted his eyes to the door through which his guests had entered, and those whose backs were toward it seemed to cock their ears in its direction, listening to each other's remarks with the thinnest attention. And well they might, for the events of the past afternoon had not been tranquilizing.

The Expedition to the Sources of the Mississippi River, dispatched by Mr. Calhoun, Secretary of War, under the leadership of General Cass, was avowedly scientific in its intentions. The members of the expedition realized, however, that in the eyes of Mr. Calhoun it had more serious things to accomplish than the collection of fresh-water shells and mineral specimens from the shores of Lake Superior and its tributaries. The British fort on Drummond Island, removed to that place after the surrender of Mackinac and the destruction of the old fort on St. Joseph's, was attracting unto itself, by gifts, flattery, and constant endeavor, the loyalty and affection of the Indians of the north, loyalty already British and slow to change since the events of 1812 and 1814. Twice since the close of the war, American military had attempted to enter the Great Lake, and twice had found it wiser to postpone the attempt, and the Secretary realized, that for all the Treaty of Ghent, and before it, the Treaty of Paris, the country beyond the Sault could hardly be considered as United States territory. Cass had received, therefore, instructions to treat with the Indians and pave the way for the founding of an American military post at St. Mary's. And for this purpose he had arrived the evening before, at sunset, with his Mackinac boat, or barge, filled with twenty soldiers, and his small fleet of canoes, at the beach between the Indian green and the Johnston house, and had there disembarked and pitched camp in the long pearly twilight between eight and nine o'clock of a summer evening. The Indians who had gathered on the shore to watch him approach fired their salute, and retreated to a distance to watch him disembark, and the ladies of the Johnston family, almost as shy, promenaded the beach in front of their house observing this rapid springing into being of a small village of canvas tents.

The expedition was encamped at the site of the old Nolin house, the Governor's markee and the tents of the "savants" occupying the most northern position, and that nearest the Indian village. To their right, as they lay facing the river, were the tents of the escort proper of the expedition,

98

under Eneas Mackey, and beyond them, still close to the river, the escort which had accompanied them from Mackinac. Little was attempted that night save the bare setting in order of the camp. The men, who had come that day from a point near Drummond, perhaps forty-five miles, without counting the added labor caused by the West Neebish Rapids, flesh drenched with sun and wind, exhausted, released, lay down at once to sleep. Young Henry Schoolcraft, in the group nearest the Indians and the rapids, lay awake for a short time listening to the drum—there was a wabbeno ceremony in progress—now heard by him for the first time, and to the rumble of the water beyond. The two sounds merged for him into something wild and romantic. He was aware that he was resting with a short rifle within easy reach of his hand because of that monotonous drum, but he was too fatigued to stay awake long to enjoy the sensation. The air, through which he had moved all day, fragrant and living, and since nightfall extremely cold, descended on him in an overwhelming flood, and he was asleep.

The Governor's markee became the scene of the council the next day. The sides were rolled up, making of it a tent à l'abri; from a short distance those outside could see quite well what took place inside. The Governor was seated before a small table, near him his interpreter, James Riley, a Saginaw half-breed, and his secretary. The gifts for the Indians were arranged on the ground beside him. The Ojibway leaders entered in due order and seated themselves with dignity on the ground opposite the Governor. They were in full council regalia, regalia not so purely Indian as that of the councils of twenty years ago. Nevertheless they were as a group sufficiently strange and impressive to the members of the expedition, and it was noted by the Americans that nearly every Indian present wore on some sort of band or ribbon about his neck a silver British medal. It was high noon before the ceremonies began, with the smoking of the pipe, noon of a day of great beauty and tranquillity. The salutations of the six directions duly completed by all the Indian delegates, Riley, the interpreter, stood up, and at the Governor's bidding explained to the Ojibways that in times past their fathers had given or sold to the French a certain number of square miles of land there at the rapids; that the British, conquering the French, had fallen heir to this land, and had no doubt also paid for it many times with gifts; that now the Americans, having conquered the British, owned this land, and that, although by the right of double conquest they felt it to be theirs without a doubt, they were willing and ready to purchase it again with gifts, and they requested the present holders of the land to make it over to them with a treaty and a grant. There was a pause in which the Ojibways seemed to confer among themselves, but more by glances than by words. At last one of the old men rose, his body naked above the hips, swathed below in a scarlet blanket, on his breast a large silver medal; in his hair, which was gray, eagle feathers, one stripped halfway down the line of the rib, one painted with vermilion. His face was lined with green and white. He said briefly that neither he nor his friends knew anything about such grants of land, and having said as much and no more, sat down again. No one else rose, but a murmur of assent passed down the triple rows of dark and gaudy bodies, and Riley, at a word from the Governor, made his speech again, in an attempt to impress upon these people, these essential warriors, the right of conquest by war. As the Indians neither assented nor protested again, but sat in a profound negative silence, the Governor instructed Riley to proceed with the distribution of the presents. The first of these, tobacco, was brought forward and dropped in a heap before the chiefs, and ignored. The other presents, strouds, blankets, traps, kettles, were ranged beyond it. The interpreter made another speech, reminding the Ojibways that their White Father in Washington wished them well, and hoped rather to make them presents of blankets than presents of bullets. Their White Father wished a little place on which to land. Would they not give it to him? The Indians conferred among themselves, this time more volubly, and the nominal head of the Saulteur band, Shingabawossin, the Image Stone, rising, made a more cordial speech. His people would, he said, be happy to give the White Father a little place on which to land, but he hoped no fort would be built, and no garrison stationed on this land, because, he concluded, significantly, if a fort should be built, he was afraid his young men might "kill the cattle of the garrison."

Cass then rose and announced that the Ojibways might set their fears at rest, for as certainly as the sun which had risen that morning would that evening set, so certainly would there be a fort and garrison at the Sault, grant or no grant. Riley interpreted, and the faces on the opposite side of the tent, which had begun to relax into a faint mobility, stiffened, and George Johnston, seated between the two groups, sighed inwardly. There was no lack of speeches now from the Ojibways. The afternoon wore on, the conference reaching no conclusion. Shingwakonse, the Little Pine, added his voice to that of the hostile element. Shingabawossin remained, as at first, conciliatory. The Indians grew a little restless, and one in the front row, reaching forward with the stem of his pipe, raked toward himself a twist of tobacco from the pile of gifts, with his scalping knife cut off a small piece and began to grind it to powder in the palm of his hand. This action precipitated into the middle of the tent a tall figure in a British officer's coat, breech clout, legging, and moccasins, who struck his lance furiously into the ground so that it quivered upright, independent, beside him, and began a harangue addressed not, at the beginning, to the Americans, but to the Indian at his feet, who held the half-mortared tobacco still in the hollow of his hand.

"It is not fitting," he announced in Ojibway, "it is not fitting that an Ojibway warrior should accept tobacco thrown on the ground like bones to a dog. It is not fitting that the Ojibway nation should accept gifts from their enemies, nor welcome them to their country. Do you wish to fill your hunting grounds with enemies that you speak of giving land to these people? It is yet only a little while since Shingwakonse led his people to fight at Mishinimackinong. It is only a little while since I, Sassaba, fought with my brother at the river they call Thames, and my brother was killed in that fight. The Americans have not covered the grave of my brother. They have not covered the graves of the people of the Little Pine. They have not built again the houses they burned." He turned here and looked George Johnston full in the eye. "They come among us asking for land. I, Sassaba, I who am a chief of the Ojibways, I say they shall have no land."

Above the scarlet of his coat, the gold of the epaulettes, his face, dark and violent, painted with bear grease, indigo, and vermilion, turned slowly from face to face of those seated in the tent, the eagle feather in his hair trembling slightly with each motion of his head. He then deliberately kicked the presents which lay before him, seized his lance, and proceeding through the center of the group, left the tent at the open northern side. The crowd outside made way for him, and he went straight to the Indian village. The conference seemed to be ended with his departure. Many of the Ojibways got up and followed him, more slowly, it is true, and most of them taking a formal if somewhat strained farewell of their host. Cass hastened to close the procedure, and in a few minutes the tent was completely empty, the presents lying there under the aqueous shadow of the canvas.

The Americans saw in the distance the figure of Sassaba descend a small gulley, mount, enter the village, disappear; but shortly after, a commotion ran through all their group as the red of the British flag mounted by little jerks a flagpole in the center of the village, where it hung slack in the windless air above the gray and silvery shaggy lodges and the bristling lodge poles.

The Governor was very angry. His clifflike face tightened and paled slightly and, nodding to Riley the interpreter to follow, he set off for the Indian camp, much like an irate parent on the trail of a refractory child. The gentlemen of his party, being armed, offered, and were anxious, to accompany him, but he waved them back, and they saw him, with a pace so different from that of the lithe and arrogant Indian who had preceded him, cross the little ravine, mount the slope, and disappear among the lodges. For a few tense moments they saw no other sign of him. They waited, fingering their short rifles; and then they saw the red flag descend from its pole. After about fifteen minutes the Governor returned, carrying the defeated emblem over his arm, and grimly humorous. He had entered Sassaba's wigwam and lectured him roundly on the etiquette of flags. He had declared moreover that if the Ojibways should ever again attempt to fly any flag but the American on the south side of the rapids he would "set a strong foot upon their rock and crush them utterly."

It was fortunate for Cass that he had gone alone. The Indians, although they admired his personal bravery, were far from convinced by his speech, and a small armed force in company with him would have been the signal for an immediate attack. As it was, the Americans at a safe distance began to clean their muskets; the jingling of the ramrods was heard as far away as the Indian camp, and presently canoes laden with women and children and some household goods began to push off from the south shore, pointing their prows toward Canada. They did not attempt to dismantle their wigwams, however, and no man left the village.

Sassaba's speech had come at the late end of the afternoon; it was now evening, daylight and darkness balanced against each other in the air, a chillness rising from the water and the dew gathering on the grass and on the sloping sides of the canvas tents. A few small fires were lighted on the high land where the Indians waited, and the Americans were also making fires. In this somewhat fictitious quiet George Johnston stopped to renew his dinner invitation to the Governor and his staff, and took the path along the shore to the Johnston house. Near the house he met his mother, who said to him:

"He is a brave man, this General, but he does not know how to speak to my people. Go back now to the village and tell the principal men to come to me here in the store. If Sassaba will come, bring him too. But bring especially Shingwakonse, Shingabawossin. Tell them to come quietly, so that not the whole village shall know they have come, nor the Americans."

So that George, sitting in his father's place at the long lighted table, had in his nostrils the particular odor, so deeply a part of his childhood, of the bark lodges in which he had found Little Pine, the Image Stone, and his uncle, the First Born, an odor of earth, smoke, and sweet grass, smoke-saturated clothing and burnt fish; and beyond the fresh, rather nondescript faces of the American guests, and the glossy curls of his sisters, he saw the strongly marked features, the long thin lips, the dark jutting brows and heavy cheek bones, of these Indian cousins of his, faces of men at once so much more determined, serious, and self-reliant than the white men, and, in certain aspects, so much more childish.

He remembered other occasions on which his father and mother had stood as mediators and interpreters between their two races. He remembered General Jacob Brown seated at this same table the year after the American attempt on Mackinac, in a house so newly rebuilt that the chips and shavings had not yet entirely disappeared from the earth about the doorstep, while his father dispensed his usual hospitality as freely and serenely as if there had never been a war; and he remembered old Nolin, the French trader, now departed, entering through the door from the kitchen, and stooping over his father's shoulder as he conferred with him in French. In landing, that afternoon, one of the General's escort had taken the ensign from the stern of the boat and planted the shaft of it in the sand, feeling, no doubt, something like Cortez; an Ojibway had as promptly flourished his hatchet and with a single blow cut the shaft clean through, so that the stars and stripes wavered and fell upon the beach, to the indignation of the Americans, who would have attacked the Ojibways then and there without considering the consequences. His father, coming up just then, had restrained them. The Indians he had sent back to their lodges, the Americans he had invited to "his bandbox" for tea. And all so easily had he accomplished this that the Americans were only amused, and their anger had dissipated itself over the teacups and among the books and pictures. Tea had prolonged itself until dinner time, and dinner had reached the stage of raisins and wine before the old Frenchman had appeared. A young Indian girl had come to him saying:

"I went to Mrs. Johnston's. They told me in the kitchen, Mrs. Johnston is giving a dinner; she cannot see anybody. So I come to you, but I cannot stay. I crept out under the back of my lodge, and I leave a bundle all covered upon my mat where I sleep, because they have put a guard all around the village and no one is allowed to leave it. They are going to kill the Americans tonight. Not soon, but when they have gone from Mrs. Johnston's to their own tents. They will kill them all."

John Johnston turned from the Frenchman and related this to his guests, smiling a little; but he concluded his explanation thus:

"I have but newly received from Montreal the guns and ammunition which I have planned to use in trade this next winter. They are at your disposal, gentlemen; my clerks will get them ready for you. And if you keep a brisk fire going tonight with a good guard, very likely there will be no trouble. I shall station my son and Mr. Holliday, my head clerk, whose acquaintance you made this afternoon, between your camp and the village, but merely for the sake of your feeling an added security."

The Americans sat up most of the night and, the impression of Johnston's easy smile lingering in their minds, were not sure but that the whole matter was a lark. George and Holliday heard whistles in the underbrush near by, but no scalpers appeared. In the morning the Americans were easily persuaded to return downstream, rather than go on their intended way into the lake.

Another time the situation had borne for the Americans an even more innocent aspect. His mother and the Indian women who helped her in the kitchen had packed for General McComb and his staff, who had then been the Johnstons' guests for a week, several picnic hampers, with cold meats and the cakes and bread and pastries at which his sisters were so adept. His father had supervised the stocking of a liquor case, and although business prevented him from attending them personally on their excursion into Lake Superior, he had sent his men to convey them, and they were to travel in one of his canoes instead of in their own more slow and clumsy vessels. The canoe was sent up through the rapids first, as was customary, half loaded, and towed from the shore with a cod line, the loading to be completed at the head of the portage. The party of officers followed along the path, chatting as they went, George and his father with them, and when they were about halfway, one of the voyageurs, a chap by the name of LeClair, came back to meet them, declaring that all things were ready for "mon général et ces messieurs." They affixed the American colors to the stern, and set off with one of those chansons without the aid of which many a difficult traverse might never have been accomplished.

La fille du Roi son vout chassan,
Avec son grande fusée de l'argent . . .

The summit of Cape Iroquois showed blue to the north across the brilliant water; the water was ruffled but not dangerous, and it was with pleasure and not a little pride that John Johnston watched the canoe swing out and take its course for Point aux Pins.

About an hour later the whole party was back in the Johnston living-room, a very excited LeClair recounting the events of the trip in a confusion of languages. "We arrive, mon bourgeois, and I leap into the water to carry ashore mon général. But I hear a grand cry from the village, a veritable war whoop, and this Indian who is drunk comes running down the shore and draws upon me with his pistol. It is no doubt because they have seen the flag, for this Indian, did he not sleep with me in my blanket one month ago? But he is very drunk. God is with me, and his pistol snaps. Dieu merci, it does not go off, and I hasten and knock him down. But they are all drunk in this village, and as I see them coming upon me, I run back into the water and push off with the canoe. I will go back alone, myself, yes, alone, but I will not go back with ces messieurs. No. Tomorrow when they are sober those Indians will be worse than when they are drunk. I am very sorry, mon bourgeois, you may dismiss me if you like, but I cannot take mon général back to that village."

He stood there, wet and stubborn, his hands spread palms out in a gesture of absolute refusal. Johnston was furious, not at LeClair, but at the Ojibways, for they had insulted his guests and made a mock of his hospitality. He wanted to send all his men in a body to chastise the village. He stamped up and down the room with his hands behind his back, uttering imprecations, orders, and apologies, like some old Scottish border chieftain, and then, ever volatile and amenable, had sent his men to their quarters, and called for the girls to unpack the hampers in the living-room. The picnic took place at the long table, and before it was over, Johnston felt, as did LeClair and Neengay, that it would be folly for the Americans to attempt to explore Superior that season. A band of drunken Indians at Point aux Pins might be dealt with; beyond Point aux Pins lay river, island, and harbor, league upon league, each increasingly remote and hostile. Johnston's indignation could not reach far enough.

The Americans, George knew, felt it discourteous to insist. They retired to bed all vastly amused, as at some well-staged play, and in the morning set off for Mackinac with many protestations of gratitude. And now as the Governor leaned forward to catch some tremulous remark of Jane's, and as Charlotte turned her pretty smile upon young Henry Schoolcraft, George thought of the old men in blankets and feathers who were waiting in the store or office from which his father habitually carried on the negotiations of the Indian trade. He wondered how much he exaggerated the risks run by these visiting Americans, and how much, secure in their status of citizens of the United States, they underestimated the danger. Certainly the power of the United States far exceeded the power of these dark relatives of his, and certainly his relatives would inevitably feel it. In the meantime they did not know that they were about to be conquered, and they were capable of doing infinite mischief. Into his concern for the safety of these men who were his guests crept a great sadness and pity for the men who waited in the log outhouse for a word of moderation and forbearance.

That evening Shingwakonse was wounded in the shoulder by Sassaba. It was the only casualty of the night, and it occurred on the path from the Johnston house to the Indian village. After the guests had departed George joined his mother in his father's office. She had already been there for some time; the council was well under way, and the small room thick with smoke. They handed George the pipe when he entered, and after he had saluted the six cardinal points and returned the reed with its red sandstone bowl and its ornaments of feathers to Shingabawossin, his mother said:

"Tell them, ningwizzis, tell them, my son, that what I say is true. The day is past for them to resist the Americans. It is now the day for them to receive them kindly and make brothers of them. It is true that many have been killed. It is time now to cover their graves with gifts. The Americans will do this. I promise that it shall be done, but the Ojibways must make gifts also."

So George made his speech. He explained that the Americans were numberless, that they would keep coming forever, that it would be impossible ever to kill them all. He said: "This is the hour in which to choose. This is the hour in which to make them friends or enemies," and ended his oration with this sentence: "The firing of one gun will bring ruin to your tribe and to the Chippewa nation, so that not a dog will be left to howl in your villages."

The room was quiet when he sat down. The faces were turned to Neengay, who was motionless, her face calm and authoritative, showing neither reproach nor fear. She did not urge them further, but she was the daughter of the man who had never counseled them wrongly, whom success had followed as the fawn the doe, and who, twenty-seven years after his death, had become for the Ojibways a legend of the utmost potency. She had, moreover, power over the white race, and these people had been her guests. At last Shingabawossin rose and, putting aside his blanket from the shoulder, held out his arm, braceleted above the elbow with a band of virgin copper, the arm extended full length before him, palm down.

"My mother," he said, "you are right. You think of the happiness of your people. Sassaba thinks only, 'I have lost a brother.' Shingwakonse will go to Sassaba, and will say to him for us, 'Stop what you are now doing, put away your war club.'" He gathered his blanket about him and sat down.

Shingwakonse did not go unaccompanied. Most of the council, including the Johnstons, followed him. They met Sassaba on the portage road, stripped of his scarlet coat and epaulettes, naked save for a breech clout and moccasins, and painted from head to foot. Shingwakonse halted him in the name of the council, and ordered him to return to his lodge. Sassaba stopped in the middle of the path, whirling his war club above his head, and declared: "Shingwakonse, you also led your people against the Americans six years ago. I now lead mine again. You cannot stop me." And, quite without warning, he brought his war club down straight before him in a terrific blow. The Little Pine dodged, without shifting his feet, and received the blow, glancing, on his left shoulder. Little Pine then addressed himself to the Indians who had assembled at the back of Sassaba, and prevailed upon them to return to their lodges. Neengay followed them into their village.

Shortly before midnight the council reconvened in Johnston's office, all the principal men of the tribe except Sassaba being present. They sent for Cass, and the treaty of June 16, 1820, was drawn up and signed. Shingwakonse, proud of having two cognomens, set his name down as Lavoine Bart. The treaty granted four square miles on the river's edge to the Americans, and it reserved for the Ojibways the right to fish in the rapids in perpetuo. The gifts which bought this priceless acreage were brought forward then and there and distributed, and George Johnston sent to the house for two bottles of wine and for tobacco, with which eternal friendship was pledged between all those present.

For the Ojibways it was the beginning of the end. They were not to be deported, like the Potawatomis, exiled into unfamiliar and hostile territory; they were to stay where they were, in their own country, to be gradually obliterated by the inevitable tide of settlers. There was one person at the council who realized the fact powerfully if dimly, and this was Neengay. She had done what she could for her people, but her heart was sad. General Cass, having thanked her personally, indited a letter to her husband, in England, praising her, and saying that the United States could never repay the debt of gratitude it owed her.

The camp between the village and the Johnston house, although greatly set at ease by the signing of the treaty, did not dismiss its guards until daybreak. The Indians of the expedition, ten Ottawas, taken along in the double capacity of canoemen and hunters, at the first threat of hostilities declared their neutrality. They would not, they said, do anything to harm the Americans; neither would they carry arms against their own people. One young Ojibway, who had been added to the party at Mackinac, came to the Governor and asked for ammunition and a musket. He asked to be stationed between the camp and the Indian village. This young savage went by the name of Buck, and Mr. Trowbridge, hearing his request to the Governor, and knowing of the refusal of the Ottawas, set him down in his reminiscences as the hero of the occasion, after the General and Mrs.

107

Johnston. It was some fifteen years before Schoolcraft discovered that Buck translates into Ahdeek, and that this particular Ahdeek was the youngest son of Waub-ojeeg, the White Fisher.

VI

July, 1822. Sassaba, stark naked save for a gray wolfskin about his middle, fastened in such a way that the brush hung down behind and beat against his thighs as he walked, paraded down the portage path, gesticulating fiercely and mysteriously to the atmosphere. He entered the French village and proceeded down its single street, stopping to peer in windows, to shake doors that sometimes opened to him and sometimes did not. There was no malice in his actions, but an intense, thwarted fury, and he occasionally beat himself on the breast. He was very drunk. The season was early summer and both the villages, French and Indian, were filled to overflowing with returned trappers and canoemen. The Indian village, increased to perhaps three times its usual winter size, was extended by row upon row of lodges and campfires; the Canadian village had built no more houses—it was simply crowded. From nearly every door came the sound of revel, although it was still morning. Billiards and cards and wine were the chief amusements. In the evening, dancing would be added to these.

On the Indian green a very lively game of boggatiway was in progress. Little naked boys, and girls almost as naked, ran whooping with netted sticks after a deerhide ball, which they caught up in the nets and flung hither and yon.

John Johnston was busy in his office, receiving visitors from L'Anse Kewenon, from Ontonagon, from La Pointe, checking off debts as certain Indians brought in their promised bundles of fur, extending credit, granting charity. The kitchen of the Johnston house, where Neengay was most often to be found, was full of Indians, coming or going, or seating themselves on their heels to wait for a visit with Neengay, or for a gift of bread. Indians who had suffered all winter with pleurisy, detained at their trapping grounds by the need of food or by the appalling white drifts, waited now for Johnston to come with his gleaming little lances to give them relief. All the tales of the winter—of death, of illness, of birth, stratagem, cheating, cowardice, hunger—were repeated to Neengay in the Johnston kitchen, and all the remedies she could devise from the traditions of her people, from practical knowledge, and from her husband's tradition and experience—herb teas, castor oil, balms, unguents, charms even—were accepted with respect and gratitude by these people who seemed to become, winter after winter, more and more susceptible to illness and disaster.

And meanwhile Americans in uniform were cutting timber in the woods, hauling logs, sharpening picket stakes; and the old Nolin house, once called the Château of the Northwest Company, was being dismembered and remodeled, for Fort Brady was under construction, to occupy the ground once occupied by the Old French Fort, then by Cadotte and the Northwest Company, then by old Nolin. The holes for the pickets of the stockade were dug four feet deep. The pickets, all cedar logs six inches thick sharpened on the ends, were planted side by side, as close as they could be placed, standing twelve feet clear of the leveled ground. Their line ran down to the water's edge and into the water in order that in time of siege the garrison should not be cut off from so necessary an article. In places the old stockade of the Northwest Company's Château was allowed to remain.

For Jane and Charlotte the Sault had become overnight a metropolis. In the tents, pitched in the form of a square between the Johnston residence and the foundations of Fort Brady, were several young American women with their small children, families of the officers of the garrison, transplanted from Sacketts Harbor, New York. They brought the latest news of fashion, the newest wrinkles in housekeeping, but they made the girls smile when they asked where they might purchase fresh vegetables and lamb chops. It was true that the Johnstons occasionally had lamb chops, that, in the winter, they had bacon and smoked ham, and, very rarely, beef, but this was only when their father made up his mind to have slaughtered one of his prized domestic herd. For the most part the meat prepared in the Johnston kitchen consisted of venison, bear meat, rabbit, or wild fowl, and as for vegetables, they had them from their own garden while the season lasted. They were happy to make the ladies a present of some, but they never sold them. In the garden, picking currants from the row of hardy bushes, they discussed the ladies minutely, and when the currants were picked Jane went into the house for a pair of shears, and began to cut fresh flowers for the vases, for at noon the new Indian agent, who was none other than that interesting Mr. Schoolcraft of General Cass's expedition, would be there to lunch with them. Her father had taken a great fancy to him, and had found in him a man to appreciate the cabinet of curios which he had been collecting these twenty years. Jane was very quiet in their presence; she doubted if Mr. Schoolcraft noticed her at all. But the flowers seemed important.

Sassaba staggered, and reaching his dark hand to the whitewashed pickets of the stockade nearest him, laid his head on his outstretched arm for a moment and wept. He was still in the French village and he was undoubtedly very drunk. Among the British his nickname had been the Count, but not since the ceremonies for the installation of the Indian agency, some eight days ago, had he worn the scarlet coat with the gold epaulettes, nor the gilt-handled sword, which had once given him so much pleasure. On that day, a day of crystal, Colonel Brady had drawn up his troops in the form of a hollow square, and inside this wall, brilliant with color and military trappings, all the important Ojibways of the village, both men and women, had been received while Brady introduced them to their Little Father, Henry Schoolcraft, who was to be the ear of the Great Father at Washington, in order that the Great Father and his children might speak together and understand each other. All the Indians said, "Hoh!" to this, in sign of their approval, and Sassaba himself found nothing very wrong with it. Then Schoolcraft had stepped forward and read the speech which he had carefully prepared earlier that morning in the privacy of his room. The Indians were well impressed by this also; the paper impressed them. This led to the distribution of presents, and to another speech by Colonel Brady in which he promised the Ojibways that he would not attempt to set his fort or any of his buildings either upon the familiar site of their village or on the high land near the eastern end of the rapids, the land which had been since time immemorial their tribal burying ground. This promise brought a chorus of "Hoh's" from the Indians, but from Sassaba it brought a brief but violent speech, which was never interpreted. John Johnston, standing, as George had stood at the council two years ago, between the Americans and the Ojibways, turned abruptly upon Sassaba and rebuked him sharply and briefly. This rebuke was not translated either. The council paused. Sassaba looked at Johnston, first with fury, then, realizing more fully who it was had spoken to him thus, with a certain surprise, and then, with an expression of greatest pride and grief, had left the council and had not returned. For the rest, Schoolcraft recorded in his journal that the event had gone off as well as he could have wished, and he hoped for increasingly cordial relations with his Indian charges. He even made a profound promise to himself to study the customs and the language of this strange people in order to be able to deal more justly and amicably with them.

Meanwhile, in Sassaba's tent, which was neither of deerskin nor bark nor woven appukwas, but of canvas, and which had formerly been his pride, the red coat lay unconsidered; and with it a bundle consisting of a sash, a

110

pair of gloves, a pair of silk stockings, a pair of English shoes, an umbrella, and two white linen ruffled shirts, once opened frequently for the edification of visitors, remained untouched, and slowly, as the summer progressed, assumed a faintly damp and moldy smell. These were not his only foreign treasures. He had also cups and saucers, knives and forks, a dozen silver teaspoons, a dozen tablespoons, and a silver tea tray. With these he put his silver British medal. The flag, in which they had all been wrapped in days gone by, was in the possession of Governor Cass. Sassaba clutched hard at the rough whitewashed wood and rolled his head slowly from side to side, face downward on his arm. Already the children were calling him My-een-gun, the Wolf, and learning to keep a safe distance from him.

At three o'clock, since the Johnstons dined at four, Jane and Charlotte were setting the table, laying the silver knives and forks on the freshly ironed damask. The sibilance of their skirts followed them from place to place, and Jane's face, as she bent above her light work, was contented and sweet. She had not been well the winter before—many unimportant infirmities, slight colds and bilious fevers, had followed each other in a too rapid succession—but the summer weather was doing her good. Before they had finished they saw, through the open window, their father and Mr. Schoolcraft enter the garden, and proceed slowly toward the house, stopping often to chat, or pausing over a plant or a flower. Since his return from Ireland Mr. Johnston had taken to using a cane. A dropsy in the leg and ankle made him limp, and he felt besides a sort of fatigue, an advancing shadow of old age, which made him find a pleasant security in the companionship of a bit of polished hickory. His hair had grayed in the last few years also, and visitors remarked merely "traces of the original Scotch yellow." He stooped a little. He had hoped while in London to obtain some recompense from the government for his losses during the war, and, meeting Ross Cox on the street while there, had declared to him his belief that he was about to have some success. His hopes had dwindled slowly. Now, two years later, he knew that the British would not do anything for him. Their reason was that he had been living on the American side. Perhaps if they had been victorious they would have been more generous. The Americans also refused to recompense him in any way for the havoc caused by the unauthorized raid of Captain Holmes, on the more reasonable ground that he had borne arms against the United States. Thus he saw himself bound to stand his losses alone. While in Ireland he sold his mother's estate of Craige, which gave him a certain amount of ready money. The business went on; his credit was as good as ever in Montreal and Quebec; his charity to his red neighbors and hospitality to his white ones as openhanded and princely as ever; but he knew himself to be heavily encumbered with debts. This was not the heritage he had been preparing for so long for his children.

He came down through the garden with Henry Schoolcraft, talking of verbs and nouns in the Ojibway language, nouns that could exist in either the past or the present tense, which had no gender but which were divided into the classes animate and inanimate—all very strange to Schoolcraft. Poor Henry! He had hired an interpreter for the agency, an Irishman by the name of Yarns who was married to an Ojibway woman and who may have spoken the language correctly enough, but who had never heard of a noun, let alone the gender or declension of one. But to talk of the language with a man who could not only speak it perfectly but also read Latin with ease was a pleasure. Neengay came from the kitchen and went to the door to meet them, her invariable custom. They waited until Dr. and Mrs. Wheaton and Captain Brant, the quartermaster, joined them from the fort, and then sat down at table, Jane, as usual, in the place of hostess, Neengay in the kitchen.

The work on the fort was going forward rapidly. They had all heard so much, these newcomers, of the swift descent and severity of the northern winter that they were somewhat terrified and were outdoing themselves in preparation for it. The old Northwest Chateau, nicknamed by the soldiers the Hotel Flanagan, was being repaired wherever that was possible and made into quarters for the officers. Part of it was fit for nothing but demolition. A few small stone houses in its precincts had been turned over to the physician and the quartermaster of the garrison. Johnston had rented such small buildings as he could spare, originally bunk houses for his men, or guest houses for the Indians who often descended upon him with their families for a week at a time. Schoolcraft had one of these, a log structure, fourteen by sixteen feet, with windows front and back and a mud-and-stick fireplace in one corner. He had rather despised it upon first glance, but had found it comfortable, and, such was the crowded state of the Sault, French village and all, with this sudden influx of soldiery and traders, he considered himself very lucky to have it.

The garrison was well disposed toward the Indians. They were there, they knew, not only to intimidate the savages and give courage to the settlers, but to make friends with this red and hostile nation. However, in less than a week they had unwittingly done two things which disturbed the Indians very much. They lacked the intuitive sense for superstition which had kept the French from wounding the feelings of the Indians. There was, between the cantonment and the wood where Brady planned to cut the most of his timber, a small rise of ground on which grew a few scattered shoots of mountain ash, or Scotch rowan, and all about the roots of this tree or trees were little piles of withered rowan twigs. Brady directed the men to construct a road sixty feet wide from the wood to the fort, and in doing so, the men, a little puzzled by the twigs, but not for long, cut down the ash and cleared away the debris. But these innocent-looking shoots sprang from the root of a manido tree, a tree sacred since before the days of the French, and the twigs and the little mound at its foot were consecrated offerings placed there generation after generation by hunters going north or south on the near-by trail. The tree, it was said, made the sound of a wabbeno drum, had made it for generation upon generation, and was very sacred. It had blown down only a few years before, but the Indians continued their offerings to its spirit, rising in young green withes. Now it was both destroyed and insulted. How could the Ojibways be sure that the manido would understand that the desecration had been performed by white hands instead of red? A few days later something even more annoying to the Indians, but more easily remedied, occurred. In time of illness the Ojibways were accustomed to cut a long sapling, peel it, and decorate it with paint, feathers, and small gifts, and erect it at the door of the lodge of the sick person, a conciliatory offering to the manido who might be causing the illness. An officer of the garrison, being in need of a flagpole, calmly appropriated one of these manido poles, stripped it of its decorations, and set it up in the fort. The owner very promptly came after it, and, in panic lest his patient suffer for the insult, redecorated it and reestablished it on the spot from which it had been lifted. The village was deeply stirred by this event, and considering the fact that the officer stood at the edge of a whole forest of flagpoles, to be had for the mere cutting and hauling, perhaps the Indians were justified in their emotion.

These things gave Henry Schoolcraft something to worry about, and he looked forward to his hours in the Johnston household, where he was always certain to pick up some important bit of Indian information. He let his correspondence slide, and spent his spare moments gossiping with Indians who were not anxious to answer his questions, and bois brûlés, or half-breeds, who were more willing, but who sometimes included a strange element of superstition in their replies, an element harking back to the forests of Brittany and the loup-garou.

He first heard from the bois brûlés and the Indians of the existence of one Waub-ojeeg, who, for a week at least, he classed with Mudjekeewis, the West Wind, and according to some stories the father of Manibush. Later, Jane brought this legendary person down to earth for him. He heard also of a sacred fire which had been kept burning at Chegoimegon since the day when the Ojibways had first brought it there from Mackinac. He heard of the enchanted canoe of Mishabou (Manibush, Manabozho, Nenbozho) which was propelled and guided by a word, and before the month was over he was impelled to write in his journal: "Nothing has surprised me more . . . than to find that the Chippewas amuse themselves with oral tales of a mythological or allegorical character. Some of these tales . . . are quite fanciful. . . . The fact, indeed, of such a fund of fictitious legendary matter is quite a discovery, and speaks more for the intellect of the race than any trait I have heard of. Who would have imagined that these wandering foresters should have possessed such a resource?"

Pushing through the copse at the head of the portage trail, followed by the two men he had requested of Colonel Brady, Henry Schoolcraft came quite suddenly upon the murdered man. The Indian lay in the grass before him, a fragrant tangle of yarrow, daisies, feathertopped grasses, and strawberry leaves. His head was incased in a sort of blue skullcap and around his brow were fastened eagle feathers in a coronal. He was dressed in his best, and the body was stretched out as if for Christian burial. He had been stabbed twice, once in either thigh, but the blow which seemed to have accomplished his taking off was evidently that of a hatchet or small tomahawk. The scar was very small, and directly between the eyes. A little farther up the shore among the still, thick bushes of scrub willow they found his lodge and his wife. His name had been Soan-go-gezik, the Strong Sky, and he had been killed by one Gaulthier when both of them were drunk. Gaulthier had fled. Schoolcraft gave orders to the men to remove the body and have a coffin made for it. He promised the woman that it should have a new blanket for a shroud and be buried at the expense of the Government.

The interment took place that evening at the old Ojibway burying ground. Before the wooden box was closed, an old Indian stepped to the foot of the coffin, and, looking down at the quiet face, began:

"Soan-go-gezik, we are sorry to have you go. We shall miss you in our camping places. You have been a good hunter, a good man to your wife, a good neejee to your people. You were sometimes drunk, like all of us, but you did not promise things that could not be so. Now you are going away. When you come to Gitche Genabik, the Great Serpent, do not be afraid, for you have lived a good life. Walk upon him boldly. Cross the stream. When you come to Gitche Oodaymin, the Great Strawberry, do not eat of it. When you come to the Lodge of Reindeer say to my son, Soan-go-gezik, that I am coming soon."

The brother of the Strong Sky then came forward, and, removing the blue skullcap, cut a lock of hair from the dead, replaced the skullcap, straightened the blanket with a touch. They covered the coffin then, and lowered it into the grave, and placed two poles side by side across the narrow trench. The same old man who had spoken before now called upon the brother of the Strong Sky to perform a brother's part by the widow, and the brother, obedient to the old man's instructions, taking the widow by the hand and treading on the two poles previously laid down, led her across the open grave. This seemed to end the ceremonies. The grave was filled in and a fire kindled at its head, the group of mourners not dispersing until the flame seemed established and steady. As the orange tongue sprang up, making visible the faces of those on the far side of the freshly broken earth, Schoolcraft was for a moment surprised to see the face of his hostess, Mrs. Johnston. He had grown used to seeing it in company with those of her children in her orderly garden or pleasant living-room; he had forgotten for the moment that she also belonged among these people. The widow did not leave the place, but stayed there through the night, tending the fire. The three successive nights, also, as Schoolcraft left his papers and books and, before going to bed, stood a few minutes in his doorway to breathe the sweet night air, he saw beyond the village the faithful fire which was lighting the Strong Sky on his perilous four days' journey.

The day after the burial he questioned Little Hawk, the brother of the Strong Sky, about the status of the widow, with the intention of making some sort of widow's dole for her. He learned, first, that she was a Jossakeed, capable of obscure magic and able to heal the sick by driving out devils, and, second, that she was a granddaughter of Waub-ojeeg. She was, then, Jane Johnston's cousin. Jane's own cousin was a Jossakeed. The thought was strangely confusing.

He moved, on the first of August, into one of Johnston's larger buildings, where he had two small rooms and one large one, a stove that would take in three-foot logs, and plastered walls. On the rear of the lot stood the smithy built the second year after Neengay's coming from Chegoimegon, and now the oldest structure on the Johnston premises. In front of him was the Indian green with its lodges, and beyond them the river. He was about a hundred yards west of the Johnston house and three hundred east of the new fort. He began to feel quite at home now. The fort library, such as it was, was lodged with him for lack of proper space in the barracks, and he was welcome to borrow books from Mr. Johnston's very good collection. Still, he had little time for reading that summer. Visits from Indians were continuous, absorbing his leisure even on Sundays, and he was not yet certain enough of his relations with them to attempt, as he did later, to enforce a respect for the Sabbath. One of the earliest visitors to his new quarters was a lean young Indian with a strangely familiar face. Upon a little questioning Schoolcraft identified him as the White Bird, Waub-ishke-penaysee, who had been guide for General Cass two years before when the General had attempted, and failed, to visit the great bowlder of native copper which lay in the upper reaches of the Ontonagon River. And well might Schoolcraft have been puzzled to identify the man, for, from a young Indian, athletic, confident, gay, Waub-ishke-penaysee was changed to the walking image of exhaustion and despair. He had come, drawn by a morbid fascination or curiosity, to look upon the face of one of the Chemokimon who had been the cause of his undoing.

After a day's journey up the Ontonagon under trying circumstances and amid great heat, for that part of the country, the General had decided to return to camp, leaving Schoolcraft to conclude the search for the bowlder. Waub-ishke-penaysee had been chosen to conduct him back to the place where they had left their canoes, the river being no longer navigable because of shallows and rapids. At this point, the manido of the copper bowlder, annoyed that an Ojibway should attempt to betray its whereabouts to a white man, had undoubtedly misled and confused the Indian, for he was unable to find the river; he could not even remember in which direction lay the great lake, and until far into the night he led the exhausted Governor through brush and bramble and over fallen logs until they stumbled on the river by chance and sat down to wait for a rescue. It was late that night before the search canoe found them and took them back to camp. The Indian had been so crestfallen, so humiliated, that at the final distribution of presents, Cass, out of the generosity of his soul, had conferred on him the special gift of a silver medal. But this medal, prized for a few hours, until the Chemokimon's canoes had disappeared down the far vista of the lake, had become for Waub-ishke-penaysee a special devil. He was reprimanded and disgraced in his tribe. Beaver and muskrat deserted his traps. His flint snapped without firing; his nets took no fish. Impoverished, hungry, having parted with all his possessions except his gun and the silver medal from which he could not part, he roamed the woods attended by misfortune. In the summer of '22 he strayed into the agency of the Sault to look curiously at Schoolcraft, then disappeared again.

Meanwhile, for Schoolcraft there were dinner parties, at Mr. Johnston's, at Mr. Ermantinger's (whose daughter was seen by a traveler of the time seated under a bush in a green riding habit and a white beaver bonnet), at the Hudson's Bay Company House—for the Northwest had the preceding year concluded its long rivalry with the older firm by becoming part of it—at the quarters of the officers at Fort Brady; and there was often dancing in the evening, and there were picnics. One, in especial, pleased the staid Henry so much that he recorded it at length in his journal. The party went by canoe to Gros Cap, stopping on the way at Point aux Pins. It was late August, the very prime and peak of summer, and the canoemen were singing *Allouette, gentil' allouette, allouette, je t'y pleumerai.* Henry wrote: "Our party consisted of several ladies and gentlemen. We carried the elements of a picnic. We moved rapidly. The water in which the men struck their paddles was pure as crystal. The air was perfectly exhilarating from its purity." At the Cap they scrambled up the steep scientific slope to the summit, and, breathless, looked down to the transparent ripples of the beach, combing the black and white pebbles into order far below. Beyond, blueness ran into blueness, and sky into water, and Jane, still gasping a little, her pale cheeks flushed and her eyes bright, said it was bub-eesh-ko-bee, a faraway-air-and-water-scene. They scrambled down the rocks again to the beach, and consumed the "elements of a picnic" with surprisingly good appetite, and on the way home the enthusiasm of the whole party persuaded the voyageurs to shoot them down the rapids. Safe in the calm waters below the falls, the "starry flag" flying from the stern and *"Allouette"* ringing once more in the air, Henry felt an almost personal pride of achievement, and his journal received the phrase "every heart beating in unison with the scene." Aye, every heart . . .

September yellowed the birches. The glowing leaves fell through the glowing air to lie silvery on the ground. Mosses, drenched in wet shadow all summer, began to receive the sunlight on their fragile emerald. A shipment of goods from Detroit reached the agency, and Schoolcraft was able to make his first distribution of presents. The entire Saulteur tribe assembled in front of the office, the Image Stone, the Man of Jingling Metals, the Bird in Eternal Flight, the First Born, an old man by the charming name of Pure Tobacco, these and their wives and children and all their various other relatives were present, and not one was forgotten by their generous Father. Schoolcraft continued to meditate on the Ojibway language, and, ever addicted to inventing names for places, devised, from the Gitchigomee of the Great Lake and Algonquin, the ethnological family name of the Ojibway nation, the word Algoma, which he wished to apply to Lake Superior. He was also having his troubles with smugglers, for it was against the law to carry liquor into the Indian country, and the Indian country included everything north and west of Fort Brady. Also, he was obliged to search all boats of traders who had been licensed at Mackinac, and to check and issue passports, permits, and licenses, since British traders, although no longer allowed within the American lines, were constantly slipping in by one ruse or another; and he could not help but note among both traders and Indians "a very thin diffusion of American feeling or principle."

Frost lay heavily upon his doorstep in the early mornings. Days were shorter, but sunsets seemed lengthened, the cold color holding the sky long. The weather became erratic. Sudden squalls struck the lake, succeeded by hours of tranquil sunshine. But on the twenty-sixth of September, as Sassaba, who was probably somewhat drunk, rose in his canoe to attend to his sail, one of these sudden gusts caught sail and Indian and capsized the craft. They were at the head of the rapids, Sassaba, his wife and little girl, and Odabit and his wife, and of the five, Odabit was the only one able to draw himself from the strong current and swim ashore. The others went over the rapids and were not seen again.

VII

Every morning the garrison of Fort Brady woke to find a world freshly deluged with white, and every morning they cleared the half-buried paths that led from building to building, the white walls rising higher on each side of the way, until they moved about in a deep network of trenches. The bugle sounded all its customary calls, and life proceeded, day after day, in a very good imitation of garrison life at Sacketts Harbor, New York. The Indians meanwhile, as the snow fell and their dwellings sank deeper and deeper into it, put on snowshoes and rose above it, going about to set snares for rabbits, or hunt deer, or spear sturgeon through the ice. At times a hard crust formed above the softer mass of snow, strong enough for snowshoes but breaking under the small sharp hooves of the deer, and then these creatures ran stumbling and falling, their narrow ankles cruelly cut by the crust, their pursuers gliding like eagles, mysteriously supported, and killing them not by the musket, but by bow and arrow and the knife.

Henry Schoolcraft dined with the Johnstons at four in the afternoon, and before the meal was over Jane brought the sperm candles—her father disliked the tallow ones—and set them on the table, for darkness came early. He stayed after dinner, usually, to family prayers, for although at that time he rather prided himself upon being something of a freethinker, reading the Bible for its literary excellence rather than as a revelation, and wondering secretly if the science of geology might not some day upset the

Mosaic chronology, the familiar, reverent words and attitudes, the pleasant cultured voice of John Johnston, the little rustlings and sighings of the young women, gave him a feeling of comfort and tranquillity, and later, returning to his quarters through the frosty blackness, the wilderness seemed less powerful, less terrifying, looming there to the north, Lake Superior and the Indian country, not seen, but rumorous in the snowy wind.

He was making an Indian grammar and vocabulary, which both fascinated him and gave him to despair. Some days he thought of nothing else, attempted nothing else, and at nightfall he reproached himself for neglecting subjects perhaps more important. The day after Christmas he spent in making out a page of verbs with the proper conjugations, pieced carefully together from the notes of many days. He left the paper lying on his table, and returned after dinner from the Johnstons' to find that young Ponty, his dog, had whiled away the hours of his master's absence by a systematic destruction of the precious sheet. Henry could not punish him. He could not even scold, after his contact with the vast and empty night, an animal so glad to see him. The remnants of the paper were lying on the floor, and Schoolcraft, collecting them, set himself to a long evening of soaking, uncrumpling, smoothing, and pasting together the chewed fragments. He did not know, himself, why so quixotic a task should seem reasonable. He knew only that he could not ask again all the questions that had made the document possible, nor had he the courage to go over the notes, partially destroyed, from which he had built up his conjugations.

After a brief spell of milder weather the mercury dropped to twenty-five below zero, and then to twenty-eight. At noon, in the full heat of the sun, it crawled up to four below, but the rapid return of evening sent it down again. There seemed to be more dinner parties than in New York; he was continually crossing the river to the Northwest Company's House, then properly the Hudson's Bay Company's, but seldom called so by the old-timers; or to Mr. Ermantinger's, the Swiss trader who had married the daughter of Katawabeda, the Broken Tooth; or to the Hotel Flanagan to dine with the officers. He seemed to be the only man at this time of year who was seriously occupied, and he had, some days, more visitors at the agency than he appreciated. However, the company of the traders and the military made its mark on him, and he began to read Harmon's *Travels*, the *Voyages* of Sir Alexander Mackenzie, and Carver's *Travels*, and accounts of the Indian wars. He was reading also Dr. Johnson's lives of Roscommon, Rochester, Phillips, Walsh, and Otway. After a disastrous evening at Mr. Ermantinger's, he swore off gaming at cards. Little by little his Indian vocabulary grew. By the end of January it contained, on paper, fifteen hundred words. Indeed, it remained mostly on paper, conjugations and all, until the end of his life. Never a ready conversationalist and always happier with a book, he found it pleasanter to record and to systematize than to speak, like the old traders, a living if incorrect version of the language, and he never, to the end of his career, dispensed with the services of an interpreter.

How it distressed him, that language! He wrote with impatience that it had "a tendency to clutter up general ideas with particular meanings," and later, "Ojibway words appear to be *glued* . . . to objects of sense." But he was happy on the day he discovered that, whereas in Persian the word *abad* signifies *abode,* the Ojibway word *abid* means *where he dwells,* and he felt himself approaching the limpid fountainhead of all language.

For a week in February, social life at the Sault outdid itself in activity and charm. Lewis Johnston arrived with a party of gentlemen from Fort Drummond. They had snowshoed the forty-five-mile distance up the river merely for the sake of paying a few calls. There were dinner parties every night, and the night before their departure a grand dinner and dancing party at Mr. Johnston's with the log-walled room full of guests, the bear and buffalo rugs pushed aside, and a little group of fiddlers from the French village playing reels and quadrilles and minuets until their faces sweated. Lewis was tall and handsome, like all the Johnstons, and his British lieutenant's uniform became him. Schoolcraft watched him dancing with his sister Jane. They made a pretty pair.

The second week in March, without warning, without commotion, the French and Indian villages on both sides of the river began to lose their population. Henry saw them going off, a family at a time, with dog trains or with sleds and horses, into the wintry woods, and did not realize at first that the maple-sugar season had begun. By the twenty-sixth, two days before his thirtieth birthday, the Sault was largely a village of deserted dwellings. Even Mrs. Johnston had been for more than a week at her camp on Sugar Island. Jane proposed a picnic visit to it, and they set off that morning in three carioles or cutters, Jane and Henry and the two younger Johnston girls, and one or two gentlemen from the fort with their ladies. Johnston saw them off from the doorstep but smilingly refused to go. The lameness in his foot troubled him, and he had been in other maple woods in other springs.

Although the sheet of snow above the river ice was still unbroken to the eye, the ice beneath it was felt to be rotting, and they pursued their way carefully, keeping near shore. Seven or eight miles down the river and a mile inland to the left brought them to a forest of silvery bare trunks almost completely free of undergrowth. Here, in a clearing, the men had put up a large temporary shelter for Neengay, and here, over a narrow fire, perhaps thirty-five feet long, some twenty to thirty copper kettles, swung from cross-poles of green maple, were bubbling and fuming, filling the cold air with a sweetness warmer than that of flowers but no less spring-like. All about were set vats made of oxhide that held the thin watery sap brought fresh from the trees, and at the foot of nearly every tree stood a small bark mokkuk into which the slow drops fell hour by hour. Neengay moved about through the drifting smoke and steam, her three-cornered red shawl folded over her shoulders, her silver earbobs tapping coldly against her strong brown cheeks, superintending the work and working also. She paused a little while to welcome her guests. As soon as the syrup thickened it was taken from the fire and stirred into a soft sugar, the sugar in turn, yet warm, was packed into large bark mokkuks, crushed down into place under the broad dark palms of her Indian helpers, and covered with sheets of bark. But the picnickers made wax, pouring the hot syrup on the snow, and candy pulls, two by two, were soon in progress.

The sky, alternately cloudy and clear, showed through the limber branches overhead, and spread the trampled snow with an ever-changing pattern of twigs, and the fire crackled, the flames thin in the sunlight, richer in the shadow. The picnic hamper was unpacked and luncheon spread on an improvised table, from which the picnickers helped them-selves, wandering about under the trees as they ate. Henry, with his cloak over his surtout, stood near Jane, a piece of cold venison in one hand and a piece of biscuit in the other. Jane, also munching on cold venison and bread, leaned against a maple trunk. She wore a little fur cap and a short fur cloak from beneath which her full merino skirt, a dark burgundy, flowed becomingly. Neengay, on the other side of the fire, watched them smiling at each other. She had grown rather to like this quiet young man who by temperament understood her people so little, but who by indus-try attempted so patiently to bridge the wide gap between himself and his charges. Even if she had not liked him, she would have said nothing of it to Jane, for although this daughter of hers, so frail, with such curious deli-cacies of taste, was at times something of a mystery to her mother, it was plain enough that Henry Schoolcraft was what Jane both needed and wanted. With hot fresh sap that had no more than come to a boil, she made tea and carried it over to them, tea that needed no sugar, and in the snow, under the clouded sky, it tasted to them like nectar.

Through April the snow lingered until the eye ached with regarding it, but as the month went on, the roar of the rapids deepened, gray ducks were seen to alight in the swift water, and here and there the naked earth appeared in rifts between snow banks. The troops at the fort set about the labor of completing the picketed stockade begun in the fall and inter-rupted by the hardening of the ground. Although on the twenty-second a snowstorm came down upon them from Superior, the feeling of spring had been in the air for two weeks, and all the inhabitants of St. Mary's felt a lightening of spirit and limb, as if an actual weight had been lifted from the flesh. Henry Schoolcraft, on the snowy twenty-second, responded to this universal sensation of release by throwing reason to the wind, and, invoking, as he thought, Reason, went on a linguistic spree in which he reformed the Ojibway language from the foundations up.

He wanted a monosyllabic Ojibway. He was willing, for the sake of rhythmic variety, to retain a few dissyllables as well. He wanted pronouns which declined themselves regularly; he wanted all nouns to form their plurals, their pejoratives, diminutives, and augmentatives* regularly, and he wished to increase the number of words expressing abstract ideas. He was willing to retain all the existing monosyllables, provided he might regulate their changes, but the polysyllables he intended to reduce. Thus, he planned to change *manido* to Eo—God.

The word *aindum, mind,* he reduced to *ain,* and by prefixing single letters from corresponding English words he devised the series: *tain, thought, jain, joy, main, meditation, sain, sorrow.* He found it necessary to add to the language a few sounds it had never contained, the English *f, 1, r,* and *v,* and when he had done so, felt himself well on the way to achiev-ing "a language of great brevity, terseness, regularity and poetic expres-siveness."

For three days he filled the pages of his notebooks with specimens of this new speech, perfectly happy in the profound sense of order which it gave him. For three days he emerged from his office and his theory only for meals. Then the snow ceased, the sun came out with added strength, he put away his notes, although he did not destroy them, and resumed the wonted tenor of his ways. Never again did he complain of the perverse-ness of the language, and, as time went by, he found in it continually new and unsuspected charm.

---

* The Ojibway says *bad dog* by adding a pejorative ending *eesh* to the word for *dog, annemoosh;* thus, *annemoosheesh.* It forms the diminutive in the same fash-ion by adding *onse,* a nasal monosyllable, *annemooshonse.* Schoolcraft invented the augmentative for the sake of symmetry. The Ojibway uses the adjective *gitche* in front of the word modified.

The winter had been in many ways a long one for John Johnston. It was now over two years since he had presented his memorial of losses to the Lord of the Treasury and, having made due allowance for the natural slowness of governments, he could no longer persuade himself that anything would be done about it. He felt now also more severely the result of the years of forest hardships imposed upon the years of Belfast merrymaking. The flesh was no longer resilient. He could not evade the thought of his financial difficulties by setting off suddenly on a journey to Mackinac. He spent long hours by the fire, and the lines of his petition to the government ran through his head.

"That your memorialist in the month of July 1814, commanded a company of militia at Michilimackinac during the blockade of the port and island by a fleet and army of the United States of America, and when Lieutenant McDonall entered the field against the enemy who had landed at the extremity of the island, the commend of the fort during his absence was entrusted to your memorialist.

"That during your memorialist's absence from home on the last mentioned service, a detachment of a hundred and fifty men with two field pieces under the command of Major Holmes of the Army of the United States of America, invaded St. Mary's Falls and plundered and destroyed the property of your memorialist to the amount specified in the statement— now before your lordship and which was in the year 1816, forwarded by Lieutenant Gore to Earl Bathurst."

The amount in the statement, as he had told Schoolcraft, was forty thousand dollars, and it was not an exaggeration of the loss. He had, on that trip two years ago, sold the estate of Craige, his last tie with Ireland, but even the proceeds from that sacrifice were not sufficient to maintain his house and his business. He saw himself running into debt. He saw the ingratitude of governments, the inglorious end of his years, and, drawing toward him a little table with writing materials, he dipped a sharpened goose quill in ink, and indited the following verses:

To Hope

Hope, deceiver of my soul,
Who with lures, from day to day,
Hast permitted years to roll,
Almost unperceived away,
Now no longer try shine art,
Fools alone thy power shall own,

Who with simple vacant heart,
Dream of bliss to mortals known.
Every effort I have try'd,
All that reason could suggest,
Cruel? Cease then to deride
One by fortune still unblest.
Ah! yet stay, for when thou'rt gone,
Where shall sorrow lay her head,
Where but on the chilling stone
That marks the long-forgotten dead.

That spring, however, having talked with Neengay about the probable plans of Jane and Henry, and also as a gesture of protest against his own recent gloom, he gave orders to his men to enlarge the house, and an ell was built on the west end having a little loft with dormer windows, a small portico built about the front door, facing the river, where there were seats.

VIII

If Henry's conversion, his abandonment of freethinking as an adequate spiritual and ethical foundation for life, was a sort of wedding gift to Jane, he did not recognize it as such himself, but gave the immediate credit to the Rev. MacMurtrie Laird, "whose life and manners resembled an apostle's." Jane's piety was as much a part of herself as her gentleness. It had been bred in her from her earliest childhood, first of all by her father, and later, in Ireland, by her father's people, and all in her that might, from such a combination of races, have become superstition was turned to an implicit Christian faith. It was for her, therefore, the greatest happiness in the world to have Henry join in her devotions, and the hours given twice a week to the services and conversations conducted by Mr. Laird were among the most cherished of the winter. They were married in October, Henry Rowe Schoolcraft and Miss Jane Johnston, and took up their residence in the newly built wing of the Johnston home, Henry reserving his former quarters for the agency office and taking his meals, as formerly, with the Johnston family. But what a different winter this was from the first! The wabbeno drum still sounded nightly from the Indian village, and, if they stepped out of doors after prayer-meeting, the strange fire of the aurora still flickered like a luminous breath against the dome of heaven, but within all was warm, secure, and Christian. Or there were snowshoe expeditions, Jane in her fur cap and full red skirt, Henry in his black cape, the snowshoe webbing patting and scuffing the powdery whiteness, and there were sleigh rides down the river, the snow packed satiny white and hissing under the runners.

Henry's new devoutness did not interfere with his enthusiasm for the Ojibway language, but rather re-enforced it, for he had the word of St. Paul "that all languages are given to men with an exact significance of words and forms . . . surely the highest warrant for their serious study." He carried on his investigations by the Johnston hearth after the day's various labors, and most especially when Neengay was free to sit with them. And often, and not for Henry's benefit primarily, while they were all seated near the fire, Johnston in his armchair with his long-stemmed clay pipe, a copy of *Paradise Lost* open upon his knee, Neengay sometimes with a bit of soft, tarry-smelling leather which she was working with quills or colored beads, sometimes with her strong hands quiet in her lap, Jane and Charlotte and Eliza busy each in some household fashion, the door would fly open, and in a whirl of snow a blanketed figure would enter to be greeted with a chorus of cries: "Ah! Here is Wayishkee!" "Here is Shingabawossin!" "Here is the Little Pine!" And the Indian, whoever he was, shaking the snow from his blanket, would come smiling into the circle of the fire and the stories would begin. How they acted the stories, the Little Pine, the Image Stone, each springing to his feet as the story became intense, mimicking the tread of the hero, the cramped and shaking gestures of the old woman, even the gestures and the voices of the animals in the stories! Henry understood now that there were Indians who, all winter long, professional story-tellers, went from wigwam to wigwam with their stories, and received food, shelter, and gifts in exchange, but these who came to the Johnston house were mostly old friends from the village wishing to pass a social evening. Jane bloomed that winter as never before. Her religion, her love for Henry, and most of all the child whom she knew herself to be carrying, set her at the core of life, blessing and blessed. Henry, who had made almost no entries in his journal from October to the last day of March, wrote,

Hope is a flower that fills the sentient mind
With sweets of rapturous and heavenly kind.

—Hetherwold

Mr. Laird had come to St. Mary's late in the fall. His labors had been rewarded in the village, although in the fort, where he was quartered, his mission met with little sympathy. As soon as the river was open to navigation, which was that year early in May, he departed. Henry also left the Sault for a short trip to the Taquimenon, where he was received by the

Ojibways in "a noble spirit of hospitality and welcome," and all this chiefly for the reason that he was now son-in-law to Neengay. Jane, at the Sault, waited for the last months to pass.

Finally, out of the long preoccupation of her body, she found herself involved one night in pain which so destroyed her personal courage, her personal identity, that at times she forgot—as she realized when it was over—the reason for her anguish and the hope that should have accompanied it. She saw, beyond the circle of her struggle, the room lit by row upon row of candles, brighter, more golden than any bedroom of her experience had ever been, and she saw Neengay standing beside her, laying her hand on the bed six inches from her own, and was powerless, but not through weakness, to move her own hand to touch it. She was as if surrounded by a substance impenetrable and absolute, delivered over to a power which left her hardly able even to wish to escape. And then, suddenly, the circle was broken; she became extremely aware, alive, and capable of effort, and the sense of pain merged with the brilliance of the candlelight; and presently she was released entirely, her body light as a girl's, her mind filled with the most pure joy she had ever known.

The next morning, more tired, but perfectly happy, she lay with the head of a strange little creature, whom she knew to be her son, against her arm, and there was Charlotte, very excited, with a basket full of little squares of white tarlatan filled with cornstarch and tied each with a blue or pink ribbon, powder puffs for the baby, and presently Henry, coming with a note from Drummond from her father. Johnston was once more on his way to Toronto in the hope of obtaining from the Lieutenant Governor indemnity for his loss in 1814. At Drummond, where Lewis was employed in the British Indian agency, he delayed for a visit with his son, and an occasion to send once more messages of affection to those at St. Mary's.

The Indians were quick to nickname this child of Jane's Penaysee, the Bird.

"What is that you have in your arms?" asked Wayishkee of Charlotte, who was holding the child for Jane.

"It's a little boy," answered the young aunt. "He has the hiccoughs."

"It sounds like a robin," said Wayishkee. "I call him Penaysee." And Penaysee he was, although his father had him christened William Henry Schoolcraft.

Henry's pride was great. He detected in his son more than ordinary beauty of lineament and mental promise," but Jane's preoccupation with her child was such that St. Mary's and all it contained became merely a green and animated background for the life of a little boy who did almost

126

nothing but eat and sleep, but did this very remarkably. Henry's fussing over the fact that he had to enter the fort to get his mail, and therefore was not always able to obtain it when he wanted it, or because he could not convince Major Cutler of the necessity of building an adequate structure for the agency, distressed her not at all. She sympathized with him gently, and went off to superintend the labors of a young Indian girl, who at the door of the Johnston kitchen was washing nainsook gowns and an indefinite number of squares of white bird's-eye cotton. Even when young Holliday, her father's former clerk and now a trader at L'Anse Kewenon, arrived one August morning with a small coffin-shaped box painted black, and showed to Henry the scalp of an American trader murdered by Ojibway Indians as a substitute for a Sioux, although she was penetrated by horror at the mere view of the box, a return to Penaysee's room restored for her completely the security and sweetness of life. From the small wooden bed where the child slept, a freshness that might have been a fragrance, that seemed one indeed, was exhaled softly. Jane, shutting the door behind her, felt herself breathe it into her very heart.

In September Henry packed them all, Jane, Penaysee, an Indian nursemaid, and Anna Maria Johnston—ten years old, and already very demure, vivacious, and pretty—on board a schooner bound for Detroit. Quite as dark as Jane but with a warmer color in her cheek, less Ojibway in appearance than Eliza, chiefly because of her manner, tall for her years, very slender in build, Anna Maria ran about the decks of the vessel, shook the cords of the rigging, stood at the very prow leaning over with her hands on the bowsprit to watch the slow curl of water at the ship's beak, or she returned to Jane, settling at her sister's knee with a flutter and billow of her muslin skirt, tucking her slippered feet beneath her. Twelve years younger than Jane, she almost associated herself with the generation of Penaysee, although feeling herself vastly more accomplished. They descended the river, familiar now to Jane and Henry and peopled with many recollections, but new to Maria, whose delight became to guess where the islands would part to let them through, and which way the channel would turn. At Michilimackinac they stopped for a short time, and then went down Lake Huron with fair weather to Detroit, where the Governor and Mrs. Cass received them, established them for a few days in the stone mansion, and sent them on their way to New York. Henry's objective was Washington, where he meant to settle a few little matters pertaining to the authority and dignity of his position at the Sault, as well as to obtain a mandate for the building of the agency. He left his little family with friends in New York City, on "Bloomingdale Road, some two or three miles from the Park."

Here Jane was a great success, and Anna Maria and Penaysee not less so. Henry's journal was starred with commendations of his wife and child and little sister-in-law. "She wrote a most exquisite hand," this was Henry's own comment, "and composed with ability, and grammatical skill and taste. Her voice was soft and her expression clear and pure, as her father, who was from one of the highest and proudest circles of Irish society, had been particularly attentive to her orthography and pronunciation and selection of words of the best usage abroad." "When I first visited Mr. Schoolcraft," their host of Bloomingdale Road inscribed, "I looked about for his Indian girl . . . not less surprised than recompensed to find such gentleness, urbanity, affection and intelligence under circumstances so illy calculated, as might be supposed, to produce such amiable virtues." New York fashionables flocked to meet the "Northern Pocahontas," a Pocahontas in black taffeta with irreproachable ringlets confined by an ivory comb.

Henry returned from the capital, all his intentions accomplished, spent a few weeks in New York supervising the publication of his *Travels in the Central Portions of the Mississippi Valley,* and in April began to conduct his little band back to the Northwest. Up the Hudson to Albany, across the country by coach, they went, stopping at Vernon in western New York State to add to their party Henry's brother James and his sister Maria Eliza, and so, like a traveling picnic, on to Detroit in May.

Jane was happy to be back at the Sault and to be established for the first time in her own home, a building to the west of the fort, known as the Allen House. Peenaysee thrived, adding the security of pounds to his small body, Maria Eliza wrote from Detroit the news of the town, Henry came and went, attending Indian convocations for the settlement of treaties, Jane selected a spot for the foundations of the agency building, which was to be her home and to contain also the government offices. She wrote grateful notes to her friends in the East, and, with Henry's permission, adopted into her family her second cousin, little Charlotte Soan-go-gezik, whose father, murdered and laid out for burial, Henry had found lying in the summer grasses at the head of the Portage trail. She wanted Charlotte to have a Christian life, and the child, as she grew older, would be a help with Penaysee and great company during Henry's absences. So three-year-old Charlotte left the lodge of her mother, who was a Jossakeed, and slept in a clean narrow bed in Penaysee's room under a geometrically patched and quilted coverlet.

When Penaysee was two and a quarter years old, Jane had the pleasure of entertaining her old friend the Governor of the Territory. Still clifflike as to countenance, still rigid in the small of the back, but less terrifying than he had been six years earlier, because of the Detroit visit, he bowed over Jan's hand, and presented her to Colonel McKenney, Commissioner of Indian Affairs, and to Colonel Croghan of the United States Army.

Jane thought, seeing her father in conversation with Colonel Croghan, "This is the man who was responsible for the burning of our house," but her father's manner showed no faintest trace of such a remembrance, as he leant on his cane, gesturing with his free hand, relating some anecdote of which she did not catch the drift. And indeed she wronged the Colonel, for although he had led the troops at Mackinac in the engagement of August, 1814, and he and her father had borne arms against each other that day, he had expressly instructed Major Holmes to destroy no private property in his expedition to the Sault. Johnston had changed greatly in the last four years; he had, like Alexander Henry, "symptoms of old age advancing rapid." The dropsy in his foot and ankle had increased so that he was often quite unable to walk, and never in fact was parted from his cane. His hair was more gray, his shoulders were decidedly stooped. In repose, his lips still met firmly, but when he smiled, the loss of some of his front teeth, and the discoloration of those remaining, from long conferences with his pipe betrayed his years. For Jane, these changes had worked so gradually upon a person continually met with and always familiar that she hardly noted them, but the Commissioner observed a man "feeble and decrepit," although possessing great urbanity and charm. The most profound sign of age, however, and one which no one noted save perhaps McKenney, was the increasing sweetness and mildness of character which tempered all that the old man said or did. The death of Lewis Saurin Johnston in the year preceding was largely responsible for this. All the affection which he would have given to his first child, now dead in his prime, Johnston bestowed quietly here and there in little parcels to each person with whom he came in contact. His bitterness he reserved for governments, and spoke of it little.

Neengay was not there, but Eliza and Charlotte had come, in dresses of striped silk made just alike, and even Anna Maria, twelve years old, had been invited because the General, remembering her in Detroit two years before, wished to see her again. It was an evening of the old man surrounded by his daughters.

The Commissioner of Indian Affairs was on the way to Fond du Lac, Superior, with the Governor and his staff, to arrange a treaty with the Ojibways, a treaty which had been planned the year before by Cass at the convocation of tribes at Prairie du Chien, which was to continue the work begun at Prairie du Chien, and also to obtain for the United States a grant to all the mineral rights of the south shore, especially of the copper, for no one had yet thought seriously of the iron. Henry was to join the expedition with interpreters, and had been placed in charge of all practical arrangements for the trip from St. Mary's on, including the commissariat, canoe, and bateau, and an equipment for removing the copper bowlder of the Ontonagon, should the treaty prove successful. This was the Commissioner's first expedition of the sort, and he had undertaken it partly out of regard for his health, which a winter of documentary labor had seriously undermined. His enthusiasm for things Indian was greater even than Henry's, and more innocent. He was enchanted with the aspect of Indian culture combined with Irish which presented itself in the persons of the four Johnston daughters; he had happy and generous ideas for a school for Indian children to be maintained by the Government at St. Mary's; he was gallant and gullible. He found the air of Lake Superior extremely invigorating, the cloud effects surpassingly beautiful, and the colors of the rainbow, after a summer shower, more glowing and pure than he had ever elsewhere observed them. The remarks of his companions on the splendor of the funeral which they intended to give him, should his fate overtake him between there and Fond du Lac, no longer fell on his ears with ominous discord. From the fourth of July until the tenth, the party loitered at the Sault, while the boats were made ready, voyageurs and interpreters engaged, and the Governor, the Commissioner, and Henry went minutely over the points to be presented and gained at the council. On the evening of the sixth they dined with the Schoolcrafts. Mr. McKenney wrote to his wife:

"We spent this evening at Mr. Schoolcraft's, where we met Mr. Johnston, the patriarch of the place . . . the genuine Irish hospitality of his heart has made his house a place of most agreable resort to travelers. In his person Mr. Johnston is neat; in his manners affable and polite; in conversation intelligent. . . . Mrs. Johnston is genuine Chippewa. . . . She is tall and large, but uncommonly active and cheerful. . . . Of Mrs. Schoolcraft you have heard. She is wife, you know, of H. R. Schoolcraft Esq., author of travels and other works of great merit, and Indian agent at this place. She is a little taller and thinner, but in other respects as to figure, resembles her sister [Charlotte] and has her face precisely. . . . Mrs. Schoolcraft is indebted mainly to her father, who is doatingly fond of her, for her handsome and polished acquirements. She accompanied him some years ago, and before her marriage, to Europe; and has been the companion of his solitude, in all that related to mind, for he seems to have educated her for the sake of enjoying its exercise. The old gentleman, when in Edinburgh, had several propositions made to him to remain. The Duchess of Devonshire, I think it was, would have adopted Mrs. Schoolcraft; and several propositions beside were made to settle upon her wealth and its distinctions; and his own friends and connexions joined to keep him among them by offers of great magnitude. But he told them he had married the daughter of a king in America, and although he appreciated, and was very grateful for, their offers to himself and his Jane, he must decline them and return to his wife, who, through such a variety of fortune, had been faithful and devoted to him. Mrs. Schoolcraft . . . would be an ornament to any society; and with better health (for at present she enjoys this great blessing but partially) would take a first rank among the best improved, whether in acquirements, taste or graces.

"Charlotte comes next in order. . . . She possesses charms which are only now and then seen in our more populous and polished circles. These are in the form and expression of a beautiful face, where the best and most amiable and cheerful of tempers . . . sits always with the sweetness of spring. . . . Her eyes are black, but soft in their expression, and between her lips, which I have never seen otherwise than half parted in a smile, is a beautiful set of ivory. . . . She sings most sweetly, but seems unconscious of it; and lest I should forget it, I will copy into this letter a beautiful song which she sings with her most enchanting effect, called the 'O-jib-way Maid.' . . . I have heard this little song sung in both the original and its [English] version. The airs are different; both are plaintive, and both sweet, but that in which the original is sung is the wildest. My opinion of Charlotte is that she would be a belle in Washington, were she there, as I find she is here. . . . Eliza is next younger than Mrs. Schoolcraft. I have never yet got her to consent to speak English. I have not, therefore, been able to judge of her improvement. She appears to be a fine young lady and of excellent dispositions. Her complexion is more like her mother's than the rest. The youngest, Anna Maria . . . is growing up, I think, in most respects like Charlotte. She certainly bids fair to be handsome."

There were, in all, not less than ten closely written pages of this account for Mrs. McKenney. The Commissioner had also from Charlotte—as if he could ever forget her!—a token to remember her by. At parting she presented him shyly with the pelt of a white fisher.

"Here is my grandfather," she said, "at least in name."

On the tenth the expedition got under way, three Mackinac boats, twelve-oared bargelike vessels pointed at either end, conveyed the military, a company of the Sixty-second Infantry, with commissariat and medical supplies, followed by four bateaux loaded with presents for the Indians. They set off with flags flying and a band playing, probably the first military band that ever went to an Indian treaty, a procession strung out for miles along the water, all the village out to wave them on their way. The day after, Schoolcraft and McKenney embarked in Henry's small canoe, which, traveling swiftly with ten voyageurs and only the two passengers, would soon overtake the heavy barges.

In March began the weather that loosened the sap in the maple roots and sent it coursing upward, sweet and thin. Waub-ishke-penaysee, he who had misguided the Governor all around the copper bowlder of the Ontonagon and had been deserted by his manidos, came in with the mail from La Pointe, telling of weather that had broken the ice on the lake and then rewelded it in extraordinary shapes. He was now in the service of the subagency of La Pointe, the official at that place being George Johnston, appointed the preceding summer by McKenney, and his manidos were beginning to pardon him. In March, the sun being warm above the softened snow, Jane and Penaysee wandered down the Portage trail, passed the Johnston homestead, and discovered under the snow the foundations of Elmwood, that was to be the agency building. It was east of Jane's old home, near the river, on a gradual rise of ground, and the view from the porch would include the whole stretch of the upper St. Mary's. They looked at the river under the snow, and saw a family from the French village traveling in a cariole to the sugaring camps, and Jane imagined, and told Penaysee, who was now Willy, about the schooners and bateaux that would be swarming on the blue water in a few more months. On the way back they stopped at the homestead, where the kitchen was warm with a roaring fire for baking, and so out across the damp snow that took the imprint of their feet like wax, past the fort, to the Allen House.

In the early afternoon the wind shifted to the northwest, coming across the broken ice and clear water in Whitefish Bay, lifting moisture from the water and chilling it into a thick white fog, and at nightfall a very frightened Jane came running through the fog with only a woolen scarf over her head, crying at the door of the Johnston house, "Neengay! Neengay! Penaysee is sick!"

The child looked up at Neengay with startled black eyes, his brow puckered as if he knew something was wrong, but could not know what, and his breath came hoarsely through his parted lips. They put a kettle on the fire, and while they waited for it to begin to steam, Neengay heated sweet oil, and touched the inside of the child's nostrils with a feather dipped in the oil, but this did not seem to ease his breathing. When the first puff of steam issued from the spout of the kettle, she took the child on her breast, and holding a blanket over his head, caught the vapor for him to breathe. Henry came in and saw her standing, a massive form with the lifted blanket hiding the child, her outstretched arm protecting and steady, the blanket falling over it, and beside her Jane, slender and dark and trembling. Jane cried when she told Henry the child was sick. Until eleven o'clock that night the place was in a turmoil, and then it was far too still, Neengay's wisdom, Jane's adoration, having been unavailing against whatever it was had assailed the little boy. It had happened so suddenly that all three of them, although only Henry spoke of it, seemed still to hear through all the rooms of the house the small high voice and uncertain little laugh of the child who would not any more return to them.

Henry was conscience-stricken. He held the death of the child to be a warning and a punishment from the Almighty because he, Henry Schoolcraft, had too much occupied himself with earthly things, the pursuit of learning and the pride of accomplishment, to the neglect of spiritual matters. This was unreasonable, he knew, and he did not ask what crimes Jane had committed to be so punished, but he could not rid himself of the feeling, and without being able to give any rational explanation of the deed, he brought his Bible, the first he had ever owned, and laid it under William Henry's pillow, under the square of white that supported the little dark head. The face was very cold and still, the eyes were slightly sunken, the hair about the face was alive and soft.

William Henry died on the thirteenth. On the seventeenth the Schoolcrafts dined with the Johnstons in order to honor St. Patrick, but it was a superficial celebration. Ten or eleven days later, unable to endure any longer the phantom of Penaysee, they closed the house, left standing all the furniture they had bought in New York State on that gay expedition when Penaysee was still an infant, and fled to the Johnston home, where Neengay established them in their old rooms. Henry never forgot the sympathy with which John Johnston drew him into the circle about the fire. He remembered the death of Lewis, and demanded little of the old man save his presence, his whimsical smile parting the old lips, the long curl of smoke from his pipe.

As for Jane, on the night of Penaysee's death a tremor seemed to enter her body like that of the aspens at the wood's edge on a quiet day. As long as she lived, any emotion, any fatigue, set her spirit to quivering. This her Irish breeding bade her hide, but it escaped always in her voice. Her mother became for her the symbol of earthly comfort, and for heavenly consolation she had the promise of seeing Penaysee again. She believed absolutely and entirely in this; if she had not been Christian before, her longing for the child would have made her so in a moment. Moreover, she was again with child, and the mystery of life beginning was constantly with her, as overwhelming as the mystery of life ending.

IX

Feet in low-heeled black slippers fastened by crisscross black ribbons to the white-stockinged ankles, feet in shoepacks, in beaded or quilled moccasins, in military boots, all morning and all afternoon stepped across the floor of the little portico which John Johnston had built facing the river, entered the living-room, entered the bedroom, and retraced their journey, as the ladies from the fort, from the village, Johnston's own voyageurs, Ojibways from St. Mary's and from encampments on the southern shore, officers and soldiers from Fort Brady, gentlemen formerly of the Northwest Company, then of the Hudson's Bay, came to pay their respects to his widow. It was a day which Neengay had always dimly known would arrive, but she sat now, between the window and the bed where her husband's body reposed, receiving with dignity the salutation of all these people, a little surprised that the day had really come. For all her wisdom, for all her patience and stability, the surprise kept flickering in her face, in the low voice with which she replied to Indian, Frenchman, or American.

Outside the window the long grass of the river front was bowed with frost and sodden with rain, although the changeable sunshine lay on it coldly and clearly. The beaches were littered with torn seaweeds, and beyond the water the distant shore was somber with leafless trees or with trees yet holding a few red leaves which the distance changed to tones of maroon and amethyst. In the living-room a fire of maple logs blazed steadily as if for a festival. Men and women gathered about it, the women laying aside their cloaks for a moment, and spoke in quiet voices. Jane, seated at her father's table, with his pen in her hand, was composing letters, stopping often to wipe her eyes with a handkerchief or to gaze absently into the crowd. An old Canadian, whose gray hair, combed back of his ears and falling almost to his shoulders, contrasted oddly with the scarlet collar of his coat and the scarlet sash about his waist, stooping, laid his hand lightly on her shoulder, and said:

"Madame, I knew your father long ago. Yes, I knew him before he married your mother, when he was on his way to Montreal to buy her a wedding gown. Yes. He was a fine man."

Jane looked up, tears in her eyes. "Merci, Monsieur Perreault."

"Jean Baptiste, Ma'ame, Jean Baptiste for you." He bowed, and slipped away into the crowd. At the door, overcome with the emotion roused by his own gallantry, he laid his arm on the shoulders of a friend, saying, "My old Piquette, what a man! There will not be another like him," and removed his arm to draw the tears from his eyes with his fingers. But it was a true emotion.

Less than a week ago Johnston had made his last journey up the St. Mary's River. He had been to New York, and in that city had contracted a "malignant fever" which had barely permitted of his reaching the Falls again. At Mackinac he had been transferred from the small sailing vessel to a bateau, and, lying half conscious on a cot in the center of the barge, had been rowed slowly upstream past the autumnal islands. He had hardly recognized any of the members of his family upon his arrival at the Sault, but, Dr. James having been called from the fort, on the day following he rallied, and was "able to converse freely." The diagnosis of the physician was "Typhoid." Johnston himself said, "Dysentery, and old age," refusing to arrogate to his demise more dignity than was necessary. The rallying had been brief. Through the next two days he failed steadily, and after noon on the twenty-second, although still conscious, had ceased to answer the affectionate questions put to him by his children. He died at eight o'clock that evening.

George was at La Pointe; there had been no time in which to send for him. And Lewis was dead, dead at Malden three years earlier, but the others were there, Will, seventeen years old, tall for his age, like all the Johnstons, and beginning to assume, both in appearance and responsibility, George's place in the family; Jane and Charlotte, differing so little from each other in feature and in years; Eliza, tall and dark, with an intense, closed face; Anna Maria, just beginning to look like a woman; and young John Johnston, not yet ten years of age, with his fair hair and hazel eyes, and something in the carriage of his head like that of his maternal grandfather. Now that the illness was over, the slow departure accomplished, they were all set free to a leisure which they hardly knew how to employ. There seemed no important business in the household, although the Indian servants went about their usual labors, and Jane set herself at her father's table to inform friends in Mackinac and Detroit of the event. People from the two villages drifted in and out, the ladies from the fort clustered about Charlotte and Eliza, and good Madame Piquette offered to take Anna Maria home with her for the afternoon. But Anna Maria clung to Eliza, feeling herself more than ever one of a unit, now that the unit itself had been shattered by the death of her father. Will had instructed the men to build a coffin.

135

Still Neengay waited while the autumn darkness settled about the figure on the bed, filling the hollows of the face, the drawn lines about the mouth, the scattered locks of gray and flaxen hair, and rose slowly about her own knees to the hands on her lap. He had lived to see the birth of his granddaughter, Janie Schoolcraft, and his own Jane happy again. He had lived to see people of his own race coming and going about the fort, about the Portage trail, he had lived to help bury old Cadotte, he had lived since the death of Waub-ojeeg. He had lived a great while. A servant, coming with a candle for the table at the foot of the bed, reminded her of the four nights' fire which burned for her father's journey to the dead, and she knew that she would build no such fires for her husband. She saw the figure of Will appear in the doorway as if he meant to enter the room, and then disappear.

At ten o'clock Charlotte had persuaded Eliza and John and Anna Maria to go to bed, and had joined Eliza where they were accustomed to sleep together in the west wing. Jane and Henry had returned to Elmwood, walking bareheaded through the sharp air of the evening. The living-room was deserted except for the firelight and the portrait of John Johnston smiling easily down from within the gold frame. Among the outbuildings it was quiet also.

The men had finished the oak coffin, which stood on trestles in the barn, where Neengay came with Will to view it. It was bare and plain and solid. She looked at it for a long time, and then turned slowly and went quietly back to the house. Her son followed her as far as the door. There, from a more than filial respect, he left her, and she went in alone. He stood there in the thin air of the autumn night, seeing the sky interrupted slightly by the ash boughs, hearing the river moving along the beach. The sky was so thickly sown with stars, minute, brilliant, white, like dust, as to appear luminous in the interstellar spaces. The coldness, etherial frost, bathed his face, entered his nostrils, electrified the fur of his cap. The house behind him, dark, quiet, and secure, was like the person of his mother. He could hear, vaguely, as he leaned against the door, the flutter of the fire in the huge fireplace, and while he stood there, listening half unconsciously, trying to fit into his awareness of the established and familiar this newer sense of catastrophe and insecurity, a small inexplicable noise struck his ear, a metronomic, silvery percussion. He pushed the door open softly and entered the livingroom. There were no candles, but before the fire on the wide, lighted hearth his mother was kneeling, beating a silver tablespoon into a thin sheet. She looked up as he approached and, speaking in Ojibway, sent him to find Henry Schoolcraft.

Schoolcraft engraved the coffin plate thus made:

John Johnston Esq.
Born Ireland August 25, 1762
Died Sept. 22, 1828
Aged 66 Yrs, 27 Days

And the men fastened it to the oak cover.

X

Seated in her father's armchair, a little more than a week after the funeral, Jane unfolded the packet of letters which Henry had given her that morning, and which she had brought, out of sentiment, to her father's favorite corner of the living-room to read. They were letters written by Johnston to Henry Schoolcraft at Henry's urgent plea for some record of his father-in-law's career, and had been delivered, most of them, to Henry by Johnston himself, on occasions when the Schoolcrafts were dining at the homestead. Jane had always meant to read them through, and always some slight household obligation, slight but insistent, had interrupted her at the first or the second or the third page. Today it had become for her a matter of filial piety to peruse them fully. Charlotte and Neengay had gone to Elmwood to keep an eye on little Jane, and Jane was alone in the house.

For a time she read without great interest in the material, enjoying the sight of her father's handwriting, and imagining it to be his voice. Her grandfather, who had swum his horse across the River Brush and perished of an influenza, her great-grandfather, who had built the waterworks of the city of Belfast, her great-uncle, the Bishop of Belfast, her cousins, the McNeils of Coulreshkan, were remote but more or less familiar figures. Her father's schooldays, his adventures as a young man in Belfast, and his early plans for seeking a fortune in India or in the Canadian Dominion interested her more. The manner of the letters was leisured and elegant, the accounts full and detailed. By the time she had come to the third letter she had a profound illusion of her father's presence.

My Dear Sir: [she read] Ill health, indolence, and the pursuit of idle amusements, which only end in vanity and vexation of spirit, have diverted my attention from writing for some time past.

And then:

In the latter end of June, 1790, I embarked on board the *Clara,* Captain Collins, for New York.

With this embarkation Jane felt her personal history begun. The letter continued:

We were detained for several hours off Carickfergus in the middle of the night, by a naval officer and boat's crew, who took possession of the ship, and made a strict search for British seamen; though then at peace with the United States. I represented to the officer the cruelty and injustice of detaining an outward bound vessel with a fair wind, especially as the captain assured him that there was not a man of the description he sought for on board; but when I saw he was determined to detain the ship all night, I addressed a letter to the Marquis of Downshire, to whom I had the honor of being particularly known, stating the circumstances. I read the letter publicly, and prepared to send it by a gentleman just going ashore, but shortly after, "the man of brief authority" gave up the ship to the captain, and having eaten a snack and drunk a pint of half and half grog, he civilly bade us goodnight and a safe passage. I had never been at sea before, though bred up on the coast, which caused me to suffer more from sea-sickness than some of my fellow passengers. I lay down on the floor of the round house, from whence no inducement could tempt me to stir for nearly two days; at the expiration of which I found myself perfectly well, and as hungry as a hawk. I got a beefsteak and some porter, and never felt seasickness after. We were four who messed together in the round house with the captain, the Rev. Charles Gray of Coleraine; the Rev. Robert Cathcart, an old friend and neighbor, and a Mr. Mathews from Edinburgh. We fared as well as people at sea could possibly wish, and had such an abundance of wine, porter and spirits, that I was enabled to bestow a large hamper of wine, spruce beer, oranges and lemons, sent on board for me by my friend Mr. Batt, amongst the passengers in the hold, several of whom were sick. Our fare was only ten guineas each, though since risen to forty; such has been the advance in living within the last thirty years! We had a favorable passage until we arrived off the Azores, where we were chased by a sixty gun ship, which having hoisted Spanish and then French colors induced the captain to believe was one of the ships of war presented to the Algerines by France. He altered his course and put before the wind, the ship repeatedly firing at us; but our vessel being a prime sailor, and light, we soon increased our distance, and the next morning, when scarcely visible, she altered her course and gave up the chase. The second or third day after, when crossing the Gulf Stream, we were overtaken by a heavy gale, which raised a tremendous sea. In the night our cabin windows were stove in; we had two or three feet of water in the floor; trunks and boxes broke from their cleatings; the poor people in the under berths were all afloat, and such a scene of terror and confusion took place as I shall never forget. Some were praying aloud, others confessing their sins, others screaming from fear and pain, whilst escaping from drowning in their berths; and at every roll of the ship dashed into contact with trunks, chests and boxes. Amongst the latter sufferers was a Mrs. Lindsey, the wife of a clergyman from the Highlands of Scotland. Whilst sprawling on the floor she was struck in the head by an iron bound trunk, which laid it open for about three inches. When candles came down, the dead lights lashed in, the scene exhibited such a mixture of frightful and ludicrous as fairly surpassed description; poor Mrs. Lindsey, who at best might have passed for one of the witches in Macbeth, now looked a perfect Hecate; her matted locks dripping with gore, and her vulgar unmeaning countenance distorted into a most unearthly grin. No one pitied her or her fanatic husband. He had made himself particularly obnoxious to me from his language to the captain when chased by the Algerine. He told him it was an act of cowardice to run away from any vessel whilst we were all Englishmen; with a great deal more of the most illiberal and vulgar abuse. The captain mildly answered that he could appeal to most of his men, who had sailed with him when commanding a privateer during the revolutionary war, whether he had ever evinced any signs of cowardice when in conflict with the enemy. But now, as accountable to his owners for the ship, and to the passengers for their safety, he only performed his duty by avoiding danger, even supposing the vessel was not what we supposed her to be. I had at length to interfere, and sent the very Rev. Mr. Lindsey to his cabin rather precipitately.

Nothing further occurred worth noting until we got in sight of Long Island, which, as we approached, the trees seemed to start one after another from the water, and the scenery every instant developed new and interesting beauties; but on rounding Governor's Island, when the city, like a splendid amphitheater, burst upon the view, I was absolutely transported with pleasure and delight. We came to our moorings after sunset, and I slept on board that I might put my foot on American ground the day of my birth; having just attained my 28th year. And as this begins a new epoch in my existence, I shall here conclude the story of my voyage.

Remaining ever truly and affectionately yours,

John Johnston.

St. Mary's Falls, 1st March, 1828

My Dear Sir: The first thing that struck me on entering New York was the kindness and urbanity of the people. I had asked my three fellow passengers to breakfast with me, and entered into the first coffee house we saw. The people told me they were not in the habit of providing meals for those who called at their house, but as we were strangers, they would give us the best breakfast they could; accordingly we had fresh rolls, excellent butter, fresh eggs, cream, tea, coffee, smoked beef and ham, for about one shilling sterling each, which I thought augured well for our future comfort whilst in the country. I then went and called upon Mrs. Sadler, in Water Street, who was a distant connection of my mother's. I found her and Mr. Sadler himself, kind, friendly and hospitable. They insisted on my residing with them whilst in town. Mr. Sadler then took me to Hill and Johnston's store, and I soon found myself in the arms of the best and most affectionate of brothers. I passed a very happy week in New York, and saw in church the great and good Washington, to whom I should have had the honor of being introduced, had I been able to make a longer stay; but my passage was taken for Albany in a fine sloop, called the *Hibernia,* Captain Moor, where for the first time I saw my national flag displayed in all its beauty. We had a delightful passage of three days, though we stopped repeatedly to put ashore passengers and take in others. The romantic beauties of the Hudson have been so often and so ably described, that any attempt on my part would be absolute presumption. Amongst my fellow passengers were several genteel well-bred ladies. The men were plain, friendly and unaffected, and I found a very agreeable companion in a Mr. Noble, who was going to visit an estate his father had lately bought near Johnstown, in the center of the state of New York.

We put up at Lewis's Hotel, then the first in Albany; where we spent four or five days very pleasantly. I one day took a stroll for about a mile up the hill from Mr. Lewis's, and saw five or six men, all armed with rifles, dash out of the wood to my left. I was at first a little startled by their uncouth appearance, but they accosted me civilly, and said they presumed I was a stranger, from my walking unarmed so far from the city. They told me they were in pursuit of a pack of wolves that had attacked a gentleman on horseback, the day before, on the very place where we now stood; when nothing but the power and speed of his horse saved him. The horse was cut in several places, and the gentleman's boots nearly torn off his legs—you may think I was very thankful for the warning. My informants entered the wood on the opposite side of the road, and I did not pursue my walk any farther in that direction. I got acquainted with a Mr. Bedient of Boston, who was on his way to Montreal, as well as myself; we therefore hired a wagon between us, there being no other mode of conveyance. We traveled through a fine but only partially cultivated country, until we came

spending a week in Montreal, I took a place with the king's courier in a calash for Quebec. We traveled day and night, so that I never put off my clothes, nor got a moment's rest, except whilst changing our voiture, or when my companion delayed half an hour to lay in a stock of bacon and eggs, or some such delicate fare, sufficient, one would have thought, to sustain a reasonable man for a week. But my friend Monsieur Labadie weighed nearly 300 pounds and was determined that neither bad roads nor the most jolting vehicle in the world, should cause the least diminution of his *en bon point*. I paid two guineas for my seat, and had the honor besides of treating Mr. Labadie to all his slight repasts. We arrived the third day, and at Frank's Hotel I soon got over my fatigue and privations. I was not sorry to find that Lord Dorchester was yet at his country house, as it enabled me to ramble over the town, the plains of Abraham, etc. etc. I had never before been in a fortified town, unless the old crumbling ramparts of Londonderry could entitle it to the name. . . .

I had got acquainted with Mr. Motz, Lord D's private secretary, to whom I gave my letters. In a few days after his lordship came to town, when I had the honor of being introduced, and was received in a very kind and friendly manner; but, as Providence would have it, General Sir Alured Clark now arrived with the commission of Governor General, and with letters of recall for his lordship; however he decided not to risk Lady Dorchester and the family at so late a season, therefore continued in office during the winter. His lordship continued very kind and hospitable to me, and questioned me as to the fate of uncles who had been his schoolfellows. He introduced me to the chief merchants of the town, and wished me to write my ideas on the practicability of opening a direct trade with Ireland. In two or three days my memoir was finished, and he again invited me along with the gentlemen concerned, to dine at the castle, when the affair was fully discussed. They all acknowledged the justice and utility of the statement I had made, but candidly avowed that their connections in London, and the general nature of their imports, precluded their taking advantage of a direct trade; though it was very evident that the products of Ireland coming circuitously through their English correspondents, cost them much dearer than they otherwise would. Thus all prospect of entering into the mercantile line fell to the ground, and I announced to his lordship my determination to return to Montreal; he then told me, as he was determined not to take his family home at so late a season, he would introduce me to the bishop of Canada, where I would spend the winter agreeably, and learn to speak the French language, and was so kind as to add that if in the interim any place worth my acceptance became vacant, I should be appointed to it. However, I persisted in my resolution, not deeming it prudent to spend my time and money waiting for a contingency that might never occur. A few days after I took my leave, and was to set off the second day after, in company with a young ensign who was going to join his company at St. Johns. But before I left town, Mr. Motz came to me with an offer from his lordship of a township on the Acadian line, but on inquiry I found it would require a considerable sum of money to make the requisite locations to secure the title. I therefore begged leave to decline the offer, as neither suiting my means or inclination. In a short time after Mr. Motz again returned—and in the most delicate manner told me he was authorized to offer me any money I might stand in need of for the winter. But as my funds were still far from exhausted, and as my determination was never to lie under a pecuniary obligation, I might not easily be able to repay, I excused myself by assuring him I had a sufficient supply for the winter. But I requested that his lordship would favor me with a letter of introduction to Sir John Johnson, of whom, and of his father, Sir William, I had read and heard enough to inspire me with admiration, and a wish to have the honor of his acquaintance. I received the desired letter in the evening, and the next morning left Quebec in a carriole, with my young Scots companion. Though early in November there was nearly a foot of snow upon the ground, and we continued the use of carrioles until we came to Three Rivers, from whence we took calashes into Montreal.

My friend Mr. Tod received me with the utmost kindness and introduced me to several officers and gentlemen of the town. Sir John Johnson was absent on an excursion to the lake of Two Mountains, but his cousin, Capt. Dease, showed me the kindest attention and hospitality, and took me with him to his house in the country, where I remained until the arrival of Sir John, on whom we called the day after, and I presented my letter from Lord Dorchester. The reception I met with has left an impression that can never be effaced from my heart; and the unabated friendship and hospitality I have ever since been honored with by him, Lady Johnson and the ladies of the family, when several times passing a winter in Montreal, shall ever remain amongst my most grateful and pleasing recollections.

As I could not think of being a tax on the hospitality of my Montreal friends all winter, though much pressed by Sir John to take up my abode with him, I took lodgings at the village of Varennes, about fifteen miles from town, on the opposite side of the St. Lawrence, at a Mr. Vienne's, where I continued my study of the French language, which I had commenced before I left Ireland, and began to speak it pretty much as a child begins to walk, stumbling at every step; but to the honor of French urbanity and politeness, my greatest blunders were corrected without subjecting me to the pain of seeing my awkwardness and ignorance the subject of mirth or ridicule.

I visited Montreal several times during the winter, and attended the assemblies, which were conducted with great decorum, and where Lady Johnson and her daughter, just then brought out, were received with every degree of deference and respect. The winter passed off very agreeably, and in the beginning of May, 1791, I returned to Montreal, to take my passage with my friend, Andrew Tod, for Michilimackinac, by the North, or Otawis river. The mode of traveling in a birch canoe, the wild and romantic scenery on each side of the river, all was new and charming to me, except the last five or six days of our voyage, when the mosquitoes annoyed us beyond all endurance. I, who had nothing else to do but defend myself from them the best way I could, was left a perfect spectacle of deformity, my eyes near closed up, and my mouth distorted in a most frightful manner; judge then the condition of the poor men, engaged in carrying the baggage over the portages with their faces, necks and breasts exposed, and the blood and sweat in commingled streams running from them. But they seemed to mind it very little, making game of some young men whose first trip it was, whom they called mangeurs de lard, or pork eaters, and treated them with great contempt if they expressed pain or fatigue. We arrived the 16th at Mackinac, and were received with great politeness and hospitality by Capt. Charleton of the 5th foot, then commanding. I had been acquainted with him in the north of Ireland, when in command of the town of Coleraine. Our meeting so unexpectedly at a distance of more than four thousand miles from home, was very pleasing to both, and called up a variety of mixed ideas, some of which to me were rather painful, as they contrasted my present situation with the time I had received him hospitably at my mother's house, when placing a detachment to guard the wreck of a ship cast away within less than half a mile of Craige. As the traders, neither from the Mississippi or the Lake Superior, had yet arrived, I had some weeks' leisure, which I employed in exploring the island and in reading. I shall, therefore, here conclude this tedious epistle with a promise that my next shall have at least the merit of novelty to recommend it.

Ever truly yours, John Johnston.

The last letter had never been delivered to Henry. Jane had found it herself in her father's portfolio. She lighted a candle and drew the writing table nearer to her chair before she went on with her reading.

145

St. Mary's Falls, June 10, 1828.

My Dear Sir: Ill health and often depression of spirits, owing to the iniquitous manner in which the Indian trade is, and has always been carried on here, and in fact, all over the continent, with the addition of painful reflections, on my own imprudence and inability to compete with opponents equally active as unprincipled, have been the cause of my letting so long an interval elapse since the date of my last. But I now resume my pen in hopes of presenting you with a sketch of the arrival of the traders, and the shifting of the scene from streets unoccupied, where dullness and silence reigned unmolested, to houses crowded to overflowing, where riot and revelry, festivity and song, swept all descriptions down its heady current with scarcely a single exception. The excuse pleaded by the traders is their many fatigues, risks and privations during the winter, and often an entire seclusion from all society, so that when they again meet at Mackinac, where they are sure to see their Montreal friends, and an ample supply of wines, spirits, etc., etc., they think themselves entitled to make up for what they call lost time, by making the most of the short interval that elapses between the sale of their furs, and their repurchase of goods for a new adventure. The chief traders and Montreal merchants keep open table for their friends and dependents, and vie with each other in hospitality to strangers. But the excess to which their indulgence is carried, seldom ends without a quarrel, when old grudges are opened up, and language made use of that would disgrace a Wapping tavern, and the finale being a boxing match, as brutal and ferocious as any exhibited in ancient times by the Centaurs and Lapythe.

But were I to relate all I have heard and been an unwilling witness of, this would become a chronicle of scandal instead of a letter, I shall therefore let the curtain drop for the present, only retaining the liberty of taking it up occasionally, as new acts of this far from delightful drama may present themselves to my recollection. The Montreal canoes began to move off with their cargoes of furs and peltries, during the month of July, and the traders whose posts were the most distant, were chiefly all off by the beginning of August, so that tranquillity and rationality began to reassume their long forgotten sway.

About the middle of August my friend Mr. Tod, fitted me out with a canoe of the largest size with five Canadian boatmen or voyageurs, to winter at La Pointe, in Lake Superior, which station I preferred to one more to the south.

This was familiar territory for Jane. It was easy to see her young father, with his fair hair and blue coat, journeying up the St. Mary's with his

Canadians. She read on, ever more absorbed, through his account of the meeting with Andriani, of the preparations for that first winter, of the desertion of his men. It was late autumn at La Pointe Chegoimegon; her brother Lewis was not yet born; her father had not yet seen her mother.

The Indians had left us for some time, and had gone to a considerable distance on their hunting excursions, all except the old father of the chief, who only went to a small river in the bay of St. Charles, from whence, however, he returned just as the ice in our bay was closing. My good neighbors rushed into the water and hauled the canoe to shore, and without ceremony possessed themselves of eight or ten beavers the old man had killed. They kept him, his two wives and a Mrs. Jayer [Sayer?], one of his daughters, who wintered with him, in a constant state of intoxication for some days, at the end of which they fairly turned them out of doors, telling them they must provide for themselves, as they would feed them no longer. Some time after the old man came to me and complained of hunger, as his wives could not go to a deposit of wild rice they had concealed at a considerable distance, the weather having become very bad, and the snow too deep to walk without snow shoes. I told him I would not see him or his family starve, though I much feared I should want food long before spring, and that he ought to recollect he had not paid me a small credit I had made him before he went to hunt. He acknowledged the fact, but said, those who had taken him to shore made him drunk, and kept him so, until his little stock of furs was exhausted, though he knew not what he had received in return, except his meat and drink for a few days. I accepted his excuse and continued to treat him all winter with great respect, as he showed me a large bugle belt, with which, and a silver gorges, he had been presented by Sir William Johnson after the fall of Fort Niagara to the British forces. He said he had kept his belt free from stain until now, and hoped his son Wabojeeg would continue to do so after he should be gone to the land of spirits.

The letter terminated quite abruptly without a signature. Jane looked again at the date, June, of the summer just gone, and laid the paper on her knee, remembering how many times her entrance into the room had halted her father at his writing, how he had set his quill into its dish of sand and risen to greet her, steadying himself with one hand on the table. She would have given the world, at that moment, never to have interrupted him, if the letter could have gone on. But the letter was ended; the voice had finished speaking.

PART THREE

Henry and George and Neengay had been sitting at the table in the living-room all the forenoon, going over the papers to the Johnston estate which Henry and George had already consulted together. The October sun was pale. Beyond the window, the garden seemed deserted, and indoors the vitality of the fire hardly reached the end of the room where the table stood with its litter of documents. Neengay's red shawl was drawn closely over her bosom. George sat with his hands thrust into his trousers pockets, while Henry shifted the papers, speaking. Debts being settled, nothing remained except the buildings, the homestead with its furnishings, and the loyalty of Johnston's men. Two years before, with Henry acting as probate judge, Johnston and Neengay had sold to Astor, Ramsay Crooks, and Robert Stuart, for the American Fur Company, three hundred and twenty acres, including land adjacent to the fort, and had received in payment one thousand dollars. Of this sum, nothing remained, and as for the legality of the sale, Congress had not as yet ratified Johnston's claim to any of the land originally awarded him by the British Crown. Johnston's books, over a period of twelve years, showed a loss of nearly forty thousand dollars in credits to individual Indians. This reckoning excluded all furs owing from the sale of liquor, and the chance that any of it would ever be repaid to the estate was, at that time, negligible. They explained these matters to Neengay, who nodded, her face quiet but not despairing, indeed so quiet and composed that Schoolcraft thought she did not understand.

"Tell her again," he said to George. "Once the debts are paid she'll have nothing but the house."

George said, "She understands." And Neengay, catching Henry's concern, said in Ojibway, "Yes, my children, I understand," her face controlled and serene as before.

Certain of Johnston's private belongings were to go to his children, silver candlesticks with the silver snuffer to George, a silver platter and a crystal cake dish to John McDougall upon his marriage, and a portrait, not the one over the mantelpiece, but one showing Johnston in a dark coat with a lapel faced with yellow satin; to Henry a very fine land-compass once given to Johnston by General McComb, his cabinets, and so on down the line. The little council had noted this before, but these were tokens, not an inheritance. After a while Neengay began to speak, gently:

"There are whitefish in the river. On Sugar Island there are maple trees. Your treaty"—she was directing herself to Henry—"gave to the Women of the Glade, to each of her children, and to each of her grandchildren, one section of land. I will choose my section from the woods on Sugar Island. Your father's children"—she was speaking to George—"will not be hungry."

She laid her dark hand on the table and swept the papers, which she could not read, into an orderly pile. Already her canoes were busy above the rapids in the bay that was then being called Wayishkee's, and at the house her women were smoking or salting fish for the winter. "In my boyhood days," wrote John McDougall Johnston, "my father had near our home a fish house twenty-five or thirty feet square. Each season he would have forty pork barrels of salted whitefish and from five to six thousand fresh fish. These were strung in pairs by their tails and hung over rows of poles. They were allowed to freeze and would keep all winter. It was nothing strange to take five hundred or a thousand whitefish at the foot of the rapids in a single night, and sometimes fifteen hundred." Many times Neengay went with the canoes in person, and, the fish house having been stocked for the season, she sold the surplus catch to the American Fur Company, to be shipped down the lakes. The second week in October she rented Johnston's office, where the treaty of 1820 had been signed, to a missionary from New York State, Abel Bingham. Knowing the deep melancholy of her race, which, when ceded to, had destroyed many of her people, a sensitive and brooding race for all their courage and endurance, an excessive grief appeared to her ignoble while there were seven living children. She put her loss aside as something which concerned herself alone, and her children's grief and need absorbed her thought. Jane and Henry saw that although the family was no longer affluent, they need not beg; Will might remain at school, and educations would be contrived for the younger Johnstons, not so fine as that given to Lewis, but still adequate for the children of a gentleman.

The first Sunday after his arrival Father Bingham conducted two religious services, one in the morning for the people of the fort and village, and one in the afternoon for the Indians. Although the Johnston children were communicants in the Episcopal Church, Charlotte volunteered to interpret for Father Bingham, and her sisters attended his first services. Sitting where Neengay had delivered her appeal to the Image Stone and the Little Pine, Charlotte folded her pale hands on her taffeta skirt, resting her eyes on them while Father Bingham preached his sermon. The room was crowded. At the end of each paragraph, she translated, the Indians listening with rapt attention, and repeating after her, at last, the prayer: "Our Father who liveth above, what you wish to be done, let it be done. Let us not play with Thy name, let Thy great power come, give us our food this day, give us our debts as we give our debtors. Do not lead us into bad things, keep us from bad things. Power belongs to Thee, and strength, forever."

On Monday Father Bingham began to teach a few Indians the letters of the alphabet. He knew something of Indian manners and customs, having spent almost seven years among the Senecas before the Baptist Missionary Board had transferred him to this wilderness, but as he wrote large a's and b's, capital and minuscule, before the wondering eyes of Shegud and his brethren, two things weighed heavily upon his mind: every male Indian in the Sault carried in his medicine pouch "poison" with which to kill his brother, and the stores and the military canteen between them were planning to dispose of fifteen thousand gallons of whiskey before spring. At least, he had been told that fifteen thousand gallons of whiskey were lodged here and there in the village, and his informant had expressed the cheerful wish that the supply might last until the next vessel up, navigation being closed for that season.

Henry Schoolcraft had a new interpreter that year, one John Tanner, recommended chiefly because of the peculiar misfortunes of his existence, and by no less a person than Governor Cass. Tanner had passed through the settlement of St. Mary's at least three times before he came with his two children to live in the outskirts of the Indian village at the Little Rapids. The first of these occasions had been when as a boy of thirteen he had followed his adoptive mother, the Ottawa woman, old Netnokway, on her journey to Fort William and thence to the Red River country. The Indians, and Tanner helping them, had stopped at the Sault to load their goods on a vessel belonging to the Northwest Company which was bound for the fort; there had been at the Sault that spring only the company's house, Cadotte's, and the French village, besides the usual cluster of wigwams. It was 1793, and Neengay and Johnston were yet at Ile St. Michel. Tanner had been bought by Netnokway from Gishgaugo the Saginaw, for a keg of rum and sundry minor considerations, to take the place of a dead child; he had been stolen by Gishgaugo from the edge of his father's cornfield in Kentucky for the same reason. Gishgaugo's mother had lost a son, and he and his father had stolen a boy of the right age to be religiously adopted as a substitute. Tanner's first adoptive parents beat, starved, and insulted him, and once his father tomahawked him and left him for dead. At the Sault, however, Tanner made no effort to escape to the traders. Gishgaugo had told him that all his own people had been killed by the Indians, and Netnokway was kind to him. No longer treated as a captive, but as a son in fact, he went with her to the Pembina, learned to hunt, learned to make medicine, forgot his own speech and his own people, married a woman of the Pembina band, and from year to year postponed the trip he had once planned with longing, to Kentucky and the junction of the Ohio and the Big Miami.

Almost thirty years later, an even thirty from the year in which he was stolen, he came through St. Mary's again. A man grown and in the prime of life, skin weathered to an Indian color, his hair long and strewn with silver brooches, his costume entirely that of an Indian, unable to speak to his own race without an interpreter, Shawshawa-benaysee, the Falcon, was going to Kentucky to find his father, the Rev. John Tanner, his brother Edward, and his sisters, Agatha and Lucy. He left behind him at the Pembina two wives and six half-breed children, three by each wife. Lord Selkirk, to whom Tanner had rendered valuable service in the struggle between the Hudson's Bay and the Northwest, then at its peak, learning Tanner's story, had advertised in Kentucky and found Edward Tanner. Shawshawa-benaysee did not see his father, who was dead eight years before his son reached Kentucky, but at Detroit he met Edward, and later, Agatha and Lucy. For the sake of these people he brought his youngest children to Kentucky, cut his long hair, and tried to learn English. But it was too late. Sleeping in a house made him ill. The food was strange. He knew of only one way to make a living, and that was by hunting, and so in 1822 he returned to Mackinac with little Martha and John, and requested the post of interpreter of Colonel Boyd, who was unfortunately unable to give it to him at that time. The two years in the south had severed Tanner from the Indians; the thirty years on the Pembina had severed him from the whites. He aligned himself with the métif class, and engaged himself to the American Fur Company for the salary of two hundred and twenty-five dollars a year and a suit of clothes. The company sent him to the Red River as a voyageur, and the Mackinac Mission opened its doors to Martha and young John.

Three years later Tanner was again in the Sault. He had left the company after fifteen months of service, and had gone on a fruitless and perilous expedition to Netnokway's band in the hope of bringing his two older daughters and his son to live with him at Mackinac. But Netnokway was dead, and his wife, the Red Sky of the Morning, tried to kill him. He came down with the traders from the Pembina when he had sufficiently recovered from the wounds received in this venture, and at Mackinac Colonel Boyd welcomed him and made him his interpreter. There he went to housekeeping with John and Martha. That was in 1825. In 1828 he was interpreter for Henry Schoolcraft.

Jane saw him waiting in the office for Henry, or accompanying her husband on his occasional visits to the Indian lodges, an erect, square-shouldered figure in a heavy tailored coat and a high stock, his hair gray and shaggy, his eyes blue and penetrating, gleaming from beneath the shaggy brows, a figure as impervious to weather as a rock. She noticed that his forehead was scarred, and his right hand also, but that the action of the hand seemed unaffected. At times she saw his daughter Martha, who did not differ greatly from other little half-breeds at the Sault except that she seemed more easily startled. Even Jane's light step, coming into the office where Tanner was conferring with Henry, brought a momentary expression of fear into the child's whole body. Jane ascribed this to a child's natural nervousness at being in a strange community, and as she passed let her hand slide gently across the little girl's shoulder.

Most people at the Sault knew a little about Tanner's history; no one knew a great deal, and some knew stories about him which had never come to pass. He was reputed by the French to be skilled in Indian sorcery, and they were afraid of him. With the white population he associated little, perhaps because he was still embarrassed in speaking English; the Indian village he sedulously avoided. To Jane he was gruffly courteous, at the store he was scrupulously honest, and he was, that first year, very seldom drunk. He entered on his duties as interpreter, as Henry himself said, with great dignity and faithfulness.

The cold of winter deepened through December, February. Winter passed, the winter of 1828, and in March Neengay went with her people to the sugar camp.

Late in August Henry left for Detroit, to attend the second session of the third legislative council, taking with him his interpreter, less with an eye to

possible Indian conferences than in the thought that Cass would be interested to see Tanner again, and that the trip might dispel an increasing
moroseness of temper which Henry noted in Tanner. There was a quality
about the man which Schoolcraft respected—a self-reliance almost Roman
in grandeur, joined to the fellow virtue of concerning himself strictly with
his own business, and because of this Henry repressed a personal irritation
founded on the suspicion that Tanner did not greatly respect his superior
as a man. A more serious cause for irritation was Tanner's scorn for all
Indians, which he troubled himself little to conceal, and which made
Henry's contact with his wards the more difficult. Henry had prided himself on his diplomacy, and Tanner's unspoken assumption that all Indians
were thieves and murderers cast a damp upon the Indian visits throughout
the winter and spring of that year. However, to Detroit they went, Henry
and Tanner, and put up at Uncle Ben Woodworth's Steamboat Hotel. The
white omnibus inscribed with gilt conveyed them from the docks, and
young Sam Woodworth, his face round and red above his tightly buttoned
green coat with the big lapels, and his brightly striped and very narrow
pantaloons, took their luggage and escorted them to the desk. The office,
the sitting room, and the dining-room of the Steamboat Hotel were shadowy, spacious, and smelled of the hay which was laid under the carpets to
make them soft. There was a barber who quoted Greek and Latin and
argued like Thomas Aquinas, there was Uncle Ben, large and square and
gray-eyed, and there were fresh-skinned country girls going about the cor-
ridors with piles of clean linen or with pillow slips stuffed full of used tow-
els and sheets, or laying out the large bone-handled knives on the coarse
white table covers of the dining-room. Here Henry Schoolcraft left his
interpreter while he attended the council. He was chairman of the
Committee of Finances, and having discharged his duties in that respect to
his satisfaction, he busied himself "with the plan of trying to introduce
terse and tasty names for the new townships, taken from the Indian vocabulary, to suppress the sale of ardent spirits to the Indian race, and to secure
something like protection for that part of the population which had amal-
gamated with Indian blood." Colonel Brady gave him a list of the officers
who had served under General Wayne in the campaigns of 1791 and 1793,
and these names seemed to him even more appropriate for the new townships than his concocted ones.

Towards the end of October, having left the council still in full swing,
he and Tanner were back at St. Mary's, and Tanner, to every one's surprise,
had brought with him as his wife one of Ben Woodworth's chambermaids,
a nice girl with bright cheeks and slow, dazzled eyes. Tanner had dined

with Governor Cass, he was employed by the United States Government, he spoke English with a foreign accent, and carried himself like a general, he was still handsome, and he had been through adventures stranger than those of Othello when he first courted at Venice; he had suffered, also. After a few weeks the dazzle changed to bewilderment, but the ladies of the fort and village said, "How nice for little Martha!" and made a point of being kind to Martha's stepmother.

Winter was no longer such as it had been in Jane's girlhood. There was now the Ahmo Society, a sewing circle which met regularly to labor for the needy. The name, which signified a honeybee, had been suggested by Henry at the request of the ladies. And there was the Mission House, completed in November, where Abel Bingham had fifty or more scholars, some of them children from the fort, most of them half-breeds and Indians; and there was Hannah Bingham with Angie, born in March in Johnston's office, the night of a grand equinoctial storm. The great social preoccupation of the village that year was religion, and Abel Bingham was preaching temperance. Henry's sister Maria had come to the Sault, fallen in love with the sutler of Fort Brady, and married him, and now this gentleman, under the combined influence of Father Bingham and Maria, was heard to declare that he would rather sell potatoes for a living than whiskey, and every merchant in the Sault had joined him in the sentiment. In fact the town went perfectly dry that winter, liquor even being poured out on the streets once as a demonstration. The new agency building was large, containing fifteen rooms and a "basement," with double windows and storm porches, the northwest wind broken by the bower of ash and elm trees which surrounded it. Early in the winter, knowing that the old man had neither strength nor provisions adequate to a long stretch of bitter weather, Henry invited Jean Baptiste Perreault and his wife to take up their quarters in the basement, sweetening his charity with the request that Perreault instruct him in French. Thereafter, every morning on the stroke of ten the old man presented himself in the upper rooms of the Schoolcraft dwelling, alert and courteous. Indians came from the Bawating band and from the nearer villages as they had come to Neengay's kitchen, and Tanner, increasingly morose and increasingly careless about his dress, presented himself regularly for his duties. Indeed his bad temper and slovenliness were equaled only by the neatness and gallantry of the old marchand voyageur, and between the two of them, Henry, coming one day from a pleasant hour with the Frenchman upon an especially bitter moment of Tanner's, lost his patience, and dismissed his interpreter. Tanner applied to Father Bingham, and that good man, thinking of Martha and the young wife, engaged him to help with the mission work.

155

Father Bingham admired Tanner for those qualities which Henry had discerned in him and praised, and he brought to the task of getting on with his new interpreter a truly Christian patience. With Dr. Edwin James and Tanner he began to translate portions of the Scriptures into Ojibway. It was Dr. James who had, before Tanner's coming to the Sault, taken down Tanner's story of his life, and who, it was believed, had sent him to New York to have his portrait engraved. Meanwhile the Ahmo Society buzzed with gossip, and Jane heard that Tanner had been beating both his wife, who was with child, and his daughter Martha.

And so the winter of 1829 and '30 wore away, and in the spring, Jane with her little new son was on her way to Detroit with Henry for what she was to remember always as one of the pleasantest times of her life. Her sister Charlotte was with her, and an Indian nurse to help her with Janie and the child. At the Governor's mansion they met all the notables of Detroit, and Henry was not so occupied with the congress that he did not manage to steal a week for a sightseeing trip to Niagara Falls. Moreover, Henry had engineered through the legislature a measure which brought a great sense of comfort to Jane's tender heart, a measure for the rescue of Martha Tanner. It was a curious law, directed purely and simply at one person, and its title read as follows: An Act Authorizing the Sheriff of Chippewa County to Perform Certain Duties therein Mentioned.

The primary duty of the sheriff was to remove Martha Tanner, daughter of John Tanner of Sault Ste. Marie, but not without her consent, to some missionary establishment or to any other place of safety he might deem expedient. Section Two of the Act stated "that any threats of the said John Tanner to injure the said Martha Tanner, or any person or persons with whom she may be placed . . . shall be deemed a misdemeanor, punishable by fine and imprisonment, at the discretion of the court." With the vision of Martha safe among the kind people at Mackinac, learning to brush her hair every night and bathe her body daily and worship the Lord, Jane rustled happily among the groups of ladies and gentlemen drinking lemonade on the broad piazza of the Cass mansion, or went for short carriage drives into the country with Miss Elizabeth Cass and Charlotte, or in sultry weather crossed to Windsor on the ferry to enjoy the river breeze and watch the gay crowds.

In August they left the steamboat at Mackinac Island, and came, all of them, up the familiar course between the summer-wooded islands, changing in mass and color under the mid-August showers. At the Sault, their attention was called first of all to the activities of Jean Baptiste Perreault, who had, in their absence, devised a remarkable boat with rotary sails, which, being moved by the wind, were to act through machinery on a set of paddle wheels. Standing on the veranda at Elmwood, Jane saw Perreault and his craft exercising on the stretch of uninterrupted water below the rapids and above the Little Rapids, and noticed that in order to come about, Jean Baptiste had often to revert to an oar. Doubtless the rotary sails were ingenious; the chief practical difficulty seemed to lie in the fact that if one had wind enough to rotate the sails and through them the paddle wheels, one had wind enough to navigate without paddle wheels. Jane suggested this to Perreault one evening, and he admitted with bowed head and an oblique smile that it was true, and then returned to a light-hearted and enthusiastic description of the wheels and ropes and ratchets by which he had so needlessly connected paddle and sail.

The second bit of news was brought her by Hannah Bingham, arriving early the afternoon of the first meeting, since Jane's return, of the Ahmo Society. While they spread out the bolts of flannel that were to be cut and sewed into petticoats for the mission children, Hannah related the tale of the conspiracy and flight of Tanner's young wife. The baby had been born shortly after Jane's departure. In a month Mrs. Tanner had gone in tears to the ladies of the fort, who made arrangements for her passage on a Detroit-bound steamer, collected a purse for her, and, taking advantage of an occasion when Tanner, arrested for drunkenness, was in jail, had sent her on her way south with her child. Tanner, released, had come home to a house empty save for little Martha, whom he had beaten, and from whom he had been able to learn nothing of what had occurred in his absence. At the end of July, the legislature had put through its Act for Martha, and only a few days before Jane's return to St. Mary's, the sheriff of Chippewa County had escorted the child down the river to Mackinac. Tanner, who could not read, and who had not been at home at the time of the sheriff's visit, had been summoned to Father Bingham's office, where the law and its contents, especially Section Two, had been explained to him. Tanner's bitterness concerning the affair was thus extended to Father Bingham. But the ladies of the fort came in for their full share, the Ahmo Society was suspect, and Tanner, knowing that Henry Schoolcraft had attended the legislative council, presently fastened the responsibility for the Act upon him, blaming him also for the disappearance of his wife and her baby.

His rancor knew no intermission. People went out of their way to avoid him, but he was hard to avoid. He had the habit of hanging about the Mission House, and one fine day Henry's sister Maria, seated in the small parlor next to Father Bingham's study, was startled by the sound of a scuffle in the next room. In a moment Tanner emerged, his greatcoat spotted with grease and filth, his stock discarded, face unshaven, moccasins making no noise on the carpet, and gazing at her from within his anger as if across a great distance, and intently, almost as if he had never seen her before, said, *"Look out for the flowers in your garden!"* He left the room at once with that motion of the body which she had always associated with the Indians, and Bingham, entering the room from his study, his hand held over his nose, found her transfixed with terror as if at the pronouncement of an oracle. He said to her mildly and in amazement:

"He tried to break my nose. He leaned over my shoulder while I was writing and *wrung* my nose. I'm not sure he didn't break it."

Tanner had said nothing to Abel Bingham, had offered no violence to Maria, but he succeeded in setting the Ahmo Society into a hubbub for a month.

Later in the year Dr. James's draft of *Tanner's Narrative* reached St. Mary's, a small volume, densely printed, with the portrait of Tanner as frontispiece. The portrait showed him in the tailored coat which all the Sault knew so well in its last degraded version, but in the engraving the coat was new, the stock was fresh, and the expression in Tanner's face was such as Jane remembered it from her first meeting with him, one of severe and self-reliant dignity. Under the picture was engraved his Indian name, Shawshawa-benaysee, the Falcon, and on the title page his name was given John Tanner, U. S. Interpreter at the Saut* de Ste. Marie, with the name of Dr. James in small type at a humble distance down the page. The *Narrative* occupied the first two thirds of the books; the last part consisted of comments on Indian customs, Indian vocabularies, and translations, with interpretations, of medicine songs accompanied by cuts of the original picture writing of the bark records. How this emblem of departed grandeur affected the John Tanner who had just had the entire legislative council enacting a measure directed against him and him alone, one cannot tell, but the book was read by nearly everybody else at the Sault, and with varying reactions. Henry read it, and coming to this paragraph in the introduction, pursed his lips, said nothing, and read on:

"It is to be regretted that he should ever meet among us with those so destitute of generosity, as to be willing to take advantage of his unavoidable ignorance of the usages of civilized society. He has ever been found just and generous, until insults or injuries have aroused the spirit of hatred or revenge; his gratitude has always been as ardent and persevering as his

---

* The old spelling.

resentment. . . . The preceding remarks would not perhaps have been haz-
arded, had not some harsh imputations been made to rest on the character of our narrator, in the district where he has for some time past resided,
in consequence of differences growing . . . entirely out of the circumstances of the Indian character . . . being indelibly impressed upon him.
However such a character . . . may excite our disapprobation . . . some
indulgence is due where, as in this case, the solitary savage, with his own
habits and opinions, is brought into contact with the artificial manners
and complicated institutions of civilized men."

Henry finished the introduction, read the narrative, looked over the
Ojibway vocabularies and comments in the back, and having noted that
Shawshawa-benaysee was in one place translated the Falcon and in another
the Swallow, and that the totem of Waub-ojeeg was given as Addik-gumaig
instead of Ahdeek, that is, as the Reindeer of the Water, the whitefish, instead
of the Deer, contented himself with remarking that James had made "a mere
packhorse of Indian opinion" out of Tanner, and laid the book aside. Jane
read it, between whiles of sewing, her hand with thimble and needle poised
above the page of fine print, a maze of darkness through which were dimly
visible the forests of the north, the smoke and stench of wigwams, of fes-
tered sores, the winter cold, hunger that made the head swim.

"When I at last came to the lodge, I immediately fell down, but I did not
lose myself as before. I can remember seeing the thick and sparkling coat
of frost on the inside of the pukkwi lodge, and hearing my mother say that
she had kept a large fire in expectation of my arrival. . . . Heavy snow and
severe cold came upon us at the Muskeeg carrying place; the trees
cracked with cold, but the water in the swamp was not yet frozen hard
enough to bear; our canoes, however, could not be pushed through. . . .
The weather was very cold and the ground hard frozen, but no snow fell;
so that it was difficult to follow the tracks of the moose, and the noise of
our walking on hard ground and dry leaves, gave the animals timely warning of our approach. This state of things continuing for some time we
were all reduced nearly to starvation, and had recourse, as a last resort, to
medicine hunting. Half the night I sung and prayed." She read, skipping
from page to page, a little here, and then, turning back to catch the drift
of the story, a few earlier paragraphs. It was a long tale of increasing disaster and enmities. In spite of the many deeds of extraordinary kindness,
even of nobility, by Indians and whites, year by year hatred closed around
him. When Jane read these pages, and when she read the long account of
his attempt to bring his older daughters to the settlement, of the treachery and suffering involved, Jane wept, and thought of Martha's bruised

shoulders, and wept again. The account of his journey to the Ohio, a stranger among his own people, also moved her deeply. She saw the peaceful Ohio farmlands, the strange figure with the long hair and barbarous ornaments, the face gaunt with anxiety, the hard mouth that spoke no English. She understood his irritation at the terror he himself evoked, and she tried to bring Henry to a greater sympathy with his former interpreter. Henry agreed with her pity, but concluded that although Tanner was unfortunate, his misfortunes gave him no right to beat his daughter or insult his superiors.

There were also people at St. Mary's who said that Tanner's book was full of lies, and Tanner, since he could not read, suspected that Dr. James had betrayed him. Before the year was out he was heard to declare in public that he meant to kill the Doctor for having made a fool of him.

II

No one kept him very well informed about the progress of the young Frenchman, and James Schoolcraft fidgeted away his time in the guardhouse at Mackinac through December, through January, Christmas, and New Year's Day, without the slightest trace of revelry, and felt that when a man's life depended upon the state of another man's health some one might have the decency to keep him better informed. James had been very drunk at a ball in one of the French houses, and had dirked a man. He supposed afterwards that there must have been a girl in the quarrel, but he could remember very little about it, and since the wounded man lingered between life and death, and no one could prophesy the outcome of the affair, James presently found himself under surveillance at Michilimackinac without having had an opportunity to inquire of his friends exactly what had occurred. When January ran into February his impatience got the better of him. He broke jail and started for St. Mary's, without snowshoes or provisions, intending to give himself up if the man was dead, and personally to solicit his recovery in case he was not. Fortune was with him, and he acquired a pair of snowshoes and some pemmican from a half-breed who did not know he was aiding a runaway, and on the fourth staggered into the Sault, exhausted, where his friend Dechaume seized upon his person and put him to bed. More than once on the journey through the February drifts he asked himself, not knowing honestly the answer, whether or not he was glad that Henry was in Detroit, but when Dechaume, embracing him, assured him that his victim was well, and that the jailbreak would surely be forgiven, he knew that he rejoiced in Henry's absence.

The Sunday following, having slept for almost three days straight, except for those intervals in which Dechaume brought him hot tea and venison steak, and assured him over and over that he had the luck of the devil, dressed and shaved, and feeling altogether elegant within and without, he presented himself at the Johnston home for congratulations. Jane was there, dining with her mother and sisters. As James entered she rose to her feet and began to weep, holding her napkin before her mouth and letting the tears run down her face unchecked. But Charlotte ran to him to take his coat, and while he was unwinding his sash and loosening his cuffs, all of them, Anna Maria, Eliza, and Charlotte, began to tell him of how Dr. James had sent the certificate of the Frenchman's recovery by the last express to Mackinac, of how Jane had sent Shegud with the express to escort James home, and of the universal dismay at the Sault when Shegud returned to announce that James had fled. Neengay had immediately dispatched one of her Indians to look for him; he was not yet back from the search. They stood about him, chattering and welcoming him, and looking so pretty that when Jane, drying her eyes, asked him seriously if he hadn't felt, while imprisoned, that God had given him a warning and an opportunity to mend his ways, he admitted that he had, although she was the only living soul who could have extracted such a confession from him.

The evening of the day following, Jane sent the sleigh and a request for him to call on her at Elmwood. James knew he was in for a lecture. He cast an appealing glance at Dechaume, but could think of no reasonable excuse for declining, and the cariole waited; he climbed in submissively and drew the buffalo robe up to his chest. Jane's lecture was affectionate and gentle. She did not blame him for his misdeeds, but pled with him to abandon gaming, drinking, dancing, and low company; in fine, to abandon the French village, and if he couldn't do that, to give up drinking for a time at least. James was pleasant and evasive. He granted that her request was wise, and vowed that he was very fond of her, but would make no promises. Fearing to push the matter too far, Jane gave over her "sage discourse," and fetching copies of the *Literary Voyager,* their old amusement, Henry's one-copy, circulating journal to which they had all, including James, from time to time contributed verses, stories, or articles, endeavored to entertain him in a manner more befitting his talents and his family.

Anna Maria, now seventeen years old, was staying with Jane in Henry's absence. She sat on a low chair on the other side of the Montreal stove, knitting a little jacket, doubtless for Janie. James, lolling with his long legs straight before him, his big, handsome frame at ease in the warmth and Henry's favorite chair, surveyed this little sister-in-law of Henry's while

Jane read, her voice silvery and low. What, he asked himself, not with great originality, occurs to a little girl overnight to make her into a young woman? No one said anything more about evil ways or reformation, and the evening grew late, pleasantly. When it was time for James to depart, Jane begged him to come again soon, and was a little surprised and greatly touched at the promptness with which he accepted. She wrote to Henry in Detroit that she wanted first to civilize his brother and after that to Christianize him, if possible, for "he is, at present, skeptical."

But Jane was not dull. However charmingly James took all her "discourses," never protesting, never arguing save in the most light and affectionate manner, it was evident that he came to Elmwood to look at Anna Maria. Jane concluded that God in his wisdom was trying a more subtle argument on James than any in her vocabulary, and found reasons to be out of the room.

While Janie smoothed down her apron and recited "How Doth the Little Busy Bee," conned from a book her father had sent her, or stood by the table to write her name, "Schoolcraft and all," and while Johnston, refusing to walk, although quite an age, hitched himself around the floor of the living-room on the seat of his pants, Anna Maria thought of James, of how big he was, how good-looking, how romantic, having almost killed a man in a moment of passion, and was immensely flattered that he spent so much time with her. Their courtship was very innocent. James's account of his trip down the Erie Canal served them for a long time. The side of the stove glowed a dull red; outside was bitter February weather. James, leaning forward, drew on the carpet the way they had taken.

Down the straits, along behind Manitouline to the mouth of the French River, in along the old Ottawa route that Johnston had taken on his first journey to Mackinac, portaging with an oxcart to Little York, not then called Toronto, up Lake Erie and across to Sacketts Harbor, where he met old friends from Fort Brady. Anna Maria remembered those friends. They conferred for a while on the early personnel of the fort; and then back down the southern side of the lake to Niagara Falls, and another portage, and so to the entrance to the new Erie Canal. They got a permit from the superintendents, and floated their bark canoe, with six voyageurs, in among the canal boats, a wild and curious sight on the level water, between the cultivated fields.

"It's only four feet deep, you know," said James, looking up without lifting his shoulders from his posture over an imaginary map, "and my, those big barges have an awful suction! We got caught behind one of them, it pulled the canoe bang up against the barge. She was going along at a good pace, being towed by three of the biggest gray horses you ever saw. The captain hollered to the driver to stop, and the driver—he was riding one horse—pulled in, and we got away. But then the driver thought that was funny and he started up again at a good clip and bang, there we were up against the barge again. Three times he did that, the captain shouting and cursing at him, and I saw the red coming up in the back of the neck of Jean Baptiste Piquette. You see, the team was going one way, we were going the other. I spoke to Butterfield in French, and he spoke to the men, and just as we were getting free of the boat the third time, he gave the word, in French, and the men came out with a regular Indian war whoop. The team started up, broke the towline and dumped the driver into a field, and old Piquette turned around to me and gave me the grin of his life. The last we saw of the horses they were jumping fences and traveling cross-lots. We didn't wait to discuss the matter with the captain."

Again: "This canal goes along just like a road through farmlands. We were singing, going through a pasture one day, and all the critters in it came over to find what the noise was about, cattle, horses, sheep, hogs, and when they saw us they didn't stay long; colts snorting, little pigs with their tails on their backs, Lord, how they ran!" He straightened and laughed, a big easy laugh that Jane heard in the next room. "Another day—maybe the same day—we came to a flock of geese that somebody put to pasture in the canal. They were yoked together with shingles and they blocked the way completely. There must have been a couple of hundred of them. 'Now how are we going to get through here?' says Butterfield. 'Leave that to me, mon bourgeois,' says Piquette. So we left it to him, and as a result, our supply of hulled corn lasted a remarkably long time."

Again: "Our worst trouble at Albany was to keep the boys from stealing pitch from our canoe. A free supply of spruce gum, they thought it was. We'd like to never to get back to St. Mary's with our canoe all eaten into holes."

He told over the names of the voyageurs, La Batt, who made the canoe, Piquette—not Toussaint—Jean Baptiste—Joseph La Londe, Joseph McLeod, La Quier, Barsair.

"I know Piquette," said Maria; "he was one of my father's men. He used to be a grenadier under Bonaparte. Justine, his daughter, comes to the mission school." "She's very pretty," said James. "Yes, but she's only a child," said Maria. After the Albany trip there was the trip to Mackinac that James made toward the end of last winter, or was it the winter before that? Jack, his horse, fell through the rotting ice; they had to rig up a cat's cradle of old harness to get him out again. It took them a week to reach the island. He thought it ranked anything of the kind this side of Alexander Henry. For days after, going down the lake on a steamer to Detroit, he went blind for hours at a time. As long as James found something to talk about, as long as Anna Maria could listen, they were happy.

Once Jane heard, from Maria, "Why *did* you stab the man?" and from James, "Old Monongahela." "Was that the only reason?" very softly, and, just as softly, "The only reason as far as I know." She wrote to Henry in cryptic underscorings that James might fancy that either a *rose* or a *lily* had taken shelter within the walls of Elmwood, and added, "Let us do our duty as Christians, and leave the rest in the hands of the Almighty."

III

In the autumn of 1832 Susan Johnston, the widow of John Johnston, Esquire, caused to be built and presented to the Presbyterian church of St. Mary's a wooden church building without a steeple. Her son-in-law, H. R. Schoolcraft, supposed it to be the first recorded instance of such a gift being made by a full-blooded Indian woman. In 1821, seeing that the approach of civilization would not be long delayed, and in order to simplify matters of inheritance, Neengay and Johnston had been married by James Winniett, who was then justice of the peace, and upon that occasion Neengay had assumed the name of Susan. Under that name in 1832 she was admitted to the Presbyterian Church, upon profession of faith, together with her four daughters and her son, George Johnston. So long after the prayers read daily, morning and evening, by John Johnston to the unbroken circle about the hearth, did she bow her head and say amen. The church was ready for occupancy shortly after the new year, and the winter was one of great religious animation. Friends at Mackinac, where there had been for some time a Presbyterian communion, rejoiced at the conquest over the old rule of wassail. Mr. Robert Stuart, of the American Fur Company, wrote, "All of us who love the Lord, were much pleased at the indications of God's goodness and presence among you." And the Rev. Mr. Ferry, "The intelligence we have received by your letters . . . of the Lord's doings among you, as a people at the Sault, has rejoiced our hearts much"; and finally, "I never think of the Sault but I wish myself there. 'It is now a happy spot—a place favored of heaven. . . . I once felt as though I could never see the place, as I always associated it with everything wicked, but now I should love to go there—the Lord is there.'"

IV

In the year 1833 Henry removed the agency to Mackinac, leaving in charge as subagent at the Sault a Mr. Audrain, and Charlotte Johnston became the wife of a clergyman of the English Episcopal Church, going across the river to live in a well-built stone house somewhat east of the Hudson's Bay House, which was directly across from the Johnstons'. As Mrs. William McMurray she interpreted for her husband at two services every Sunday, conducted a Sunday school for Indian children, and taught the Christian hymns to their elders. The Indians were always very deeply moved by the singing. They had fine voices, many of them, musical and sweet though not strong; there were old men who in singing the wabbeno or Mide chants could begin the repetitions in a high pure voice and descend, as the song progressed, smoothly and easily two full octaves, finishing in a grave dark sequence of intonations. As a rule their voices were true, but they lent always something mournful even to the most cheerful of Christian promises. Conversion by rational explanation was often difficult; McMurray realized this soon after his installation at the Sault; but Charlotte's hymns seldom failed to cause a state of humble grace, sweet, although often temporary.

Mr. McMurray was in charge of the spiritual welfare of the Indian village on the Canadian side in especial, as well as in charge of that of the wandering Indians of the north shore. And to be in charge of an Indian's spiritual welfare was also to be in charge of his temporal; McMurray's house became promptly a haven for the needy, for the ill, for the unhappy, for the merely idle, as Elmwood had been, as before that Neengay's kitchen had been. Many an Indian not yet ready to place himself beneath the dominion of the Christ was quite willing to place himself beneath that of the Woman of the Wild Rose.

"Ogene-bugoquay," said an old pensioner, who, before rolling himself up in his blanket to sleep beside the stove in her kitchen, was enjoying an evening smoke, "it is this way. Once there was an Indian who became Christian. He threw away his Mide bag, he stopped making prayers to the Master of Life, he never gave any more tobacco to Nokomis the earth. He came to Bawating and sang hymns with Ogene-bugoquay, very nice hymns. He thought he was pretty good Christian. So one day he died. He went to Christian heaven, and when he get there they say to him, 'This is Christian heaven. The Master of Life he has a very good heaven for Indians. You better go there because you can't come in here.' So he start off to the Lodge of Reindeer. When he comes to Gitche Genabik he can't get across. Gitche Genabik says to him, 'You throw away your Mide bag, you never make any offering to our Grandmother the earth. What make you think you can cross Gitche Genabik?' So that Indian, he wander around like Wahwahtaysee. I think maybe he turn into Wahwahtaysee. He carry his little light around, he never fly very high, he never get very far away from earth, he has no place to go. You see, Ogene-bugoquay, I am afraid to be like that Indian."

With the Sunday school, with the singing, with the two long sessions as interpreter each Sunday, with guests in the kitchen, and in the living-room too, for that matter, with her concern for the welfare of her mother's people, at the end of a year Charlotte became quite ill from overwork. When she was recovered, she abandoned the church sessions. McMurray hired himself an interpreter and Charlotte continued with the music, the Sunday school, and the day-long hospitality, which was really sufficient even for Charlotte's resilient strength.

V

That summer when Charlotte gave Thomas McKenney the skin of the white fisher, saying, "Here is my grandfather, at least in name," and when Henry had recounted for him the old story of how her Grace the Duchess of Devonshire had endeavored to persuade Jane to stay in England, wishing to adopt her, that summer when the three barges of military and Henry and McKenney in the canoe allège approached the meeting place at Fond du Lac with flags flying and the band playing "Hail, Columbia!" and the council was held under a bower covered with green branches, the Ojibways of Lake Superior and the upper reaches of the Mississippi River ceded to the United States, as a token of their goodwill, all mineral rights to the great lake basin, promised to maintain the lines drawn the previous summer at Prairie du Chien between the Sioux and Ojibway grounds, and promised not to carry on further warfare with their ancient enemies. By this treaty, also, one section of land was given to the Woman of the Glade, to each of her children, and to each of her grandchildren, to be chosen wherever they might wish among the Ojibway lands, and Henry hung forty silver medals of the first, second, and third classes about the necks of the more important chiefs.

The existence of copper on the southern shore of the lake had been well known since earliest times. The most careful survey on the subject to date had been made by Henry Schoolcraft under General Cass in 1820, but just where the copper mines might lie, and how marketable the metal might be, not even Henry's scrupulous report had indicated. At all events the Government knew that neither survey nor promotion could be carried much farther without the consent of the Ojibways, who held curious and

166

uneconomic opinions regarding copper, its quality and its uses. For a long time that afternoon the Ojibway consent hung in the balance, while the light filtered through the leaves upon the incongruous assembly and the Ojibways wrestled with their manido.

It was Shingabawossin who settled the matter, rising from his place among the delegates from the St. Mary's band, five feathers in his hair, three feathers pendant from his right earring, three falling from little threads to the left of his head, the hair bound with a narrow scarlet band, his face, with the broad high forehead, arched nose, and narrow chin, the wide mouth with narrow lips, determined and serene. At the council in Johnston's office he had worn a blanket. At Fond du Lac he wore a blue coat with buff facings, a red vest with a high collar, and above it, a black neckcloth, but the voice was the same:

"My relations, our fathers have spoken to us about the line made at the Prairie. With this I and my band are satisfied. You who live on the line are interested. To you I leave the subject. . . .

"My friends, our fathers have come here to embrace their children. Listen to what they say. It will be good for you. If you have any copper on your lands I advise you to sell it. It is of no use to us. . . .

"My brothers, let us determine soon. We, as well as our fathers, are anxious to go home."

In the western branch of the Ontonagon River the copper bowlder, an irregular mass of virgin copper, partially faced on one side with mottled serpentine dotted with milk quartz such as was later found at Presque Isle, and having grains and pebbles of this stone variously scattered through it, lay at the edge of the shallow river bed, between the water and the steep clay hillside, so that the reddish water raved it and, in the spring, rising, scoured it with sand and ice, giving it a perpetual metallic luster. Three feet and eight inches at its longest, three feet and four inches at its greatest width, averaging a foot in thickness, and weighing on an estimate twenty-two hundred pounds, it had lain there since glacial times, perhaps, while the river took its three leaps downward through the seventy-foot drop, joined the eastern branch, and ran, ever less rapid and troubled, to a gently moving flood at the lake's level. The men commissioned to remove it for the inspection of the Government at Washington tried first to hoist it with levers, trucks, crowbars, and ropes, and were unable to stir it. They then, under the misguided notion that they were to transport the copper and not the copper bowlder, hacked it here and there with axes and chisels, piled the fallen trees of the river valley upon it and set fire to them, and when the metal was heated, threw water upon it from the river. They succeeded thus in cracking off a

167

part of the green serpentine. Finally they wearied of these endeavors, and left it. This was in 1826, shortly after the Treaty of Fond du Lac.

In 1831, Dr. Douglass Houghton, a small man, compact and finely built, and an extraordinarily brilliant physician, botanist, and geologist, a doctor of medicine at the age of nineteen and in 1831 but twenty-two years of age, ascended the Ontonagon with George Johnston and Melancthon Woolsey, and found the copper bowlder lying in its old position, the somber and burnished mass as patient and enduring, in spite of insult, as the god the Indians supposed it to be. He did nothing to disturb it, but included an account of it in his report to the Secretary of War, recommending that copper mines be sought for, not at the Ontonagon, but under the Green Rock of Kewenaw Point. He again pointed out the fact that although extraordinary masses of the native metal did exist in various places along the southern shore, no mines had as yet been discovered. His ascent of the Ontonagon was a moment in Schoolcraft's Expedition to Lake Pepin and the Mississippi, for the triple purpose of intercepting Ojibway war parties against the Sioux, of vaccinating the Indians against the smallpox, and of making a geological survey with special attention to the appearances of copper. Dr. Houghton's report appeared in the appendix to Mr. Schoolcraft's *Narrative of the Expedition,* and was not overlooked by gentlemen who spent their leisure in calculating the cost of transportation and possible profit from copper in the undiscovered mines.

VI

Anna Brownell Murphy was Irish by birth and by nature, the daughter of a miniature-painter and designer of enamels, a small, fair, blue-eyed person with a taste for traveling in Italy and reading the English poets. Her fortune did not permit her to travel independently; her first journey was made as a governess, and resulted in the publication of the *Diary of an Ennuyé.* When she was perhaps twenty-five she met an English barrister by the name of Robert Jameson, who fell in love with her. She evaded her fate successfully for a time. There was an engagement, the engagement was broken, then mended. In 1825 she married him, thus becoming the Mrs. Anna Jameson of English letters, and a few years later when he was appointed puisne judge to the Island of Dominica, she let him go alone, resuming her foreign travels, this time with her father as companion. She haunted the picture galleries of Florence. She traveled in Germany and met the great Goethe. She wrote a series of essays on the characteristics of Shakespeare's women, which were published in 1832 and well received in the States as well as in England. In 1836, Robert Jameson, having been appointed Chancellor of the Province of Toronto, wrote to her from Canada, begging her to rejoin him. In her forty second year, therefore, having a forgiving heart, a sensible disposition, and a longing for domesticity in spite of her literary and artistic habits, she set out across the Atlantic to repair a marriage so long in disrepair.

At New York, things began to go wrong. The season was late, she had a very vague idea of the geography of the country, and she was unduly disappointed that Robert had not come to the city to meet her. It was some time before she realized why he might reasonably have been excused from such a devoir. She proceeded up the Hudson to Albany by boat, from there to Buffalo by coach, the coach proving to be a springless wagon and the roads unspeakably bad. The weather grew daily more inclement. She was transported across the lake a day earlier than she was expected, and found herself at the end of her journey, wading alone through mud and slush ankle-deep from the steamboat landing to the Chancellor's mansion. All the way up the forlorn street, past houses that looked raw about the edges, she reminded herself that this sad welcome was none of Robert's fault. But it was too late. The damage had already been done, or perhaps it had been done eleven years earlier when the daughter of an Irish artist married an English barrister. She could not enjoy Toronto, she could not enjoy her husband's company. She climbed into bed under a mountain of quilts, suffered from chills and fever, but mostly chills, and when she was better devoted herself to the German poets in the seclusion of her chamber.

As the weeks went by she did make an effort to observe the picturesque in this new landscape, and to learn something about her husband's newly adopted country. She visited Niagara Falls, then pillared, banked, sheeted with ice, but roaring downward nevertheless in their ageless fashion; she visited the Chamber of the Assemblies, read a great many journals on the development of the province, and observed with real pleasure the red muffler of a Canadian who drove past her house seated on a pile of logs behind a team of oxen. But it was all rather a cold and doomed effort. New Year's Day, with the English Colonial statesmen attempting to observe the old French custom of New Year's visits, was the dreariest occasion of the winter. In the spring some one suggested a tour of the West, and she seized upon the opportunity for decorous flight. The Chancellor wrote letters, provided funds, did everything in his power to assist her in her project. The Chief Justice gave her a whole sheet written full of traveling instructions and advice. Every one was as kind as could be, so much so indeed that she almost regretted the notion of flight, and in the middle of June, although still insecure in health from the illnesses of the winter, she drove down to the steamboat landing surrounded by her luggage and her friends. There, at the moment of embarkation, her physician hurried on board to introduce her to Mr. and Mrs. McMurray, "the missionary from the Sault Ste. Marie and his Indian wife," who had just arrived at Toronto. Two minutes of conversation lost Mrs. Jameson's heart to Charlotte Johnston, lost Charlotte's to Mrs. Jameson, and resulted in the urgent invitation for Mrs. Jameson to visit the McMurrays at the Sault. Mrs. Jameson wrote:

"I must confess that the specimens of Indian squaws and half cast women I had met with, had in nowise prepared me for what I found in Mrs. McMurray. . . . Her figure is tall . . . rather above than below the middle size, with that indescribable grace and undulation of movement which speaks the perfection of form. . . . Her dark eyes have a sort of fawn-like shyness in their glance, but her manner, though timid, was quite free from embarrassment or restraint. . . . It seems there is some chance of my reaching the Island of Michilimackinac, but of the Sault Ste. Marie I hardly dare think as yet—It looms in my imagination dimly described in far space, a kind of Ultima Thule."

Nevertheless, one morning towards the end of July, 1837, Mrs. Jameson did indeed find herself standing on the deck of the *Thomas Jefferson* in the harbor at Michilimackinac, with Ultima Thule but seventy miles or so up the river and straits. She had been awakened in the dark, the vessel having been for some time at anchor, and the captain anxious to be again on his way. She dressed hurriedly, in the back of her mind the confused recollection of a very stormy passage across Saginaw Bay, of fainting, and of waking again in the darkness of her berth and, having collected her packages and drawn her mantle about her shoulders, emerged into a world just at the point of dawn.

"A scene," she wrote to her friend, "such as I had never imagined, such as I wish I could place before you in words,—but I despair, unless words were of light, and lustrous hues, and breathing music. . . . We were lying in a tiny bay, crescent-shaped, of which the two horns or extremities were formed by long narrow promontories projecting into the lake. On the east, the whole sky was flushed with a deep amber glow, fleckered with softest shades of rose colour—the same intense splendour being reflected in the lake; and upon the extremity of the point, between the glory above and the glory below, stood the little Missionary church, its light spire and belfry defined against the sky. On the opposite side of the heavens hung the moon, waxing paler and paler, and melting away, as it seemed, before the splendour of the rising day. Immediately in front rose the abrupt and picturesque heights of the island, robed in richest foliage, and crowned by the lines of the little fortress, snowwhite, and gleaming in the morning light. At the base of these cliffs, all along the shore, immediately on the edge of the lake, which, transparent and unruffled, reflected every form as in a mirror, an encampment of Indian wigwams extended far as my eye could reach on either side. Even while I looked, the inmates were beginning to bestir themselves, and dusky figures were seen emerging into sight from their picturesque dormitories, and stood gazing on us with folded arms, or were busied about their canoes, of which some hundreds lay along the beach.

"There was not a breath of air; and while heaven and earth were glowing with light, and colour, and life, an elysian stillness—a delicious balmy serenity wrapt and interfused the whole. O how passing lovely it was! how wondrously beautiful and strange!"

Well, there she stood, quite lost in the spectacle, every idea of disembarking quite gone from her mind, until the Bishop of Michigan appeared at her elbow, seized upon her packages, and hustled her on to the pier.

She breakfasted with the Bishop, Colonel Hugh Brady, the aide-de-camp of the Colonel and two Indian traders, the hostess of the inn being a fat, greasy, half-caste Frenchwoman, and the breakfast consisting of coffee, tea, fresh eggs, whitefish, and rolls, all prepared to perfection, and costing twice their price in the best hotel in New York. The Bishop and Mrs. Jameson were old friends by this time. They had spent many an hour together on board the *Thomas Jefferson,* beneath the shade of the awnings on the upper deck, conversing with the son of Daniel Webster, the great politician, or with a charming woman who turned out to be the sister of Governor Mason, while on the lower decks the children of the emigrants to Illinois climbed over and under the two-wheeled oxcarts, or played with the emigrant chickens and pigs. "Our English idea," said Mrs. Jameson, "of the exterior of a bishop is an old gentleman in a wig and lawn sleeves, both equally *de rigeur;* I was therefore childishly surprised"—at the Episcopal service in Detroit—"to find in the Bishop of Michigan a young man of very elegant appearance, wearing his own fine hair, and in a plain black silk gown." Ever and anon in their conversations they were passed by Colonel Brady, so military in appearance, and so deeply sunk in reverie that she had never mustered up courage to speak to him until this morning. In the large cabin, hung with blue silk and carpeted with blue of the same shade, had lounged the other one hundred and eighty passengers, a small load for the *Thomas Jefferson,* as the Captain had explained; the summer before he had not made a run with fewer than five hundred souls on board. A very fine craft was the *Thomas Jefferson,* "a magnificent machine, admirably appointed in all respects, gaily painted and gilt, with flags waving," and those who had traveled upon her from Detroit to Mackinac, with or without speaking, felt themselves of a company. Breakfast was therefore a pleasant affair, and at its conclusion Mrs. Jameson parted from the gentlemen with a feeling of regret.

The hour was yet far too early to permit with propriety of a call upon Mr. and Mrs. Schoolcraft. With her sketchbook under her arm, Mrs. Jameson set off for the Indian village, a small, sensible, amiable figure with a house-wifely gait and countenance, yet very definitely a lady, and with an added personal distinction which may have come from a subdued knowledge of her capabilities in the arts and letters. Far off toward the Straits she saw the *Thomas Jefferson* steaming into the azure, small and black under a huge black plume, and she hoped with all her heart that Mrs. McMurray had not forgotten to say some word of introduction for her to Mrs. Schoolcraft. The island was crowded with visitors; the inn controlled by the greasy half-caste woman had not a room to spare, and, from rumor, neither did any other house. Mrs. Jameson might have to sleep on the stones.

The Indian village was occupied with breakfasting, where it was occu-pied at all. A few ambitious souls were preparing to go fishing. A few women were grinding corn in long mortars made from birch logs, but the greater part of the population was lounging. Every individual was natural and picturesque, and Mrs. Jameson, sitting herself down in the shade of an arbor vitae, observed them with the eye of an artist. She did not however take out her sketchbook, but gave herself over to the leisure and charm of the hour.

When the morning had advanced to its full warmth and brightness, and she was assured that the moment had come to seek out Mrs. Schoolcraft, she found her way to the agency building where it stood, high enough on the slope for a fine view of the bay, close under the sheltering cliffs. The gar-den was surrounded by a sixfoot picket fence. She passed through the grounds by a driveway bordered with fruit trees to a house with a wide veranda. She noticed plum trees and currant bushes towards the cliff, and, beside the veranda, an elaborate hotbed. A very beautiful mountain ash grew in front of the house, and all things, grass, flowers, and leaves, and even the gravel of the drive, seemed fresh and radiant under the downpour of sweet thin air and sun. A deer, which had been lying among the bushes, rose and followed her a short distance, neck extended, sniffing curiously, and left her within a few steps of the porch, but with no appearance of fright.

She waited for some time in the living-room after the Indian maid left her, hearing at a distance household sounds, and household conversations, in which were mingled children's voices, carried on in Ojibway. She had a great sense of the charm of the garden through which she had entered, of the spacious and invigorating views from the pathway, of the orderliness and regularity of the menage into which she had entered. At last Henry appeared and received her gravely, said that he had been made acquainted with the fact of her arrival by friends, that a room had been prepared for her, her baggage sent for, and that Mrs. Schoolcraft greatly regretted her inability to welcome their guest; she had for some days been confined to her bed by illness. Mrs. Jameson expressed the deepest dismay, concern, and thankfulness, and was installed in "a nice little room with a wide comfortable bed," and in a few hours Jane felt sufficiently recovered to meet her distinguished visitor. Said Mrs. Jameson:

"I am charmed with Mrs. Schoolcraft. When able to appear, she received me with true lady-like simplicity. The damp, tremulous hand, the soft, plaintive voice, the touching expression of her countenance, told too painfully of resigned and habitual suffering. . . . In the course of an hour's talk, all my sympathies were enlisted in her behalf, and I thought that I perceived that she, on her part, was inclined to return these benignant feelings. I promised myself to repay her hospitality by all the attention and gratitude in my power. I am here a lonely stranger, thrown upon her sufferance; but she is good, gentle, and in most delicate health, and there are a thousand quiet ways in which woman may be kind and useful to her sister woman. Then she has two sweet children about eight or nine years old—no fear, you see, that we shall soon be the best friends in the world!"

The following morning Mrs. Jameson, alone in the Schoolcraft parlor, was turning over the pages of the *Wisconsin Gazette*, reading, with much amusement, an invitation from the Wisconsin bachelors to the "downeast girls" to come to Wisconsin and be wooed, when a darkening of the windows caused her to look up. She had wished to see Indians; to see Indians she had penetrated the American wilderness—and here the Indians were. She hastened to the porch and found herself immediately surrounded. On the trim lawns, the gravel walks, leaning against the pillars of the porch, well behaved but making themselves very much at home, were some thirty or forty specimens of the "wild and lordly savage," men, women, and children, Ottawas and Potawatomis, festively arrayed, who, seeing the fairhaired woman on the porch, greeted her with a chorus of "Bo-jou, bo-jou," and approached her to press, but not to shake, her hand. The Ottawas were neat in their appearance, the Potawatomis less neat but just as bravely attired. She saw one young man who wore "a common beaver hat, all round which, in several silver bands, he had stuck a profusion of feathers, and long tufts of dyed hair, so that it formed a most gorgeous helmet." Another, evidently

173

a Potawatomi, had his face painted, "the upper half . . . vermilion, with a black circle round one eye, and a white circle round the other; the lower half a bright green, except the tip of his nose, which was also vermilion. . . . He had armlets and bracelets of silver, and round his head a silver band stuck with tufts of moose hair, dyed blue and red. . . . Over his shoulders hung a blanket of scarlet cloth, very long and ample, which he had thrown back a little, so as to display his chest, on which a large outspread hand was painted in white." The women were some of them very pretty, their faces unpainted, their hair parted in the middle, smooth upon the forehead, and "twisted in a knot behind, very much *à la Grècque*." And all around her was the wild smell, the Indian smell, which had frightened the horses of the early settlers.

At tea time she learned that she had happened upon the beginning of a grand Indian conclave; she could hardly have done better for herself, in the matter of observing the aborigines, had she planned. Jane, on the opposite side of the tea table, in black taffeta and lawn, her ringlets as glossy and impeccable as when Henry had first seen her in her father's living-room, explained to Mrs. Jameson the annoying question of the "goods offer."

Hardly more than a year ago, Henry, as Commissioner, had completed at Washington the treaty which he considered the crown of his career, the Treaty of March 28—his birthday—1836. By this treaty, the Government purchased from the Ojibways and the Hurons territory in the lower and upper peninsulas amounting to over sixteen million acres, at the price of twelve and a half cents an acre. A system of annuities had been arranged for the actual payment of the money, a task in itself, for every man, woman, and child of the tribes concerned was to receive a specified individual share; and the first of these annual payments had taken place the autumn before, at Mackinac.

"How I wish you could have been here then!" said Jane. "There was never such a gathering. Four thousand Indians at the very fewest were here, and a body of the military as well, and a great many more traders than were ever here before at one time. We were quite a metropolis. And every one was so happy—it was like the millennium. The Indian debts with the traders were all settled, some of them debts of thirty years' standing, and every Indian received money and gifts besides. They went away with their canoes loaded."

"But they have lost their land," interposed Mrs. Jameson wisely.

"Not entirely," said Jane. "They will have the same use of it as they have always had until it is actually needed for settlement. By that time this generation will be gone, and the next generation will learn to be agricultural.

There is enough land reserved for every person in the nation to have a little farm, if he likes. You see," she spoke very earnestly, "my people are like
children. They do not know what they need, and they have to be planned
for. They are becoming Christian very slowly, and they will learn to become
good farmers. Their land is no longer fit for hunters. The fur trade has
impoverished it. You do not know," she added sadly, "what it would mean
to them to have to leave their country and go into the West like exiles. Their
country is part of their souls."

Her sadness had brought her a long way from the "goods offer." Mrs.
Jameson reminded her of it, and helped herself from the sugar basin.

"This year," said Jane, "the Government is unable to meet the annuities.
Henry has been instructed to offer the Ojibways half of the payment in silver, and the other half in goods. The traders, of course, are anxious to have
the Indians accept—it would be excellent for them—but I hope that the
Indians refuse it. Most of them are already in debt to the traders. They made
their purchases at the beginning of the winter on credit, as they always
used to do, and they counted upon having this money to settle with their
creditors, as my father's Indians counted upon having furs in the spring. If
they refuse, the Government will pay them in full next year in specie. All
this is very difficult for Henry and very unfair, for it makes people think that
he has joined with the traders to fleece the Indians. However, it will all be
settled in the council tomorrow."

An Indian maid came into the room with a basin of hot water and a clean
linen tea towel, and Jane began to wash and dry her delicate cups. Henry
had left them some time before. The two women were alone in the room.
At a distance they heard the light voice of Janie Schoolcraft, and her light
step on the gravel, as she escorted one of her Ojibway acquaintances to the
kitchen door.

"Ah," exclaimed Mrs. Jameson after a meditative silence, placing her cup
in her saucer with precision and handing it to Jane, "what a fortunate
woman I am! I shall have such a chance to see these people as few of my
countrywomen have experienced, and not only through my own imperfect
vision, but through your understanding and affection." And she smiled a
truly radiant smile at Jane that brought a flush of pleasure into the ivory
face, for although Mrs. Jameson spoke with an unusual elegance, she meant
what she said, and her blue eyes surveyed Mrs. Schoolcraft with the utmost
affection.

Mrs. Jameson attended the council. The number of Indians on the island
had been continually augmented, and not all of those camping on the beach
were concerned with the goods offer. The British Government was also

making payments and presents in August at Manitouline, and Indians from the north shore of Superior, on their way to the British payments, paused for a few days at Mackinac. However, one afternoon a fleet of thirty or forty canoes with blanket sails came skimming into the harbor, and their arrival seemed the signal for the convening of the delegates in Mr. Schoolcraft's office. There were fifty-four of them in the building and some two hundred crowded close around outside, peering through the windows, all very orderly and courteous but very eager. There were approximately fifty-four pipes soon lighted, the crowd about the doors and windows obstructed the ventilation, and the day was late in July. In spite of the interesting faces, venerable or young, the costumes, the orations, Mrs. Jameson could not stand it for very long. She saw that the Indians were disposed to object to the offer, and then, as gracefully as she could, retired to the garden walks. On Sunday she attended services in the mission church. The twenty Christians of the town were there, and a few Indians, most of them loitering on the porch. The Bishop of Michigan conducted services.

"Immediately before me," she wrote, "sat a man who at once attracted my attention. He was an Indian, evidently of unmixed blood, though wearing a long blanket coat and a decent but worn hat. His eyes, during the whole service, were fixed on those of the Bishop with a passionate, eager gaze; not for a moment were they withdrawn: he seemed to devour every word both of the office and sermon, and, by the working of his features, I supposed him to be strongly impressed—it was the very enthusiasm of devotion: and yet, strange to say, not one word did he understand. When I inquired how it was that his attention was so fixed, and that he seemed thus moved by what he could not comprehend, I was told, 'it was by the power of faith.'"

She had seen this man before. Jane's duties had been greatly multiplied by the visits of the delegates. There were also the children's lessons to be attended to, and Henry's usual wants to be considered, so that during the early part of the day she had been obliged to leave her guest pretty much to her own devices. Mrs. Jameson, never at a loss, had "stepped out freely about the island," and found much to engage her attention. Her mantle on her arm and her sketchbook under it, a little bag of crayons swinging from her wrist, she crossed the agency piazza one morning after breakfast, and descended the drive between the plum and cherry trees and the lilacs, which had been pruned more to resemble trees than bushes. The weather was, as on the day of her arrival, indescribably clear and fresh, and the view charming. Nimmi, the deer, followed her, an attention to which she had already become accustomed and which she would have missed, and as she approached the white picket gate, she met an Indian on his way to the house. He had just entered the garden and was turning to fasten the latch behind him, the oddest of figures. Perhaps in his youth he had stood over five feet; now, in what seemed an extreme old age, he could not have been more than four and a half feet tall, and he was withered and narrowed through all his frame proportionately. From beneath the black felt hat with the wide brim, his hair fell in two ashen braids. His coat was blue, with wide lapels and yellow brass buttons, his cloth trousers and vest were of a darker color, and he wore moccasins. He turned his head sideways as she approached and smiled up at her with what struck her as the strangest blend of malice, wisdom, and gentleness. His small dark face was finely lined, but his eyes were very bright. She seemed to see in them gleams of a rich brown, as in a trout stream, and reflections, or little darts of green, like reflections of hazel leaves overhanging such a stream. As he moved aside for her, his small feet in the richly decorated and fantastic shoes flickered upon the gravel light and deft as leaves. She addressed him cordially in a firm, bright voice, and thought, after he had left her, that she had rather expected her "Bo-jou, bo-jou" to perform the office of a cockcrow in dispelling something of the supernatural.

This was Chusco, the jossakeed, known as the Muskrat. He was an Ottawa, he lived on Round Island, and he had, until one spring seven years before, performed remarkable things with the aid of the spirits of the crow, the tortoise, the swan, and the woodpecker. His wife had become a Christian, but no prayers of hers had had any effect on him until one day in the sugar bush when he was filled with such agony of soul as if the Devil himself had entered into him; he had no peace until he also was baptized. After his conversion he took unto himself the name of Zachariah, perhaps in memory of the fact that he had once been a prophet, gave his medicine bags, his drum and rattles, with which he had been accustomed to invoke the Mudji Manido, to Mr. Schoolcraft, indulged no more in the use of whiskey, and became a most exemplary Christian. Every summer, before digging his potatoes, he knelt in his potato patch, together with his old wife, and thanked the Lord for having prepared him a harvest. He believed implicitly in the atonement of Christ, and never failed to answer, to those who asked him, that he had worked all the wonders of his Jossakeeding directly through the agency of the Evil One. All this Mrs. Jameson learned from Mr. and Mrs. Schoolcraft at late tea Sunday afternoon. What a pity, she remarked, that no medicine man could be got to tell the truth about his witchcraft, for undoubtedly many of their remedies would be valuable. Henry replied that Chusco had in fact told the truth. He intimated that he himself was writing, for *The Literary and Theological Review,* an essay on

177

the works of Satan in the vicinity of Mackinac. Had he informed Mrs. Jameson that he was about to include a report on the activities of his Satanic Majesty for the summer of 1837 in his governmental report, he could hardly have surprised the lady more.

The conferences went on, and on the twenty-fifth were terminated, to Henry's relief, by the Indians' refusing the goods offer, accepting the Government's promise to pay the lacking half of the annuity in specie the following year. The next day he saw Mrs. Jameson, Mrs. Schoolcraft, and the two children off for St. Mary's, where Mrs. Jameson was to visit Mrs. McMurray, and Jane her mother.

The trip was made in a Mackinac boat with a crew of five Canadians. The first night they drifted in Lake Huron under a starry sky, the children asleep on the floor in the center, Mrs. Jameson and Mrs. Schoolcraft alternately slumbering and waking on the two lockers, which remained very hard in spite of the buffalo robes, blankets, mats, and capes with which they were upholstered; four of the Canadians asleep among the oars, the youngest, a boy of nineteen, awake at the helm and more than willing to tell Mrs. Jameson strange tales in the intervals of her slumber. The next morning they rounded the Grand Detour, and would have spent the next night at Encampment, had the mosquitoes permitted. As it was, Mrs. Jameson, with the aid of a douceur, persuaded the men to row all night, so that they reached St. Mary's at dawn. All this she described in detail and very charmingly for the benefit of her English friend, who undoubtedly enjoyed the American mosquitoes in literature almost as much as Mrs. Jameson suffered from them in life. She ended her account thus:

"But whenever I woke from uneasy, restless slumbers, *there* was Mrs. Schoolcraft, bending over her sleeping children, and waving off the mosquitoes, singing all the time a low, melancholy Indian song; while the northern lights were streaming and dancing in the sky, and the fitful moaning of the wind, the gathering clouds and chilly atmosphere, foretold a change of weather. This would have been the *comble de malheur.* When daylight came, we passed Sugar Island . . . and just as the rain began to fall in earnest, we arrived at the Sault Ste. Marie. . . . I went to bed—oh! the luxury!—and slept for six hours."

At St. Mary's there were quite as many delightful subjects for correspondence as at Mackinac, quite as many ways in which to forget the miseries of Toronto. She was welcomed so graciously, so affectionately, into all this close, happy family life after a winter with no affection whatever; the scene was so beautiful, so new to her experience; small wonder that her enthusiasm grew with every little adventure. She was taken to call upon Neengay early in her visit, and also upon Wayishkee. She spent a great deal of time wandering about the shore of the rapids, or seated with her sketchbook open on her knees while Wayishkee's oldest daughter, the pretty Zahgahsee-gayquay, whose name signified The Sunbeams Breaking through a Cloud, held an umbrella over her head, and one day, at George Johnston's instigation, she resolved to risk her life upon those glancing, snowy waters. Seated on the floor of the canoe, a pair of crocheted zephyr slippers on her feet, her mantle drawn loosely about her to protect her from the wind and spray, a wide-brimmed straw hat tied on her head with a veil, Mrs. Jameson felt herself borne on the waves with all the poetry of Anadyomene in the shell. They came down the descent, three quarters of a mile, in less than seven minutes, and before she knew it Mrs. Jameson, breathless, exhilarated, was telling Neengay of her exploit. Neengay laughed softly, clapped her hands together, and embraced Mrs. Jameson on both cheeks. Jane declared she should have an Indian name, and Neengay entitled her Wassahjewun-equay, Woman of the Bright Foam. Nothing could have pleased her more. She had all along been envying these women their beautiful Indian appellations. What matter if the names were not in common use? To be in private, to oneself and one's family, the Woman of the Wild Rose, as Charlotte was, could not but give one a secret satisfaction like that of wearing a beautiful pendant, a love token perhaps, on one's breast, buttoned out of sight. Eliza Johnston was the Woman of the Morning Star, Wahbunnung-oquay; Anna Maria, the Woman of the Red Leaf, Omiskabugoquay; and Jane, the Woman of the Sound the Stars Make Rushing through the Sky, Obahbahm-wawagezhagoquay. When Mrs. Jameson heard this last name, she promptly exclaimed, "The music of the spheres!" Neengay, Charlotte explained for her was, literally, The On-the-Green-Prairie Standing-Alone Woman.*

And so Mrs. Jameson became one of the totem of the Reindeer.

They sat in the portico facing the river, to converse, Mrs. Jameson, Neengay, and Jane, Jane's hand folded in that of her mother, her face

---

* This is the translation given by the living members of the Johnston family. The word *prairie* evidently came through the French, and meant a meadow, and almost certainly a meadow in a forest. Since prairie is now generally understood to mean a vast expanse of treeless plain, and since John Johnston's vocabulary was more English than American, I have taken earlier the perhaps unwarranted liberty of shortening the name by dropping the "green," and have used "glade" instead of "prairie." Schoolcraft gives The Woman of the Green Prairie, but misspells the Ojibway in four different ways. McKenney gives The Daughter of the Green Mountain. Michel Cadotte might have called her La Dame du Pres Vert, the most correct translation of all.

animated and happy, interpreting for the other two. Mrs. Jameson had remarked at Mackinac Jane's longing for her mother. It had amounted, as the Irishwoman thought, to the unspoken declaration, "I would be well if I could see my mother today." In fact, Jane had not seen her mother all winter, the Schoolcrafts having passed the season in Detroit, and now, seated beside Neengay, she did begin to blossom and revive. She came forth with whimsies and little quiet jokes such as had never appeared at Mackinac, and when they were all together in the big living-room, the four daughters and their mother, she provoked the others to merriment with which she did not attempt to compete.

Mrs. McMurray imitated with great humor the deportment of a tipsy squaw, dragging her blanket after her, with one corner over her shoulder, and singing, in most blissful independence and defiance of her lordly husband, a song, of which the burthen is—

"The Englishman will give me some of his milk! I will drink the Englishman's milk!"

The talk was not always of Indians. Correggio and Goethe had their part, and the actresses of the continent—Sophie Müller, Madame Arneth, Anna Krüger, names then so radiant, women of whom Mrs. Jameson spoke with intimacy and charm. And always Neengay presided over the table or over the room, her "nindannis," "my daughter," falling alike on Charlotte or Jane, Eliza, Anna Maria, or their guest. Happy hours, and all too soon over. On July 31, Mrs. Jameson wrote in her diary: "This last evening of my sojourn at Sault Ste. Marie is very melancholy—we have all been sad. . . . I am sorry to leave these kind, excellent people, but most I regret Mrs. Schoolcraft."

It had been arranged that she should accompany the McMurrays to Manitouline, whither the greater part of Mr. McMurray's flock had already preceded him.

"August first. The morning of our departure rose bright and beautiful, and the loading and arranging our little boat was a scene of great animation. I thought I had said all my adieus the night before, but at early dawn my good Neengai came paddling across the river with various kind offerings for her daughter Wasahge-wonoqua, which she thought might be pleasant or useful, and more *last* affectionate words from Mrs. Schoolcraft. We then exchanged a long farewell embrace, and she turned away with tears, got into her little canoe, which could scarcely contain two persons, and handling her paddle with singular grace and dexterity, shot over the blue water, without venturing once to look back! I leaned over the side of our boat, and strained my eyes to catch a last glimpse of the white spray of the rapids, and her little canoe skimming over the expanse between, like a black dot; and this was the last I saw of my dear good Chippewa mamma!"

Mrs. Jameson also wiped the tears from her eyes.

The plums ripened in the shelter of the cliff at Mackinac; Captain Marryatt visited the agency and was dubbed, in private, by Henry a "perfect sea urchin"; troops arrived from St. Mary's to garrison the fort and keep order during the annuity payments; and by the twentieth of August Jane received a letter from Mrs. Jameson, now in Toronto:

"If I were to begin by expressing all the pain it gave me to part from you, I should not know when or where to end. I do sometimes thank God, that in many different countries I possess friends worthy that name; kind hearts that feel *with* and *for* me; hearts upon which my own could be satisfied to rest; but then that parting, that forced, and often hopeless separation which too often follows such a meeting, makes me repine. I will not say, pettishly, that I could wish *never* to have known or seen a treasure which I cannot possess: no! how can I think of you and feel regret that I have known you? As long as I live, the impression of your kindness, and of your character altogether, remains with me; your image will often come back to me, and I dare to hope that you will not forget me *quite*. I am not so unreasonable as to ask you to write to me; I know too well how entirely your time is occupied to presume to claim even a few moments of it, and it is a pity, for 'we do not live by bread alone,' and every faculty and affection planted in us by the good God of nature, craves the food which he has prepared for it, even in this world; so that I do wish you had a little leisure from eating and drinking, cares and household matters, to bestow on less important things, on me for instance! poor little me, at the other side of the world.

"Mrs. McMurray has told you the incidents of our voyage to the Manitouline Island, from thence to Toronto; it was all delightful; the most extraordinary scenery I ever beheld, and the wildest! I recall it as a dream. I arrived at my own house at three o'clock of the morning of the 13th, tired and much eaten by those abominable mosquitoes, but otherwise better in health than I have been in many months. Still I have but imperfectly achieved the object of my journey; and I feel that, though I seized on my return every opportunity of seeing and visiting the Indian lodges, I know but too little of them, of the women particularly. If I had only been able to talk a little more to my dear Neengay! how often I think of her with regret, and of you all! But it is in vain to repine. I must be thankful for what I have gained, what I have seen and done! I have written to Mrs. McMurray, and troubled her with several questions relative to the women. I remark generally, that the propinquity of the white man is destruction to the red man; and the farther the Indians are removed from us, the better for them. In their own woods, they are a noble race; brought near to us, a degraded and stupid race. We are destroying them off the face of the earth. May God forgive us our tyranny, our avarice, our ignorance, for it is very terrible to think of!"

Estimable lady!

VII

1838. June. The conference had begun shortly after noon and was wearing on through the four o'clock dinner hour to which the Johnston family, in spite of their changed circumstances, resolutely clung. The hostility between the two men was of such long standing and had been so diffused between the social units which they represented, that they were neither of them conscious of it; but it was there nevertheless. Franchère was exercising a proper business caution. He kept saying: "We must arrange this. For my own part, you are an old friend, and I know you to be a man of honor, but we must make arrangements for the company." George, on the other side of the table, was well aware that he was a man of honor. It was the principal emotion of the hour for him. He developed it in his mind and in his bearing, and Franchère was subtly irritated by the constant minute reminders—the motion of the hand by which this man lifted or laid down a paper, the slight inclination of the erect head—that his vis-à-vis was of the nobility of two nations. George was not always considered, by those who knew him, a handsome man, but the studied distinction of his manner escaped no one. Moreover he was well educated. The manner, the education, the ancestry, of Gabriel Franchère were those of the typical coureur de bois. He was now about to grant a favor to George Johnston, and was deriving therefrom a more than neighborly pleasure.

Franchère, returning from Astoria, had passed through St. Mary's a few days after the burning of the Johnston home by Colonel Holmes. He had heard then that John Johnston was a renegade of the worst sort, having served as Collector of the Port for the Federal Government that same year in which he had borne arms against it. This slander had been corrected and forgotten when Franchère returned to the Sault as local representative of the American Fur Company, but it left a slight stain. Franchère could always remember that he "had heard things about the man." While John

Johnston lived, the American Fur Company held the Johnston family a rival to be reckoned with; after his death, partly because of the inheritance of debt which he left to his children, partly because the fur trade was no longer in its palmy days, the family fortunes began a slow but certain decline. Today George Johnston wished to go, as interpreter, with James Schoolcraft to the headwaters of the Osage, where James and certain Indian delegates, in accordance with Henry's treaty of 1836, were to make an inspection of the terrain. If the land was found suitable, the Saginaw Indians, at the expense of the Government, would be transferred to it in a band. George now found himself in the annoying situation of having to ask permission of Franchère before he could leave St. Mary's.

They sat in the office of the American Fur Company at the Sault, and having repeated "We must make arrangements for the company" a sufficient number of times, Franchère presented a document to George to which George duly affixed his signature, as he had done more than once before to various other documents in this same office. He waited, while Franchère reached under the table for the greasy old letter-copy book, and, while Franchère transcribed slowly into the book the note which he had just prepared, sat with arms folded, gazing in complete detachment through the window at the June landscape. Franchère completed his copy, closed his book, folded the letter, and handed it to George, who put it in the inside pocket of his coat. At the door, George turned and bowed, hat in hand, and Franchère, rising, returned the courtesy.

"Bon voyage!" he said, with a lift of the hand.

After almost a week of steady rains the sky was cleared. The June meadows were lush, dry on top but thick with dew at the root. Clover, red and white, was in bloom, and the air was full of its cool honey. George, pausing on the steps of the office a moment, drew a long breath that was half resignation, half relief, and threw back his head. The hour of humiliation was over. The letter in Franchère's copy-book ran thus:

"June 5, 1838. Gabriel Franchère to Samuel Abbott of Mackinac. Mr. George Johnston, the bearer hereof, is about proceeding with Mr. James Schoolcraft on a tour of the Missouri. He being in our debt, I have come to the conclusion of allowing him to go on his giving me a bond and mortgage on his property to the full amount of his debt, he has besides offered to give me a power of attorney to dispose of his interest in the Forsyth farm at Detroit in which Mr. Henry R. Schoolcraft has invested for his account two thousand dollars."

1838. August. Angie Bingham was returning from the Johnston house, where she had delivered a message from her mother. The day was fine, the sandy path was dry. She walked adroitly, keeping to the grass because the sand drifted into the instep of her low black slippers. She was pleased because her message had been to Mrs. James Schoolcraft, whom she adored in secret, because she had been able to loiter a moment between the rows of bachelor's-buttons and sweet william in the Johnston garden, because she had curtsied to Miss Eliza, who was in the shady kitchen beating up a sponge cake, and had been rewarded by a charming smile from that severe lady, and because it was always a pleasure to be admitted to the elegance of the low, sunny living-room in that house, where the heavy beams of the ceiling, the broad gold frames, the silver on a table against the wall, were all gleaming softly from frequent polishings. She adored Mrs. Schoolcraft for her dark, foreign beauty—Indian, she had heard it called, but it was not like that of any Indian in the mission school—and for the regal way in which she swept down the aisle of the mission church on Sunday mornings, gathering up her full and gracious skirts with one dark hand. Angie played with the fair-haired Schoolcraft children and envied them their mother, feeling no disloyalty to her own parent, who occupied quite a different place in her imagination. She was pleased also this morning because she had, as she felt, for a little girl, quite an insight into the social affairs of the moment. Mrs. Schoolcraft—the other one, the frail one—had arrived from Mackinac. There were three children with her, her daughter, her son, and a niece, and also an Indian maid. They were all going on a camping picnic up the lake with Mr. Schoolcraft. They might be gone a month and a half. She naturally connected Miss Eliza's sponge cake with this expedition, and she followed the sandy path with seemingly erratic steps, thinking of white damask cloths spread on the pine needles far to the north, beyond Point Iroquois, Vermilion Point, beyond Les Grands Sab, as she called them. Her eyes sought the north and she saw a person approaching the Portage trail from the woods, indistinct among bushes. She did not make out who it was; she could not decide, either, whether it was an Indian or a white man, but the individual interested her greatly because of the burden he carried. Since he stopped often, turning to look back at some one or something indiscernible to her, she had a fine view of the object, which seemed to be neither more nor less than a great eagle. It was hung over the man's shoulder by a cord attached to its feet. The body and the ominous head fell limply down his back and the wings drooped, one of them partly over his shoulder upon his breast, and the other halfway down his back to the knee. The feathers were a soft golden brown, blurred here and there with black. When the trail passed between bushes which hid the moving feet, the torso of the man and the wings of the bird seemed to advance like a strange monster. As his path and the Portage path presently converged, she met the man, and, making no question of her curiosity, and the stranger slackening his pace a little, they walked on side by side, Angie staring upward with all her eyes, the man looking down at her with a removed, speculative gaze. She saw a face weather-beaten and lined, the lines cut, almost, into the leather of the skin; she saw a gray stubble about a singularly hard and bitter mouth; she saw a pair of acute and very brilliant blue eyes. The face was surmounted by an old bearskin cap, greasy and worn. The dull red woolen of the skirt was blackened with grease. The naked yellow claws of the young eagle were pulled heavily over the shoulder, knotted about with dark rawhide. Where he had trapped the eagle she hardly thought, or what he was going to do with it. She was too preoccupied with the perception of the limp and feathered power, the rank, terrifying smell, like that of a crow, and the intent blue gaze.

He said, "You are Abel Bingham's little girl." It was a statement, not a question. She nodded, and they went on in silence. As they approached the Mission House, she removed her fascinated gaze from the eagle and the man long enough to see a familiar figure in a long black cape mounting the steps. A fragment of adult conversation came into her head, and she remarked wisely, "There goes Uncle Sam's Pet."

The man turned his head abruptly. "Who?" he demanded. "Mr. Schoolcraft," answered the little girl.

The man halted, staring down at her sharply, and then burst into a laugh, very loud, very staccato, and that, for a reason she could not name, frightened the child to the bottom of her soul. He turned then and left her, striding off in the direction of the Little Rapids, the wings of the eagle flopping slightly with each step. When she turned again to the Mission House, Mr. Schoolcraft had disappeared within. The door was just shutting slowly. Such was Angie Bingham's first conscious encounter with John Tanner.

Henry was on his way to the north shore for the purpose of checking Indian improvements, for all of which, even to the last apple tree, the Indians were to be compensated by the Government in the taking over of the Indian land by the State. It was one of the stipulations in the Treaty of Washington. He had, as Angie Bingham had been informed, brought Jane and Janie and little Johnston with him in order to make pleasure out of business. He was not at the Falls so frequently these days but that he was glad of a chance to call on his friends at the mission and the fort, and to see his brother James. While Jane was visiting with her mother and sisters,

185

Henry dropped in on Pastor Bingham for a quarter of an hour, interviewed Mr. Placidus Ord, and persuaded him to join the expedition as recording secretary, and stopped in at a long shed on the water front where one of the home band was making a canoe to order for him. Although the day was one in the early part of August, he wore his old black cape thrown loosely over his shoulders, and carried the heavy walking stick which had by this time become a part of his sense of personal dignity.

The shed was empty, the grassy floor strewn with shavings from the cedar ribs, rolls of faulty bark tossed here and there, coils of wattap, and a little tin pail half full of unmelted balsam pitch set near the wall. The frame of the canoe, with stones set upon the curved ribs and the huge rectangular sheet of bark set loosely under the frame, occupied the greater part of the space. It was shady and cool, a little more dim because of the occasional rifts of sunlight that filtered through the roof. Henry walked slowly along the side of the frame, peering intently at the binding of the thwarts to the gunwale, swinging his cane, noting the quality of the bark and of the cedar ribbing. It was a thirty-foot canoe and was to be fitted with a mast. He heard steps behind him which were certainly those of feet clad in moccasins, and turned expecting to see his canoe-maker. It was, however, not an Indian, but Angie Bingham's companion of the morning, John Tanner. The man had been quite out of Henry's mind of late, and now had come exceedingly near without speaking, two circumstances that, joined to a hasty perception of Tanner's countenance, sent a series of rapid shocks through Henry's nervous system which left the ends of his fingers and the soles of his feet sharply stinging. He swore afterward, when relating the experience to Jane, that he saw in Tanner's eye the cold intention of murder, and in Tanner's hand, which was dropped by his side, the blade of an opened knife. The shed was near the river. The little ripple of water on the sandy beach came to them, and the wind turned over a roll of bark, shaking the loose bark mantle of the unfinished canoe, and ceasing before Henry lifted his heavy walking stick and, brandishing it in the face of the old hunter-interpreter, declared roundly that he knew Tanner meant to kill him, that he considered him a dastard and a sneaking thief, and that he would have the law on him if he ever attacked him again. Tanner said nothing. He retreated slowly, a step at a time, backwards, without removing his eyes from Schoolcraft's countenance, and avoiding as if by a sixth sense the various small obstacles over which he might have blundered. When he reached the sunlight, he turned and walked away, his dull red shirt, old bearskin cap, and grizzled visage distinct in the full summer light for a moment, framed by the entrance to the shed. Henry remained in the shadow by the odorous bark to remove his hat and wipe his forehead meticulously with a white cambric handker-chief.

VIII

The garrison of Fort Brady had a way of lounging up and down the inclo-sure in flannel jackets and shirt sleeves, muskets over their shoulders, looking, as Mrs. Jameson remarked to Charlotte McMurray, more like a troop of plowboys going to shoot sparrows than the defenders of a nation. However, on the morning of May 13, 1839, a company of thirty regulars under Captain Johnson left Fort Brady, fife playing, muskets and bayonets shining, in a rapid and orderly march, and, proceeding in a westerly direc-tion along the Portage road, arrived at a spot near the upper end of the rapids where, on the banks of a small mill race, some fifty workmen with shovels and picks, according to the instructions of Contractors Weeks, Smith, and Driggs, of Buffalo, were making the first excavations for the canal and locks which a sanguine State government had considered war-ranted by the increasing trade with the upper peninsula. There were to be three locks tandem, each with a lift of six feet, each measuring a hundred feet in length, thirty-two in width, ten in depth, and approached by a canal seventy-five feet wide. These gentlemen had undertaken to do the work for $112,544.80, the estimated cost, and Mr. Weeks had imported his men, implements, rations, and other necessary equipment in the schooner *Eliza Ward,* seventy tons burthen, arriving at the rapids on May 11.

It was a fine day for the inauguration of such an undertaking. The rapids, swollen with melted snow and ice, raced and tumbled and flung their wreaths of foam into the sweet spring air, and at their foot mallards, green-winged teal, helldivers, and little grebe splashed and dove and called to each other. Captain Johnson halted his regiment with drawn swords upon the brink of the mill race and called upon the crew of workmen to disperse. A short but pithy correspondence having passed the previous day, which was Sunday, between Captain Johnson and Mr. Weeks, the issues were well defined, the workmen had received their orders, and were not surprised to be thus interrupted, and, while they stood to their picks, and the thirty regulars flourished their sabers, briefly, the situation was this.

Mr. Weeks, surveying the ground in a leisured stroll on Saturday evening, had observed that the line of the canal which was stipulated in the contract of Smith and Driggs of Buffalo crossed an already existent canal serving as mill race to the United States Army sawmill, and had on

187

Sunday sent a note to the Commander at Fort Brady explaining that it would be necessary to check the flow of water through the mill race in order to construct the lock canal. The Commander, strong in the possession of a certain letter from the War Department, informed Mr. Weeks that he could not tolerate any interference with the highly important mill race. The letter in question was from the Acting Quartermaster General, and read as follows: "It could not, it is presumed, have been the intention of the Legislature of Michigan in contracting for the opening of the canal around the rapids of St. Mary's, authorized by that body, to interfere with the improvements made by the United States at your post, amongst which the mill race is regarded as one of the greatest importance. You will therefore apprize the contractor that he cannot be allowed, in the execution of his contract, to interfere in any way with that work." On Monday morning Mr. Weeks instructed his men to commence work at the point of intersection of these disputed waterways. And on Monday morning Captain Johnson, since the foreman of Mr. Weeks's gang did not disperse his men nor cease work, engaged in a hand-to-hand battle with the foreman, wrested his spade from him, and, resolutely backed by his regiment, drove the fifty workmen from the field. And that was the end of the proposed ship canal and locks, for the year 1839 at least, and for the twelve years to follow.

The driver of an oxcart which was conveying a load of hay and flour to the upper end of the portage, observed the battle and applauded. Before nightfall the action was well known in town, and not so well approved. Mr. Weeks, having been forcibly prevented from fulfilling his contract, considered it canceled, and dismissed his men, who, having nothing else to do, went fishing, and by the first of June were causing not inconsiderable competition and damage to the fishing business of the American Fur Company. For since beaver had grown scarce, the American Fur Company was shipping the incomparable whitefish by the thousand, and the oily and indigestible but none the less valued siscowet, three hundred barrels at a shipment, to Detroit and other ports down the lakes. To the annoyance of disappointment thus was added the annoyance of fifty free-lance fishermen, and members of the American Fur Company were mean enough to remind Captain Johnson that the highly important mill race had been out of use for a number of years, in fact, ever since the sawmill had gone up in flames. The United States Army seemed in no hurry to rebuild the sawmill.

IX

A little later in that same year, 1839, Henry Schoolcraft gave his sister-in-law, Miss Eliza Johnston, two small brownish volumes entitled *Algic Researches,* inscribed to herself with the respectful compliments of the author. Although she said little to him at the time, she was greatly pleased. The book was more than a personal possession. Jane's name was on the page of acknowledgments, and those of George, William, and Charlotte (Mrs. McMurray of Dundas), and Anna Maria (Mrs. James Lawrence Schoolcraft of Detroit)—the contents being the Ojibway tales these people, or others, but chiefly these, had related to him on winter evenings at St. Mary's. The name of Neengay was not recorded, neither was that of Miss Eliza—she had never been much given to social converse with her brother-in-law; he frequently annoyed her by what seemed to her a condescension toward Jane's Indian ancestry—but she knew that Neengay's memory and her own had aided and prompted many a recital of the stories here recorded, that if she had not purveyed the stories she was at least very near the fountainhead, and she felt in the book all the interest of a maiden aunt for a very presentable nephew. Most of the prettier stories of her childhood were there, those of Ojeeg, the Summer Maker, of Mondawmin, the Indian Corn, of the Robin, Opeechee, a group of stories about Manabozho and his brother, the gentle Wolf; the history of the Storm Fool, Paupukeewis, and others more strange than beautiful, like the story of the Undying Head. The whole collection possessed for her a fascination which she was unwilling to admit, and it gave her pleasure to see them acknowledged publicly, as it were, printed and bound.

Many things in these stories, Henry was aware, did not make sense. The tales in his notebooks made even less sense, often repeating and contradicting each other in a bewildering manner. When he begged of Neengay some elucidation, or some additional story for the Manabozho series that might perhaps straighten matters out, she shook her head, professed ignorance, evaded him gently, and finally gave him an innocent and charming little allegory of Spring, the Young Man, in the wigwam of Winter, the Old Man; with which he had perforce to be content.

Nevertheless he also was greatly pleased with the volumes, more so than with any of his earlier and perhaps more serious publications. He had spent fourteen years in collecting these stories, and had lavished care upon the rewriting of them, struggling to make his language pure and graceful without losing any of the aboriginal simplicity. It is only fair to credit him with an ethnologist's desire for accuracy. In regard to a letter from Washington Irving he had written in his journal, "I have never regarded these manuscripts, gleaned from the lodges with no little pains-taking, as mere materials to be worked up by the literary loom, although the work should be done by one of the most popular and fascinating American pens." He valued these stories for their "Doric truthfulness," and for the insight they gave "into the dark cave of the Indian mind." The cave, in spite of his long associations with its borders, was dark indeed to him; the stories were dark, but not so dark and wild as they might have been had they not been filtered, like spring water, through the pure and gentle mind of Jane Johnston.

Meanwhile the Hebrew lessons with Johnston and Janie went on, or Henry strolled up over the cliffs with the children, in the early May weather, to find the first miskodeed, the pale small blossoms veined deli-cately with pink, chill against the winter-washed leaves, drooping there-after in the small warm hands, to find the first violets and adder's tongue. In January he slaughtered an ox and packed it in snow for winter beef. When the thaws began he made cuttings from his currant bushes for Shabowawa and the St. Ignace village. He read his mail, answered letters, conducted family prayers before breakfast, performed his duties as an elder in the church, and continued to train his wife in the essentials of philology. During the first ten or eleven years of his stay in the Indian country, that is, during the time when the agency was situated at St. Mary's, his domestic life had been greatly interrupted by journeys West; the years at Mackinac were broken in upon by trips to Detroit, Washington, New York, even Chicago, the muddy little village at Fort Dearborn, where on the sand dunes and prairies the wild flowers were profuse in June.

For a man so devotedly domestic and regular in his personal habits these trips were something of a trial. A member of his family was once heard to remark that she believed that if the food eaten by him on any day in the year were weighed, the amounts would always tally to the ounce. No trip had been made, however, without its definite purpose and definite accomplishment. He had been associated, in one way or another, with and personally present at every treaty made with the Ojibways since 1820. In 1825, the second summer after his marriage, while Penaysee was yet an actual high sweet voice and living body, with his delegation of chiefs from St. Mary's he took the Green Bay-Fox River route to the Wisconsin, and having portaged to this stream, descended it to its confluence with the Mississippi and the meeting place of the tribes, Prairie du Chien. It was late July. The plains Indians as well as the forest-dwellers had been sum-moned to the conference. Above and below the village on both banks of the river, and on the island in the river, their lodges were set, pointed leather tepees of Dakotas and Winnebagos; wigwams of bark and appukwa, conical, and bristling with lodge poles—Ojibway and Menominee. Keokuk, with his iron-tipped lance and his high crest of feathers, naked and painted, had brought with him a band of Sauks and Foxes with shaved heads and plumes of red horse-tail, their naked backs printed often in white clay with the mark of a man's hand. The Yankton chief Wanita wore a robe of buffalo skin worked curiously with colored porcupine quills and sweet grass. Iowas, Sauks, Foxes, Ojibways from Fond du Lac, from La Pointe, from Lac du Flambeau and the St. Croix, Menominees from Buttes des Morts, Potawatomis and Ottawas from the more southern shores of Lake Michigan—for a full month, under the supervision of General Lewis Cass and General William Clark, they drew maps of tribal boundaries in the sand, or on bark, the naked bodies and crested heads bent peaceably hour after hour above the tracings, while agreements were arrived at and sworn to, for the purpose of the conference was to settle the lines between the nations and bind them in peace with one another. Remarkably, the United States were asking for nothing by this treaty. In the middle of August the final document was signed; the Indians were greatly pleased. Mongazid, the Loon's Foot, an Ojibway from Fond du Lac, made an oration: "Truly, it is a pleasant sky above our heads this day. There is not a cloud to darken it. I hear nothing but pleasant words. The raven is not waiting for his prey, I hear no eagle cry—'Come, let us go. The feast is ready—the Indian has killed his brother.'"

Henry returned by the way he had come. Near Pine River on the Wisconsin, he overtook Shingabawossin with the other delegates from St. Mary's, who were waiting for him in order to enjoy his company and protection while in the neighborhood of their co-signers of the treaty, the Winnebagos. The journey home was personally memorable to Schoolcraft because of a premonition which descended upon him among the wild-rice fields of the Fox River that something was seriously wrong with his family at St. Mary's. While flock after flock of blackbirds rose at the approach of the canoe along the twisting waterway—"The birds of heaven shall vindicate their grain"—the fear settled about his heart like the weakness of a fever, and all the rest of the trip he struggled against it with reason and with prayer. He was detained at Mackinac by the effects of an ague fever on two of his men, and the drunkenness of the others. At Point aux Outards he was halted by contrary winds, and held there the greater part of three days, while the waters of Lake Huron swept by him with a dizzying rapidity. Jane had been ill so great a part of the time during the last year that he hardly

191

knew whether to think of her as going tranquilly about the duties of her house or as confined to her room. While the wind blew, the rain poured down and ceased and poured again, he thought of her safety and of that of Penaysee, and, walking in a lull of the rain along the stony shore, watching the gray water washing furiously landward, he fancied the pleasure it would be to meet her coming toward him, until, with a start, he realized that he was actually looking for her. The next morning, at the eminent risk of drowning himself and all his crew, he got away from the point and up the straits to the Grand Detour, where, turning to the northwest, he entered the St. Mary's River, and found the water sheltered, the wind favorable, and remembered what an Indian had once told him, "That river is called Jewedaywenoning, because when you come into it from the Lake of the Hurons it is like getting home." A schooner downward bound was there at anchor, from which he procured a whitefish and the happy news that all was well at St. Mary's; a passenger on board had been the previous day in the Johnston house.

The next summer occurred the Treaty of Fond du Lac, in which the northern tribes agreed to the lines settled upon at Prairie du Chien, ceded the mineral rights of the Lake Superior region to the United States, and asked that an Ojibway mission school be established at the Sault. The Senate, in ratifying the treaty, struck out the school, but retained the magnificent gift of copper, silver, and iron.

Fond du Lac was followed in 1827 by the Treaty of Buttes des Morts. Beside a conical green mound, twelve feet high and a hundred feet in circumference, a calm memorial in a green meadow at the foot of Lake Winnebago, the nations assembled for the final settlement of those agreements begun at Prairie du Chien. A band of Iroquois deported from the Eastern States, and the forlorn band of exiled Mohicans known then as the Stockbridge Indians, were there, and Potawatomis, Ottawas, Ojibways, Menominees, Winnebagos. The commissioners had caused to be erected a log mess house, and a canopy of green branches beneath which the council was to be held. Seated in orderly ranks on the grassy earth, the delegates listened and assented to all the propositions introduced by Governor Cass, while beyond the shadow of the boughs their women came and went, their children played, and in the low green pyramid the bones of Foxes slaughtered by Iroquois long before the days of the French grew slowly more compact with loam. Like the two earlier treaties, this treaty was signed in August, and by it the United States received nothing.

For a time the Indian Department felt that something permanent had been accomplished by these negotiations, but in 1831 rumors from the country of the St. Croix and Chippewa rivers were such that Governor Cass instructed Henry to proceed to the headwaters of the Mississippi and "visit as many Indians as circumstances will permit." He was to take with him a surgeon to vaccinate the Indians, and for this office he selected Dr. Douglass Houghton. George Johnston he took with him as interpreter, and Melancthon Woolsey was appointed to aid in keeping records. A small detachment of troops from Fort Brady completed their company. Late in June they set out, and as far as Point Iroquois Jane and the children, the Miss Johnstons, and Lieutenant Allen accompanied them as for a picnic.

Henry made all possible speed along the southern shore, reached the Burntwood River, but learning that the water was too low to admit of canoes as large as those in which he was traveling, returned along the lake shore to the entrance to the Mauvaise, and ascended this to the grand portage over the height of the Porcupine Mountains which led to the upper forks of the Chippewa River, called by the French the Folle Avoine. At Larch Lake he managed to intercept a war party of Ojibways from Lac Courtoreille, who were bent against the Sioux, and, proceeding to Lac Folle Avoine, held a council there with Ojibways, who told him that the agreements of Prairie du Chien were being violated by American squatters who had built sawmills "within the lines." He continued down the Chippewa to the Missouri and Lake Pepin, the scene of the murders which had caused the delivery of the little black scalp-coffin to his office at the Sault in the year 1825, and so down the Mississippi to Prairie du Chien. Having continued as far as the Galena River, he sent his canoe, with Dr. Houghton and George Johnston, back to the Wisconsin, and went himself in a light wagon to visit the lead mines of the region, rejoining his party a week later at Fort Winnebago. He may have prevented by this trip alliances of the Ojibways with Black Hawk, and the Black Hawk War, which broke out within the year, was probably less terrible than it might have been because of Henry's prolonged geologizing and botanizing among the farther slopes of the Porcupine Mountains.

The expedition of 1831 was followed the next summer by that of 1832, in which, having been led there by the hand, as it were, by an Ojibway from Leech Lake, Henry Schoolcraft discovered the true and final source of the Mississippi River in Lake Itasca. Dr. Houghton and George Johnston accompanied him on this journey also, and for the sake of the souls of the Indians he included a missionary in his party, the Rev. Mr. Boutwell. Young Mr. Melancthon Woolsey had died in the course of the winter.

All these travels performed by canoe and portage, involving such inti-mate acquaintance with the aspects of changing weather, with the texture of water, either spread grandly and liberally in the lakes or spun to glass over a mountain rapid, seeping through woven grasses or descending from heaven through pine or alder boughs; sunshine in all its vexation or charm; the necessity of sleeping in a quaking bog with one of those tufts of grass for a pillow which the voyageurs called têtes de femme; the minute and immediate vision of fur, feather, scale, and claw—one of the men, at Pointe aux Beignets, caught a kingfisher by clapping his hand over an orifice in the clay bank, and afterwards took from the subterranean nest six eggs—the pattern of the feathers distinct and accurate in the hand, the smell of the bird, the small bright angry eye—these things, one might think, would have weathered Henry as they did his old black cape. But although in after years a certain painless stiffness impeded his movements, especially in his legs, his temper remained always as exact and routinaire, and he did not grow into the forests so as to be held by them.

Henry was not without a good measure of personal courage—a virtue to be added to that of his perserverance—in proceeding so many times and with so small a guard into the heart of the Indian country. For although he was always received by the Indians with courtesy, although Christian grace had made itself known as far west as the Sault, and although, in New York, Professor Anthon, Henry's sometime correspondent, was preparing his ample edition of the *Carmine* in true Horatian leisure, in 1838 a short distance west of the Mississippi, Pawnee Indians sacrificed at the ceremony of the Spring Corn Planting a young Sioux woman, a captive, and, cutting her flesh into very little pieces, buried each piece with suitable mysteries in a hill of corn. There were also the Lake Pepin murders and kindred events to be considered.

In 1836, having been appointed Superintendent of Indian Affairs for the new State of Michigan, Henry felt himself privileged to remove his headquarters during the winter to Detroit, placing a subagent in charge at Mackinac, and reserving that favorite post for himself in the summer. Jane's health, he felt, also would be benefited by a less rigorous climate. Thereafter he spent but one entire winter on the island, his interests and inclinations carrying him more and more frequently to the East, where there were publishers to confer with, old friendships to renew, a fine ethnologist like Albert Gallatin with whom he might spend an occasional morning.

In November of 1835 the Ottawas of the lower peninsula, being as a nation greatly in debt, and realizing the poverty of their forests, without conferring with their agent, sent delegates to Washington to talk of territorial sessions. Schoolcraft, at Mackinac, hearing of this, hastily packed his bags and followed them, and, finding them in the mood to make some final and sweeping settlement with the United States, had sent for delegates from other important tribes, Ottawa and Ojibway. Negotiations were suspended through January, February, and March, while delegates arrived from the Ottawas of the Grand River, from the Ojibways of the southern peninsula, and from St. Mary's, headed by Wayishkee, until late in March a treaty was concluded which gave to the United States the greater part of the territory of the State of Michigan. The land was paid for equally, muskeg, sandy waste, rich arable soil, all twelve and a half cents an acre, an act of justice, it was felt, not to say generosity, on the part of the Government, and provisions were made for schools and blacksmiths for the Indians. In May a delegation of Saginaws, Gishgaugo's band, the captors of John Tanner, straggled in and desired to sell their reservation, having sold all else and being still in debt. Henry carried on the negotiations, and the reservation having been delivered over to the United States, plans were made to transfer the Saginaws themselves to the headwaters of the Osage, in Missouri. A few days later, Ojibways from Swan Creek and Black River came in, also anxious to sell their reservations. Henry again took charge of the negotiations and concluded a separate and satisfactory treaty.

He returned, at the end of May, to Mackinac, accompanied by bands of rejoicing delegates. All Indian debts were to be paid by the Government. Yearly the Indians would receive, each man, woman, and child, a little pile of silver. The land would belong to the Great Father at Washington, but the Indians would continue to live on it as they had always done, because they could not imagine any other situation. Even Henry felt that all was for the best. Hereafter Henry's relations with the tribes were chiefly concerned with payments, readjustments of treaties, appraisals of values; until his resignation of the post a continual struggle to see that his charges received all that was due them, in spite of a defaulting Government, and a population which in general considered Indians a nuisance and an Indian treaty an agreement to be kept by the Indians and wriggled out of by the whites. The war with the Seminoles in Florida broke out that winter, apparently a war of extermination. Also, while the Ojibway delegates were still at Washington, the Senate was completing arrangements for the deportation of the Cherokees from their fertile lands to lands unknown to them across the Mississippi. When the time came to move, the Cherokees were unwilling to travel. It took the imminent presence of General Winfield Scott and his army to get them under way. So that, all things considered, the Ojibways were probably fortunate. Meanwhile Henry had become something rather more than an obscure Indian agent at a remote post, something more, even, than Superintendent of Indian Affairs for the State of Michigan. For four years he had served as representative in the territorial legislature. He had published, from time to time, *A View of the Lead Mines of the Missouri;* the *Narrative Journal of an Expedition to the Sources of the Mississippi River in 1820; Travels in the Central Portion of the Mississippi Valley; A Narrative of the Discovery of the Actual Source of the Mississippi River in Itasca Lake, in 1832;* and the *Algic Researches. Algic* was here an invention of Henry's to shorten the word Algonquin. He had contributed to the *North American Review, The Literary and Theological Review,* and other magazines; he was the author of an essay on Ojibway syntax, which, being translated into French by Mr. Peter S. Duponceau, received a gold prize from the National Institute of France. He was one of the founders and the first president of the Algic Society, an institution devoted to increasing the physical and spiritual welfare of the Ojibway and Ottawa nations, and to collecting information, social and ethnological, concerning them. He had been appointed a regent of the University of Michigan; he had been president of the Michigan Historical Society, vice-president of the Society for the Diffusing of Useful Knowledge, honorary member of the Royal Geographical Society of London, co-founder of the American Ethnological Society, member of the American Philosophical Society at Philadelphia, member of the American Lyceum, a corresponding member of the Hartford National Historical Society, honorary member of the Pennsylvania Historical Society, of the Georgia Historical Society, and member of the Royal Society of Antiquarians of Copenhagen.

Jane accompanied him one winter to Washington, the children having been placed in school, Johnston at Princeton and Janie at Philadelphia. They spent a part of a winter in New York City, and then an entire winter, returning always to Mackinac in the summer. Finally Henry completed arrangements for his dearest personal plan, a journey to Europe. Jane preferred not to go. Perhaps it was impracticable financially; more probably she dreaded the thought of being so far from Neengay and the children. After Henry's departure she went to Niagara, Canada West, to which place Mr. McMurray's Bishop had promoted him from St. Mary's, for a long visit with her beloved Charlotte. Henry traveled through France, Belgium, Prussia, Germany, and Holland, making comparisons between the fair champaigns, the orderly woods and villages, each finished like a piece of embroidery and thrifty as a cupboard, and the prodigal wild Bangles which surrounded the upper lakes, making comparisons and taking notes. He wrote, "This visit was one of high intellectual gratification," and during his absence, at one o'clock in the afternoon of May 22, 1842, Jane died in

Charlotte's fragrant, tranquil, white-curtained bedroom, thus bringing to an end her long forebodings during every trip he had ever made without her, that the separation was to be a final one.

<h1 style="text-align:center">X</h1>

Jane was dead in the spring. In the summer, at St. Mary's, John McDougall Johnston married Justine Piquette, daughter of Jean Baptiste, whose beauty James Schoolcraft had admired. She was then twenty years old. Her mother was an Ojibway woman, her father had been a grenadier in Napoleon's army. James Schoolcraft had taken over the cutler's store at Fort Brady, and on the occasion of John's marriage, offered him the position of head clerk. The John McDougall Johnstons began housekeeping on Portage Avenue, Madame Piquette and old Jean Baptiste living with them. Eliza was still unmarried, increasingly aloof in manner and often unaccountable in temper. Angie Bingham still loved her, a little cautiously indeed, as did most of the children of the village. She exacted of them the most scrupulous courtesy and rewarded them with strange tales and pieces of warm sponge cake. She had begun to be an unchangeable figure. In winter when she walked abroad she wore "a long blue pelisse, or cloak with wing-like capes, a square of plaited folds at the back trimmed with velvet; a copper-colored satin bonnet with round, high crown and broad front; a long green barege veil tied over the front with a ribbon, always drawn to one side, and held back by her right arm. In summer she wore a blue-black silk gown, a bonnet with a heavily embroidered black lace veil, drawn over the face and reaching nearly to the feet, or a large green silk calash made like the top of a covered buggy, with rattan cords shirred in, to fold up or let down, managed by a ribbon attached to one side." In one hand she twirled always a sprig of sweet-smelling green, eglantine, wintergreen, or whatever bud or blossom matched the season; in the other she carried a blue-beaded bag. Wherever she went, winter or summer, she was followed at a respectful distance by a little Indian maid, to whom she spoke always in Ojibway, and who was known to the community as "Miss Eliza's Equay-zonse." She lived alone with Neengay in the old house.

In November, 1843, Neengay died. Whether her death was caused by apoplexy, as Henry Schoolcraft had prophesied, or whether Jane's passing had been a sort of signal to her, a release, no one could know. For fifteen years she had survived the loss of her husband, for eighteen the loss of her first-born. That she died in the full hope of heaven and the resurrection, all her children were certain. She was buried beside her husband in the cemetery of Fort Brady, and the James Schoolcrafts came to live with Miss Eliza.

XI

When the new butter arrived, the cook on the *Independence* packed it in with the old, achieving a curious mixture of pale and deep yellow, which he dished up in a massive hunk and set in the center of the bare table in the dining-room. The *Independence* lay at the dock above the rapids, taking on passengers and cargo for Kewenaw Bay. Her passengers were miners, surveyors, and settlers, her cargo provisions for the mines, mining machinery, hay, and flour. She was a black little tub with one mast, more efficient than the schooners which had been wont to sail from Whitefish Bay for the fur companies, but not one half so graceful. She had been built to transport grain to England, and only one thing prevented her from fulfilling this mission: she could carry only enough coal to get halfway across the Atlantic. Consequently, she had been transferred to Superior, where the coaling stations were less far apart. When she came down from Kewenaw she would be loaded with copper directed to Henshaw and Ward and Company, Boston, care of John R. Livingstone, agent of the American Fur Company, Sault Ste. Marie; care of Biddle and Drew, Mackinac; care of Degarmo Jones, Buffalo. Some of this copper was found and brought down in pieces weighing as much as seventeen hundred and fifty pounds. It was the pure metal. It seemed to have solidified from a fluid mass, and might almost have been cut and minted then and there. The passengers for Kewenaw saw such masses lying on the shore. They admired it, and went down into the dark little cabin, their heads full of copper dreams, and all their conversation of lodes, outcrops, and alloys. One of them assailed the cook's butter, and perceiving its curious appearance, called out, "Hey, what kind of butter do you call this?" The Negro answered, "Boss, that's conglomerate butter with spar veins."

Or if it was not the *Independence* at the dock, it was the *Ocean* or the *Merchant*, all new steamers and all hauled over the Portage within the last year, by "grease and perseverance," the *Ocean* boasting in her walking-beam the first piece of iron from the Jackson Mountain and Cleveland Mountain Iron Mines. The *Swallow*, the *Algonquin*, the *Napoleon*, and the *Chippewa*, the remainder of the Superior fleet, all steamers, and all new on the lake that year, plied the blue water or the leaden, trailing their smoky plumes and burning, most of them, timber cut from the shores they passed.

Six years earlier, John McDougall Johnston had portaged the first of the copper emigrant families to the harbor in Whitefish Bay, taking their household goods in his two-wheeled oxcart to be loaded on a steamer bound for Copper Harbor. He had hauled, also, the first steam boiler to go over the Portage, seventy-five hundred pounds on a flat car drawn by a team of horses, the flat car being part of the equipment of strap railroad which ran from the steamboat landing below the rapids to the head of the Portage. The railroad was called strap because the rails were wooden, strapped with iron.

The Sault was crowded to overflowing, and the Van Anden House was doing heavy business. Luke's Best whiskey sold for twenty cents the gallon, and many were the gallons that went north to Copper Harbor, Copper Cliff, or Eagle River. As the old Frenchman said, "In this life we need it to cook our vittles in our stomachs." And still the fishing canoes floated at the foot of the rapids, and Father Bingham, in spite of his sixty years, in his red boat with the white sail went to Taquimenon, to Goulais Bay and Batchewana, preaching the gospel, caring for the sick, as if copper and iron in quantity on the shores of Lake Superior had never been heard of.

James Schoolcraft was in high feather these days. His luck, such as had brought back from the edge of the grave the young Frenchman he had dirked, manifested itself in little things which gave him great satisfaction without materially augmenting his fortune. Somehow or other his consignments of goods from Detroit always arrived a good ten days before those of Livingstone and Crooks, a source of particular annoyance to Livingstone, since it enabled James to take his pick of the furs for the season. The Indians of the village, if they had fish to sell, went first to James. James underbid the American Fur Company in the contract for firewood for Fort Brady. He was full of plans. As agent, he was trying to persuade the Indians to build a gristmill, the grain to be shipped north from Chicago—a fantastic idea to most people. He believed in the increasing value of land at the Sault, and since, as Livingstone said, "the whole town is nothing but one huge preemption claim," James was homesteading land to the south of the agency, clearing it, and selling the timber. Moreover, he looked lucky, with his magnificent physique, the vitality and vivacity of his bearing very little changed since his courting days. The Temperance Society, the Baptist Church, the Methodist Church, the Methodist Mission, Wednesday evening prayer-meetings, and three regular church services on Sunday had passed lightly o'er his head. He took pride in marching down the aisle of the Baptist Church four times a week, provided he was in town, with the handsomest woman in the Sault on his arm.

199

At thirty-two Anna Maria had still the gracious way of gathering up her black silk skirts which had charmed Angie Bingham six years before. Her figure had grown a little fuller, her forehead was a little lined, and since her mother's death she had become accustomed to wearing black almost entirely. Jane's death had touched her sadly. She never forgave Henry that he had left her sister alone in her last illness, and she missed Jane as a second, younger mother. When her mother had been dead a year, to please her little daughter she set some sprays of scarlet embroidery in the bosom and about the tight cuffs of the dress, and since it became her greatly, and pleased James as well, she made it a habit to touch all her black frocks with a little scarlet or rich red. She had the deep ivory pallor and dark eyes of all the Johnston women, and the costume emphasized the quality in her face that Angie Bingham thought of as foreign. She was still undoubtedly very beautiful, and in spite of her griefs, her domesticity, and her preoccupation with the Baptist Mission, she had never lost the sauciness, which, joined to a manner so gentle and so good, had first charmed the young James.

The Fourth of July fell on a Saturday in 1846, and the Hudson's Bay Company was keeping wassail that evening. Since Anna Maria was in Pontiac with the children, visiting relatives, there was no reason for James to remain at home. He would doubtless have gone over anyway, for Maria kept a loose rein upon her husband. He had never "given up the French village," but his drinking, his dancing, and his occasional gambling had not broken her heart, as they might have broken Jane's under like circumstances; she loved him, as at first, and stood between him and the severity of Father Bingham. On the evening of the Fourth he stepped into the store for a minute's visit with John McDougall, a fine figure in his white blanket coat and trousers, his vest of coonskin, a pair of beaded moccasins on his feet. Fifteen minutes later John saw him crossing the inclosure in company with Major Kingsbury and Lieutenant Tilden, both very brave in gold braid and gilt buttons. The store being within the stockade, a box within a box, John had no view of the water or of the town, but, watching the daylight fade on high, seeing the ground of the cantonment growing dim with massing shade, and feeling the early chillness of the night, he fancied he heard, across the perpetual soft roar of the rapids, the salutes and shouting with which the party across the river began, and later, through the darkness, he heard quite plainly the music of the violins. He was keeping the store open late because of the day, but most of the business was going to Portage Avenue and Water Street, the Van Anden House, and the billiard tables of the French village. Towards ten o'clock John Tanner came in, asking to have some bills changed for coin. He made no purchase, and while John counted out the silver dollars, he stood biting at his underlip, leaning against the wooden counter and staring before him in a sort of daze. He had reassumed his Indian costume completely of late years, even to the string of wampum hanging against his hunting shirt.

Although John McDougall was one of the Johnstons, and therefore had always been included in the hatred which Tanner bore to Henry Schoolcraft, John had always shared a great deal of Jane's pity for the man. As Tanner stood now, spreading the silver coins before him in groups of three with a finger stained and stiffened by many years of woods life, yet still adept with trigger and net, he looked so old, so lonely, that John felt moved to do him some kindness. Having arranged and rearranged the groups of silver for some moments in silence, Tanner asked that some of them be changed into quarters and some into half dollars. John did as he was asked. Tanner had his gun with him, and a small bundle. He was evidently prepared for a departure.

John said, "Going far?"

"Perhaps," said Tanner. He wrapped the coins in three separate pieces of cloth and put the parcels so contrived, two in his trousers pockets, one in his belt, a woolen sash. John hesitated to question him further, but watched him pick up his gun, pick up his bundle, and leave the store, his kindness yet unperformed.

After Tanner's departure there were few visitors. At midnight John shut up shop and went home, hearing, as he took his way along the Portage, ever more distinctly the sound of violins at the Hudson's Bay, and the laughter and sudden nasal shouting of the merrymakers in the French houses. He was taking off his coat, standing near the darkened window, when he saw a red glow begin along the eastern horizon, and knew it was not the dawn. It was like a large and very intense bonfire. As it soon reached its maximum and did not increase, he concluded it was nothing to bother about and went to bed.

Justine knew that it would be useless to attempt to interview James on Sunday—doubtless he had no more than got into bed before the sun rose that day—but on Monday she made an errand to the old homestead, taking a bag of calico scraps to Eliza for a quilt, in the hope of hearing about the party the night of the Fourth. It was good haying weather, had been so for a week. The long grass on the edge of the woods was dry, and the turf between the stockade of Fort Brady and the homestead, where the sheep had been cropping, was sunny and close, a dry sweet carpet. In front of the house she found Miss Eliza, who, her hands encased in an old pair of leather gloves, was cutting back the rosebushes. James was in the living-room, seated in John Johnston's easy-chair, his legs stretched out before him, a pair of light moccasins on his feet, his gray flannel shirt open at the neck, finishing an after-breakfast smoke. He had risen late and made a luncheon of his breakfast, and was then trying to persuade himself to useful action. Justine sat down on the sofa opposite him, and opened negotiations for a full account of the Hudson's Bay festivities by delivering her own piece of news.

"John Tanner's house burned down Saturday night. They say he laid a train of gunpowder all around it and then set it off. They say he's gone off to the Red River again. John saw the blaze as he was coming home from the store."

"So that was it," said James, taking his pipe from his mouth and holding the bowl of it curled in his hand. "It made a famous blaze. We thought some one was celebrating Independence."

"I guess he was," said Justine. "I think he was tired of civilization."

"Well, if you want to call it that," said James. "What becomes of Betsey Gheezha-goquay?"

"Betsey left him a year ago, at least," said Justine. "You're far behind the times."

James smiled at her. "You're still my prettiest sister-in-law. I suppose I am. For an up and coming man I'm far behind the times. Also, for a popular man, I've entirely too many people annoyed with me." He sighed, and drew his feet up, the slippers scraping softly over the carpet. The garden beyond the windows was full of sunlight, the room was shadowy. The woodwork which Miss Eliza had polished with beeswax shone softly, and two little specks of light sparkled on Justine's jet earrings. She pressed her hands hard against the sofa on either side of her, beginning to smile at what she guessed from James's manner was coming. "Do you know," he continued with elaborate melancholy, "at the shindig the other night Lieutenant Tilden announced to the world that he would have my scalp? Not only that, but he promised me personally he'd take it." "Why?" said Justine.

"I think on account of a certain Séraphine LaBadie. He likes her, you understand, and she makes eyes at me."

"Oh, you," said Justine, "they all make eyes at you. Tell me some more."

"I can't," he answered, shaking the ashes out of his pipe against the cold stones of the fireplace. "I'm a busy man. I'm going haying." He stuffed the pipe in his trousers pocket, picked up a big straw hat that was lying on the table, set it rakishly on his head, and stopping long enough to rub

Justine under the chin with his finger as if she had been a kitten, he went outdoors. She followed him, saw him speak to Eliza and pause to salute Madame Piquette, who was just then coming into the garden, and then watched him, smiling a little, as he took the path that ran past the agency, Jane's Elmwood, to his hayfield.

Madame Piquette, dressed in black-and-white calico with a high neck and a tight bodice, like a French-woman, came into the garden and began to speak to Eliza in Ojibway, meanwhile reaching her hand to her daughter as to a child with whom one is too busy to speak. Hand in hand, and with Eliza, who was folding her big shears, first cleaning the blades of scraps of leaf and bark with her gloved finger, they drifted to the portico and stood there in the shade, the older women talking, Justine half listening, her mind on James and Séraphine. They had parted from Eliza, who had gone into the house, and had left the garden, were on the dry turf by the river, when they heard the shot. It was plainly in the direction James had taken, over by the alder swamp and the hayfield. Why she did not presume it to be some one shooting at rabbits in the swamp, or some one in the agency garden driving away a thieving squirrel, or shooting for any other innocent reason, Justine did not know. A gunshot was nothing strange to the Sault of those days. For some reason never understood, she thought at once of James, was frightened, and began to run desperately down the hayfield path. She had left the group of buildings about the Johnston house, the barn, the smithy, the men's quarters, and was running on a sandy path opposite the Indian green. The sand impeded her, and she took the side of the path, running on the grass or leaping, half instinctively, from one stretch of firm ground to another. She was running in the bright sunshine, her long skirt beating against her legs. She pulled it up to her knees, crossed the band of lush grass, and plunged into the shadow of the alder swamp. The path swept downward, crossed the stream at the bottom of the ravine where a few logs and sticks were thrown to make a sort of bridge, and rose, twisting through the alders, on the far side. Near the head of the far slope lay James, face downward, his arms flung over his head.

How she got to him, how traversed the intervening ground, she scarcely realized, but she was presently beside him, laying her hand first on his shoulder, then, since he did not answer, turning him gently on his back, and lifting his head into her lap. He was warm, but she could not tell if he was breathing; the illusion of life was yet in the face, and in the relaxed hands. She looked quickly toward the spot where the path ran again into sunlight, wondering if the men in the hayfield would have heard the shot, and if, hearing it, they would have attached any significance to it. But no one was coming; she was alone with him in the luminous shadow of the alders. A little way down the path stood his moccasins, exactly as his feet must have left them. He must have leapt like a stag when the shot struck him. Cautiously she moved her hand to the damp place on his breast where the fibers of the shirt seemed to have been beaten into the flesh. There had been a similar stain on his side, low under the arm and toward the back. The path was damp, a black earth beaten smooth, obstructed here and there by the small roots of the alders. In the water grew marsh marigolds with coarse green leaves. The margin of the stream was thick with dead leaves of a year ago, rotting slowly. The thicket was a favorite place for violets in early May, and she remembered hunting there for the flowers while a young horse, his coat shaggy from the winter, cropped the new grass along the margin of the field. She was not alone with him long. Madame Piquette appeared, touched him, said at once that he was dead, and hurried on to tell the men in the hayfield. Justine still sat with his head in her lap, her eyes, so dark as to appear black, opaque yet soft, filling with tears and overflowing, the damp fragrance of the thicket surrounding her head, her hands, the body of the man who had so recently carried into the thicket on his hair, his face, the surface of his clothing, the dry warmth of the sun; surrounding all these with a cool, impartial felicity. The men came to carry the body to the house before the curious stiffening of the flesh began.

In the Johnston living-room there was confusion. James lay on the sofa where Justine had been sitting less than an hour before. Some one had brought his moccasins and the straw hat which had fallen from his head and laid them on the table near by. Dr. Bagg, the surgeon from the fort, was probing for the bullet. Some one at John Johnston's writing-table was making a diagram of the scene, and some one else, searching the path, had found an ounce ball in the packed mud. John McDougall had been sent for, and Father Bingham. Major Kingsbury hurried in. Justine heard him saying, "Tilden threatened to kill him the night of the Fourth. Some row about a woman," and she interrupted him hotly, "It was all a joke, all that. He told me so himself."

"Who told you?" said the Major.

"James himself, this morning. It was a joke."

"Tilden sounded damned in earnest," said the Major shortly. But Father Bingham had already suggested the name of Tanner. Justine heard her husband protesting, but the evidence continued to pour in. Every one there had heard Tanner threaten James. Since Henry had left the country, James was the only Schoolcraft within reach, and Tanner had Indian notions about revenge. He believed, and all the world knew it, that a man might be punished as well by the death of a member of his family as by his own death. Like an Indian, also, Tanner would consider it fair to shoot from ambush; indeed most Indians would have considered it pure folly *not* to shoot from ambush. And Tanner was gone.

"No, Father Bingham," said John, "he's not gone. Henry Shegud saw him this morning near your house."

It developed that Henry Shegud had seen him an hour before the murder. "He was sitting on a log. He had a gun across his knees and a little bundle beside him on the ground."

Men were sent to look for him, and could not find him. The white chimney and a pile of ashes and charred stick were all that remained of his house. Some one said that he had borrowed a musket at the fort that morning. A soldier came and testified to the fact.

Dr. Bagg, having finished his investigation, rose from his knees and announced that the wound had been caused by three buckshot and an ounce ball, of the type then used by the army, that one of the buckshot had been flattened against a rib, that the ounce ball had passed clean through the heart and body, and that the wadding was evidently the torn leaf of a hymn book. The scrap of bloody paper was examined, and identified by Father Bingham as a leaf from a Baptist Hymn Book, such as were in use at the fort. The ounce ball was examined by Major Kingsbury and identified as army shot. Lieutenant Tilden had come into the room at the beginning of the doctor's pronouncement. He had stood quietly near the door, listening to the identifications and comments, and heard the repeated remark, "John Tanner borrowed a rifle from tile fort this morning." Across the heads of those who stood between him and Father Bingham, Father Bingham standing with John near the fireplace, he announced coldly and clearly, "I also borrowed a rifle of the guardhouse this mornin'." His face was grave and defiant.

Major Kingsbury said, "What did you do with the rifle?"

"I went to shoot rabbits."

"Have you it still in your possession?"

"I returned it to the sentry in charge about an hour ago."

"Do you realize that you are being questioned by your superior officer?"

"I do."

The soldier who had testified to Tanner's borrowing a gun, testified also to his part in Tilden's story. Tanner had returned his gun soon after Tilden. There was a short silence. Then Tilden said, "If Major Kingsbury will appoint a detachment of men to go in search of John Tanner, I will be happy to lead the force."

There was another silence, Tilden and Major Kingsbury eyeing each other across the room. Then the Major said, "I will appoint such a detachment."

So began the hunt for Tanner. Search parties from the town joined those of the fort, Tilden directing their operations, which went on all night. Eliza, lying awake in the west bedroom, the one built on to the house the year of Jane's marriage, and nearest to the fort, heard the return of the various groups, fresh groups setting out. At morning a band of Indians from the south shore, on their way home from Manitouline, learning of the event, pitched their camp on the Indian green and joined in the search. All the threats that Tanner had ever made, all the strange attitudes assumed by him, recurred constantly to the minds of the inhabitants of the settlement. Particularly did Angie Bingham wake suddenly at night, as the torso of a man draped in the feathered wings of a young bald eagle entered her dream and stared down at her through darkness with eyes of a cold and penetrating blue. People said that Tanner had only begun the vengeance of which he had talked so many years. A guard was set about the Bingham residence both day and night, and although the search parties were disbanded after a few weeks, the guard was not withdrawn. Neither did the constant presence of a soldier in a flannel jacket with a long gun across his knees if he were sitting, or with the muzzle dropped in the crook of his arm if he were standing, succeed in removing that eagle-draped visitant from Angie Bingham's dreams.

Justine, having talked with her husband on the matter, was not convinced of Tanner's guilt. Nor was it easy to bring herself to believe in the guilt of James's boon companion, young Tilden. After a week it began to seem to her unimportant whether some one were convicted of the murder or not. One thing she decided upon firmly: Maria was not to return to a village babbling of her husband's infidelity. She stuck to her first involuntary protest to Major Kingsbury, "It was a joke. James himself told me so."

Maria, sent for, returned to St. Mary's the latter part of the month. Justine, who loved her especially and who had named for her the little girl, her first daughter, met her in the Johnston living-room and embraced her, and then led the Schoolcraft children into the bedroom, to remove their traveling wraps and console them. Father Bingham and John remained in the living-room with Anna Maria. She had laid aside her bonnet but not her cape. Grave and sweet and pale, and very tall in her long cape, she stood beside the table and listened to Father Bingham's account—how they had found James, brought him home, and laid him on the sofa; her eyes moved to the sofa—the detail of the hat, of the moccasins, of the ounce ball and buckshot, of the subsequent conversations and decisions—the good man told her all, gently, honestly, believing firmly himself in Tanner's iniquity. In the end he gave her the three small pieces of lead, the heavy ball, the bloodstained wad of paper, placing them carefully on the broad, delicate palm. The long fingers closed over them, and the hand went to her bosom, where she held them as if they were a treasure. Father Bingham kissed her on the forehead and left the room. John, dropping his hand a moment on her shoulder, said that if she wanted him, she might send Justine. He would be in the store. She was left alone in a room in which, whether she looked toward it or not, James lay upon the sofa near the table, bare-headed, slipperless, a small stain on his breast. She leaned her forehead against the pane of a window, looking into the garden, trying to remember what she had been doing the day and the hour when James was killed—without success. The days of her visit remained a blank. There was no reality save what was here with her in the room. Finally, unable to bear it longer, John and Father Bingham having some time since disappeared from view, she slipped out of doors, and, in order not to take the path to the hayfield, turned toward the river, westward, and walked a little way along the grassy bank.

It was then between three and four o'clock, past the first vigor of the afternoon, and the light had begun to soften on the surface of the water. A short distance before her the stockade of Fort Brady intercepted the way, coming down to the river's edge, the most northerly pickets being awash at some times. It cut her off from the village, the steamboat landing, and the crowds of prospectors and half-breeds. Little ripples crept up the sandy beach with an hypnotic regularity, each with a small burden of luster which it dropped on the wet surface. Drifted reeds, pale gray, lay on the upper margin of the beach where the sand gave way to grass. Almost directly across from where she stood was the Hudson's Bay Company Post, set in an indentation of the shore, and to the right, on higher ground, Charlotte's old home, and farthest to the right, beyond the waters, the head of Sugar Island, with the green shapes of trees picked out roundly by the afternoon sun. From where she stood, almost in the shade of the pickets, the light on the Canadian shores and on Sugar seemed more intense and fair than on the American side. A meadow, high on the slope above Charlotte's house, glowed like emerald, a small suave stretch where there were sheep and cattle at pasture. Mr. McMurray's stone church was there; it had been a great pride to him. Her little daughter had been baptized

207

there by a bishop of the Church of England who had been traveling through this country with Lord Morpeth. On that day even the Baptists and Methodists of the two settlements had attended the Episcopal service. McMurray's Folly, some one had called the church. Now it was full of hay, the lofted grasses. Over Hay Lake she had gone with James and the others to the meadows on Sugar Island where they had mowed. Walking slowly, pausing now and again to look across the river, she found herself relaxing, until she paused with her feet in the shadow of the stockade, her head and shoulders in the sun, and became aware that she still held her fingers tightly locked over the mementos handed her by Father Bingham. She smoothed out the paper. It was, as he had told her, a scrap torn from a Baptist hymnal. She did not need the page number to identify the few words, the concluding words of the hymn. She had played it too often at the square rosewood piano in her father's house, Justine, Eliza, and herself singing the treble, her brother John the bass, and James himself carrying in his easy tenor the familiar words:

On Jordan's stormy banks I stand
And cast a wistful eye
To Canaan's bright and happy land
Where my possessions lie.
Could I but climb where Moses stood
And view the landscape o'er,
Not Jordan's stream nor death's cold flood
Could fright me from that shore.

She lifted her eyes from the paper. Across the water they lay, the fields of Canaan in the afternoon sun, there, where her mother and Jane, Jane's little son, her father, her brother Lewis, and now James, were gone. "Oh, not Jordan's stream nor death's cold flood!" she said, and the tears began to run down her cheeks.

Tanner had not been found, but it was believed that he was lurking in the neighborhood. An Indian woman reported seeing him in the woods below town, where she was gathering moss. She said that he was creeping along on his hands and knees, and that he had tied bunches of grass and leaves to his clothing so as to be practically invisible. He had been known to disguise himself in that fashion when hunting, and the story was generally credited, the woman's terror lending it added veracity. Again, a hunter told of finding a hollow in the woods which looked as if it must have been Tanner's camp, and vacated but recently. Anna Maria let her friends persuade her to take refuge in the fort, which she did the more willingly since Lieutenant Tilden had been ordered to the Southwest to take part in the Mexican War. The summer went slowly on. There was an unusual number of forest fires, and often the air was hazy with smoke. The odor of burning leaves was in the nostrils, a perpetual reminder of some disaster, at times remote and half forgotten, at times sharp and pungent. Those who climbed Gros Cap or the upper meadows on the Canadian side for any reason, saw small fires starting here and there all through the woods, and the Indians and half-breeds were assured among themselves that these were set by Tanner in his malice. Speculators in copper, bound for Kewenaw, continued to throng the town, and another steamer for the Superior fleet, the *Julia Palmer,* a thick side-wheeler, was being hauled over the Portage. Stumps were cut close, and small hills leveled to make way for her, and every morning saw her a little farther along on her arid cruise. The townspeople warned strangers not to go into the woods alone for fear of Tanner.

Still the white chimney, all that was left of Tanner's house, waited behind the thicket of young balsams at the Little Rapids, plainly to be seen from the river, like a monument. In the autumn, Indians who had gone out to their trapping grounds told of hearing him at a distance in the woods, beating a drum and singing Indian songs, and Indians coasting along the shore of the lake reported seeing his campfire. He appeared in this manner in widely different places, and at odd times, but no person ever saw him distinctly or spoke to him, save that it was rumored that an Indian from the Red River country had said, "In the moon of snowshoes he came among us, and after a few moons passed away." He seemed to have vanished into the supernatural.

Through August and September Anna Maria followed her children with a careful eye, letting them play but seldom without the inclosure, and then only on the Indian green or the beaches, within plain view of the fort. She did not know whether she believed Tanner to be the murderer or not, but the words he had once addressed to Maria Schoolcraft, Henry's sister, recurred to her constantly—*"Look out for the flowers in your garden!"* After the leaves were fallen, and the snow came, the woods seemed less of an ambush, the children were less eager to penetrate them, and she had less fear in her heart. This was the Tanner Summer.

Late in the next spring a Frenchman by the name of Gurnoe found a skeleton in the woods above the Sault. Gurnoe was hunting for a lost pony among the charred trees and fireweed of a region that had been burnt over the previous year. The bones he found were in a tangle of fireweed and bracken. He scrambled over a fallen pine, whose half-burnt branches projected like bayonets, blackened and sharp, and crouched beside the skeleton, parting the mauve and purple flowers. He found two barrels of a musket from which the stock had been burned, a flint, and what might have been a few strands of wampum, but these last were so scattered through the sand that they might have been bits of broken shell. There was also a number of silver coins; some of these had melted and were stuck together. Gurnoe collected these relics and took them back to town. John McDougall inspected the coins and identified them as those he had given John Tanner the night of July fourth the year preceding. Apparently Tanner had not spent any of his money. The musket was believed to have been his own. It was known that he had returned the gun he had borrowed of the fort. It remained as much of a puzzle as formerly to John why Tanner had ever borrowed a gun; he thought it a strange way to "divert suspicion."

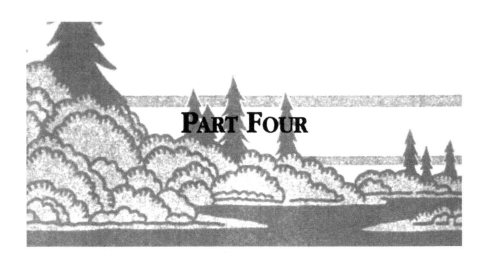

PART FOUR

The house was of squared cedar logs, whitewashed, and square in shape, having downstairs three bedrooms and a large living-room, and upstairs, reached by a narrow staircase at the back, more bedrooms, low beneath the eaves. It stood just below the Point on what was already variously known as Rains or Encampment Island, where the river channel turned abruptly from a northerly to a western course, narrowed between Encampment and St. Joseph's. The ground sloped smoothly and swiftly down about it, leveling somewhat toward the Point, breaking in a surfed edge above the narrow sandy beach. The beach in turn fell away swiftly into deep water where a schooner might lie at anchor within ten feet of the grass. Across the river a steep grassy hill was crowned with limestone rocks and round clumps of arbor vitae. Upstream, the channel led to the Middle Neebish Rapids, unpassable, and to the channel through Bear Lake to Lake George and the Sault. Downstream, below the foot of the island, the water widened out of sight through Muddy Lake. The house stood in a natural meadow, the only clear space on the island. It was said to have been built by a certain Black Anthony, a trapper, who had lived there with his friend Le Sens. At that time the house could have been only a low fortress of logs, without the upper storey. Black Anthony and Le Sens went trapping on the north shore of Lake Superior one winter. In the spring Black Anthony returned alone to the Sault with a remarkable number of pelts, saying that he had last seen his partner at such and such a place near Batchewana River, and that Le Sens had been having good luck. He did not know what had become of Le Sens. Whereupon the sheriff packed a month's supply of pork and flour and went north on a fishing trip. He

211

found an Indian who had seen both Anthony and Le Sens. Yes, he had sold furs to these men. He had sold them to Le Sens before meeting Anthony. The sheriff asked him if he could identify any of the skins. Yes, said the Indian, he could identify an otter skin which he had torn and mended. He further pointed out to the sheriff the place where he had last seen Anthony and Le Sens.

The ashes of the campfire were enormous in quantity. The sheriff, with the help of the Indian, sifted them, and found three metal buttons and eight inches of femur. After that, the Indian returned to the Sault with the sheriff and identified the torn and mended otter skin in Anthony's pack. Black Anthony was sent to jail in Jackson, and the house remained in its green meadow by the waterside without an owner.

There was, about that time, a retired English Major living on St. Joseph's Island at a point farther south and a short distance inland, who had a notorious and interesting history. He had been pointed out, metaphorically, to Mrs. Jameson as she passed down the river with the McMurrays towards Manitouline, as a magistrate and justice of the peace who had two Indian women living with him, sisters, and a family by each, and William Cullen Bryant, visiting the Sault at the time of the first excitement over copper, had also, in passing St. Joseph's, had this gentleman designated to him as a "long-nosed English Major on half-pay" who had come to the Island with two wards, English girls, and "married" them both, leaving meanwhile his true wife in Toronto. The Major kept two establishments, one of which was on a small but lovely lake on the highland above Point Fort St. Joseph, ever afterwards known as Loch Rains. The story of the English wards was the correct one, and about the year 1833 a Jesuit priest, passing that way, had conversed the Major and the family at Loch Rains, legitimized and baptized them. In 1854 the Major decided to move this family to the shore of St. Joseph's opposite Black Anthony's house. There was not a cleared field on St. Joseph's, not even a meadow for a house. The nearest approach to a meadow was the steep grassy slope directly across from Black Anthony's, and that was so broken with rocks as to be unsuitable for farming. But Black Anthony's house was uninhabited and unowned. Therefore the Major moved in temporarily, built a loft over the main structure with bedrooms, and the narrow stairway at the rear, and set about clearing himself a field on the Canadian island.

Whatever moral oddities he may have possessed concerning marriage, William Kingdom Rains was a man of integrity and perseverance. For eight years he lived in Black Anthony's house, cutting and selling timber to the steamers which were then beginning to ply the waters of the St. Mary's

River, clearing his Canadian field and building his home. It took him the full
eight years of labor. Meanwhile the schooners and steamboats anchored at
the wharf he had built a hundred yards down river from the house, loading
their decks with the short resinous lengths of white pine, and in the house,
Edith and Alice, Constance, Alma, and Linda performed the tasks that fall to
frontier women. A son, Owen, married, and brought his wife to live with
them, and set about clearing fields adjacent to his father's on St. Joe. The
young couple had two rooms to themselves in that crowded house. The
Mary Scott, the *Illinois,* the *John Jacob Astor,* and the *Ramsey Crooks*
went up and down the river, stopped at the Major's dock. The *Julia Palmer*
of the copper-rush days was tied up at the Sault, and serving as part of a
wood dock; the *Independence* had exploded, also at the Sault. Major Rains
planted poplar trees in front of Black Anthony's house from slips brought
to Lake Simcoe from England, and, as the story goes, from Milton's grave.
The transmuted flesh of the magnificent moralist murmured in leaves like
silk above the comings and goings of the Rains family.

The poplar trees were of ten years' growth when John McDougall
Johnstone brought Justine and the ten children to live in Anthony's house.
Molly, the namesake of Anna Maria Schoolcraft, the oldest daughter and the
second child, was a young woman of twenty, tall and very slender. She had
the face of her grandfather Waub-ojeeg, narrowed and made delicate to fit
a woman. Her hair, black and fine, parted in the middle of the head and
brought down smoothly over her ears to a braided knot at the back of her
head, this hair, which was the gift of Justine, framed the forehead of Waub-
ojeeg in a series of precise scallops, and the damper the cool sweet river
air, the more precise the frame. Her sister Charlotte was seventeen, her sister Eliza fifteen. With Justine, they set out beds of mint and sweet william
by the kitchen door, to the south of the house, planted lilacs to the north
and in front, and roses to the south, in front, thick-stemmed, with long
curved thorns, and single blossoms of a deep damask red. They made some
ornamental raised flower beds by piling bowlders in a circle, and in back,
at the foot of the steeper slope, planted a kitchen garden. John McDougall
and the boys built a veranda across the front of the house, screened a little
from the river by the young poplars and by the picket fence which surrounded the yard. Towards the back, the property was inclosed by a rail
fence, running zigzag up the hill through the grasses and young poppies.
John McDougall built a lean-to against the back wall of Anthony's structure
which housed a kitchen and more bedrooms. Mallows bloomed in the
deep angles of the rail fence, mullein, with yellow blossoms and coarse velvet leaves, on the hill slope, and in autumn, sumach and red hew on the

Point. Gold or green, and smooth with distance, the cleared fields of William Kingdom Rains shone on the high land of St. Joseph's, surrounded by the heavy first growth of beech, maple, ash, and white pine. On Neebish Island, above the entrance to the creek which divided Encampment Island from Neebish, a deep bay called by river captains the Dark Hole, and known as a watery cul-de-sac, a trap, Madame Cadotte, wife of a descendant of Johnston's old friend, had built a oneroom log house. These were the John McDougall Johnstones' only neighbors between Drummond and the Sault.

John McDougall Johnstone, like the Major before him, cut white pine from the surrounding shores and sold it to the river steamers. At fifty, he wore a full beard, blond and wiry, and brushed his hair back from his forehead as his father had done. He pronounced his middle name McDouall, spelled it usually McDougall, and had added an *e* to his surname. There were Johnsons at St. Mary's with whom he wished not to be confused.

The three girls, just coming to maturity, and especially Molly, might have been expected to miss the sociability of the village more than they did. Molly was even at twenty very shy and devoted to her family, and after all, a family of twelve was something of a village. She taught her younger brothers to read and write and figure a little. Will, a brown-haired boy with a fair skin, who was six years old when they moved to Anthony's house, was her especial charge. Howard Lewis Johnstone was four years older, very dark of skin, with eyes as dark as Molly's, and hair as dark; agile and slender and erect, exceedingly like his father in carriage and expression. James was the red-head of the family. They were all, indeed, fairer than Howard and Molly. Eliza's hair was a pure black, Charlotte's more brown, and Charlotte's eyes were a soft brown, not black. Their faces, and the faces of most of the other children, were broader than Molly's, less Indian in appearance. Molly and Charlotte went to pick strawberries in June, raspberries in August, in places on Neebish where fire or ax had thinned the woods. In August also they went to the rocky islands between Sugar and the northern end of St. Joseph's where the blueberries grew thick along the seams of the glaciated rock. Once, in a raspberry patch, they met a bear. The girls screamed and ran; the bear ran also. Afterwards, telling about it, Molly said, "I don't know which of us was the most frightened, the bear or me," and hid her face in her hands in embarrassment before she looked up smiling.

In winter, Justine made shoepacks of canvas for her men, leather being less easy to procure than in her mother's day. She went with her husband and her sons to the sturgeon fishing in the spring, and supervised the smoking of the fish, remembering how when she was a girl she had gone with the men in the canoes to help handle the nets and lines, and how a speared fish had sometimes run away with a canoe and an excited girl. Molly milked the cow, tended the chickens, pieced quilts with Eliza, boiled soap once a year in a place behind the barns where the ground was trodden with chips and ashes, scoured her grandmother's copper kettles with wood ashes and sand, and went yearly to the high land on Sugar Island or on the Neebish to make sugar from the thin pale sap of the maples. On Sunday afternoons at Anthony's house there were hymns sung in English or Ojibway from the collection made and translated by Peter Jones, with Charlotte playing the melodion, and leading the singing in her pretty voice.

> Nuh go shuh a zhe
> Pah pe nain duh mowod,
> Ke zhe mon e coon ken wahb mah jig. . . .
> How happy are they
> Who their Saviour obey
> And have laid up their treasure above,
> Tongue cannot express
> The sweet comfort and peace
> Of a soul in its earliest love.

This was Howard's favorite hymn. Days when the great thunderheads appeared suddenly beyond the cedars on St. Joseph's, darkening the water and the islands with apocalyptic shadow, the Major's green fields remaining lit with sun, then suddenly gone somber under the purple light, Molly, from the shelter of the porch, watched the rain sweep across the river, or ran to close windows and doors, while the rain, continuing its progress, trampled the white dry sand below the Point, bent the mallows, and assailed the thick shelter of leaves at the forest's edge. The manido of metal lying under the rock of all that region drew to itself inevitably the accumulated electricity of heaven. Spring was announced always by the crackle of the bright fluid through the air, the roar and rumble of its airy wake. There were calm days of summer when the river seemed as tranquil as water in a china cup, sunny days when the river ran under the northwest wind, a succession of whitecaps above the Point, still water below, or, the wind having changed its direction, Mud Lake was unpassable and above the Point all was tranquil. There were days in winter when the snow drifted from the hill toward the roof of the kitchen with scarcely a

215

droop in the white line, when every drop of water used in the house had first to be melted from ice or snow, when the men brought in immense logs, rolling and bumping them along the kitchen floor, to be used in the Montreal stove, and days when the house stood alone in a white whirl-wind, no river, no farther shore. And then again, the spring, sudden and late, and the summer wind plunging through the lilacs, spinning the poplar leaves, whitening the grass, and, when it was gone, water and meadow still beneath uninterrupted light. No sinister shadow, either of the old Major's immorality, the dark end of the trapper Le Sens, or the still darker reputed end of Anthony, who was said to have been hanged on a pine tree in back of the house, fell across these days of Molly Johnstone's young womanhood.

Still, she remembered a day in spring, when navigation had been open but for a short time and every vessel was still an event. Her father brought the Captain of a steamboat to the house for a visit while the boat was load-ing. It was one of the intensely warm days of early May, a seasonal acci-dent, a full release into summer before one had done full time with winter. The doors of the house stood open, and Molly, coming into the livingroom with the fresh cake and pitcher of milk her father had asked for, heard the men at the dock talking to each other, the thump and roll of the logs, sounding hollow across the dock. The Captain, indistinctly seen because of the sunlight at the windows, was a Chicago man who had a cousin in Seattle; she heard him saying so to her father, and that the cousin in Seattle sent him the town papers regularly. Molly, listening to hear more about Seattle, heard instead of a second lieutenant who had been stationed at Fort Brady in the year 1846.

"There was quite a piece about it," said the Captain, "and knowing about your sister, I cut it out. Thought you might care to see it." He began searching in the inside pocket of his unbuttoned coat.

"Molly," said her father, "I wish you'd take the children down by the river."

Later she learned, but not from her father, that the clipping contained the deathbed confession of Lieutenant Tilden that he had ambushed and slain, on the morning of July 6, her uncle, James Schoolcraft, because of "a quarrel over a woman." After the Mexican War, he had been transferred to a post near Seattle; from that place his confession had at last come home to the people most interested in it. Anna Maria herself was dead, had been dead since Molly was twelve years old, and Henry Rowe Schoolcraft had died the first year that the John McDougall Johnstones spent at Encampment. Perhaps because of the phrase "a quarrel over a woman" neither Justine nor John McDougall could ever be brought to discuss the matter at any length. It became for their children a family mystery. Molly, partly because she was named for her aunt, and partly because of a natural shrinking from such a subject, followed the example of her parents and never spoke of the affair if she could avoid it.

And once she went with Howard across the river to see the performance of a Jossakeed. Opposite the Dark Hole, a little farther upstream, an Ojibway family had settled. The place was a mile and a half or two miles from Anthony's house. They went in a small rowboat, Howard at the oars, Molly in the stern with a paddle to guide their progress. Molly was then in her thirties, as slender as ever, capable and erect, without great physical strength, but with grace and distinction in her bearing. She wore a printed calico, a white ground with a fine magenta figure, a gray calico sunbonnet on her head, shading the dark smooth cheeks, hiding the even scallops of her hair. The sleeves of her dress were long, covering her wrists and the upper part of her hands, which were like the hands of her aunt, Anna Maria, not small hands, but very beautiful. The fingers, a copper bronze, closed firmly around the silver-gray wood of the paddle. Occasionally she shifted the blade from one side of the boat to the other for a better purchase against the water, and the water dripped in a train of large drops across the sunny, sandy boards of the flooring. Facing her, Howard bent forward, straightened, bent again, his hands reaching toward her with the shafts of the oars, drawing back towards his chest, in a short rapid stroke almost as brisk as walking, a stroke for a short oar and a light boat, very little lengthened from the tempo of a paddle stroke. Under the shadow of his straw hat his face was bronzed and lean, the cheek bones high and pronounced, the jaw long, the chin firm, the nose slightly curved, the eyes well set. He wore a silky black mustache, but his face was unbearded, like that of an Ojibway. He resembled his father, he resembled Molly also. He wore a blue cotton jacket over a white shirt, and as he rowed, his glance turned from side to side, alert and easy, gauging his progress and the direction he was taking from what he saw beyond the stern of the boat, while he advanced backwards into the familiar unseen. They had lived almost ten years at Encampment. Howard was planning to spend the next year at St. Mary's, perhaps as a lock hand. They crossed the river at the Point, where it was narrow, going directly over until they were beyond the force of the current, and then turned north. They passed Major Rains's house and clearing, and his dock, running out across a stretch of sandy shallows, and continued north, the water smooth and bright, the sun hot, the shores all wooded to the water's edge except the green fields on St. Joseph's and the meadow behind them, beyond the Point, where Anthony's square white house stood with its veranda and lean-to among shrubs and flowers.

The Jossakeed was a man from Potoganissing. The Ojibway who had sent for him, after three days of struggle between his Christian inclinations and the habits of his race, was the father of a little girl whom Molly knew as an occasional shy beggar at the Johnstone kitchen. The child had been ill for a week with a high fever and a cough, the fever alternating with chills in the morning. Her family lived in a small house walled and thatched with cedar bark; there were no windows They kept the child on a pile of old quilts in the corner, as far from the sun and air as possible. When Molly and Howard arrived, the father was standing by the door of the house, weeping, and the Jossakeed was within, speaking to the child. After a little, he came out, a man of medium stature, in his late middle age, an Ottawa type rather than an Ojibway, with a broad face. His hair was black, and fell to his shoulders, unbraided. He wore a black felt hat, and a black sateen shirt which was not tucked into his trousers but fell over them, like a tunic, and was belted by a red, fringed sash. His leggins of red cloth were bound at the knee with narrow strips of beaded cloth, fringed at the end with beads. He wore moccasins. When he saw Howard and Molly, he came to them and shook hands. He was not a prepossessing man nor was there anything strange about him. He said that he was very sorry the father had not sent for him earlier; he was afraid that the child would die. He would do the best he could, however.

He had brought with him rolls of birchbark and bundles of poles of varying sizes. He cleared three spaces in the flowered grass in front of the house, carefully tossing away any little rock or stick that he found, smoothing down the grass in three circles. In one circle he put his moccasins, in the next largest his legging, and in the largest of all his drum and pipe. He moved about in his bare feet, his black trousers hanging down to his ankles, building a small lodge over the moccasins, and a slightly larger one over the legging. These were true Ojibway lodges, domed at the top, and had no doorways. He built the third lodge high enough to accommodate a man seated, and when it was finished, asked for tobacco, which was given him by the father of the sick child. He then crept inside the third lodge and drew a piece of bark from within across the opening. For a while he smoked, and then began to beat his drum and sing. It was mid-afternoon. Molly and Howard, at a little distance from the lodges, walked about or stood, but did not speak. Owen Rains was there also, a small man with rosy English cheeks, his shoulders already stooped from hard work, although he was in the prime of life. Except for the three small lodges, and the fact that no one was speaking, the scene was as commonplace for Molly as well could be. It seemed strange to her that it should be so commonplace. She looked down the river to Encampment Island, rising under its mantle of trees to a low ridge, she looked at the sandy, ripple-marked beach where their rowboat lay half drawn up, and at the grass at her feet, full of mallows with silky, faintly ruffled mauve corollas, with powdery yellow, thick pistil heads. The drumming and singing went on for some time, then ceased. The sunlight continued undisturbed by any cloud or wind. Owen Rains was standing, leaning against the bark wall of the house, coatless, his thumbs stuck through his braces, his shrewd pleasant face mildly speculative. The father of the child sat crouched in the doorway. Then Howard touched Molly on the arm, and she looked, as he was looking, at the smallest lodge. She knew that the moccasins were in that lodge, and nothing else, yet the lodge was shaking. It trembled as if a storm were within it, not merely the bark of the sheathing trembling, but the framework of the structure, the bent poles, which had been firmly planted in the ground, shaking violently. The shaking continued for perhaps five minutes, in silence, in sun, then it ceased, and, after a short interval, the lodge in which the leggins had been placed began to tremble, and shook as violently as the smaller lodge had done. This demonstration ended, and was followed by the trembling of the lodge in which the Jossakeed himself was hidden. Molly said afterward, "It did not look as if he were touching the lodge." When the lodge was still again, after a little while the bark shifted from the doorway, and the Jossakeed crept out. He appeared very fatigued. He turned to the father and said: "It is too late. It makes me very sorry, but my spirits say it is too late. You should have sent for me before." While he was still conferring with the Indian, Molly and Howard went down to the boat, got in, and pushed off, neither of them wishing to stay longer at the place nor to speak to the Jossakeed again. Nor did they have anything to say to each other until they were halfway home.

Molly had never denied the existence of the supernatural. What troubled her now was presently expressed by Howard, who, resting his oars, and holding the balanced shafts both under one hand, took off his hat and passed his free hand slowly over his forehead. The sun was mild, it was half-past five at least in the afternoon, there was no reason why he should longer wear a hat. He said, after a moment, with a shake of his head, as if he had come to the end of a long spoken argument, "No, sir, it wasn't the Devil." Then, persuasively, the gentle, cultured timbre of his voice as persuasive as his manner, "That man might have been ignorant, but I don't believe he was *bad*. Didn't he come to try to do good?" It was the conclusion of a long family discussion, a discussion beginning years before his birth when Henry and Jane Schoolcraft had decided that Satan was actively present in the magical works of Chusco, the Jossakeed who had received grace in the sugar woods. What the spirits were that shook the small bark lodges, Howard could not say. He was certain, however, that Satan the great myth—or the great truth, evil being a reality—had not stood among the mallows in the sunlight. Yet the existence of evil was something he did not deny either, and during the rest of the trip Molly was troubled by the remembrance of an incident of which Howard had once told her. An Indian woman living at Drummond had once, in her childhood, been forced to pick up a toad towards which she had been seized with a sudden and unaccountable aversion, the aversion being not against the toad as a toad, but against the animal as a particular individual. Her father had forced her to lay her hand over the creature and lift it from the ground. She laid it down again almost immediately, yet too late, for, as the story declared, the change had occurred the moment she touched the creature, all that was good in her nature as a little girl passing into the body of the toad, and the pure evil in the toad, which had warned her from it, passing into her own body and nature. From that moment on she was known as a transformed person, unaccountably malicious. The day when Howard and Molly rowed across the river to see the Jossakeed she was living at Drummond, a woman who abused her children and was dreaded by her neighbors. A part of Molly saw the toad exactly as the Indians at Drummond saw it, a part of her protesting meanwhile, and protesting also against the shaking of the lodges.

She supposed that her decision was much the same as Howard's, and yet there remained the supernatural—something that was the Devil, or if it was not the Devil was certainly not the Christ, and also the Christ himself, an aspect of the supernatural so familiar, so sweet and sane, that she sometimes did not think of it as such at all. For days after the Jossakeed's performance she went about her tasks deeply confused and troubled.

Except for such intervals as these, the years in Anthony's house were for Molly all "earliest love"—affection for her mother, for Charlotte and Eliza and the younger children, for her father, for the place itself, river, house, and garden, and for the hymns sung at the melodion; all "sweet comfort and peace." When she was thirty-two, John McDougall removed his residence to a farm near the Sault, returning to Encampment only for the summer months.

220

II

Immediately upon his return from his brief schooling in New York State, John McDougall Johnstone had become interpreter for Henry Schoolcraft; since then he had been almost continually in the service of the Government as Indian interpreter for one agent or another. Two years he spent as Indian farmer at the mission at Grand Traverse Bay, George being with him there as Indian carpenter, and George's second wife, a Boston gentlewoman by the name of Mary Rice. The mission was a part of Henry's plan to make good agriculturalists of the Ojibway hunters. As interpreter, again, in the summer of 1838, John went with James Schoolcraft and George and the delegation of Ottawas and Ojibways from Saginaw to overlook the lands west of the Mississippi which were to be given to the Saginaws in exchange for their lands in Michigan. Down the Mississippi to St. Louis they went, then up the Missouri to the headwaters of the Osage and the heart of the Indian territory, James with his two interpreters and the thirty delegates. The territory was then occupied by three nations, the Osage, the Oshawanos, and the transported Delawares, to whom were to be added the transported Saginaws. The nations held a council during the visit of the Saginaws to which James and his interpreters were invited by courtesy James declined, thinking it wiser to do so, and George remained with him, but John attended the council. He found himself that night in a lodge one hundred and fifty feet long and fifty feet wide, having three central fires. Opposite the fires on a staging were seated the principal men of the three nations, and near them the musicians with every sort of instrument, both new and old. The dance around the central fires which opened the ceremonies consumed three quarters of an hour. Later, the women danced alone, nearly a hundred of them, each wearing a black beaver hat ornamented with two broad bands of silver and with black fox-tails, a blanket of fine cloth garnished with silver brooches, and half moons of silver, and moccasins worked with colored beads. As they danced they sang, keeping time with a slight motion of their feet, and the silver flashed, the black plumes swayed in the firelight. Outside, a guard of thirty young men on horseback patrolled the prairie, the dull beat of the hooves breaking, now and again, through the beat of the music, and John McDougall, remembering why they were there, and that his hair was blond, and that he could understand neither the Osage nor the Delaware language, felt in his pocket for the small dagger which Henry had given him before he left St. Mary's.

Afterwards, in the sunlight, riding through Kansas on the way home from the survey, he reined his horse beside a cornfield and, standing with one foot on the saddle, the other on the top rail of a fence, reached as high as he could and broke off eighteen inches of rustling stalk. This cornfield was owned by an Indian.

Frequently, while he was clerking for James, he was sent in charge of a bateau of goods to La Pointe, the place of Indian payment for those years, as the Sault had been earlier and was to be again. Franchère, in 1837, impatient over a consignment of goods which had not arrived, wrote, "The Indians will receive $5,000 at this place [St. Mary's] next August, and you are fully aware that they will spend every cent before they leave the Sault." James, like the other traders, found it advantageous to reap what harvest he could from the conditions of Henry's treaties, and John McDougall, as his father had done before him, approached Ile St. Michel with his packages of needles, of vermilion, twine for nets, ax heads, strouds, blankets. Once, from a point near the Yellow Dog River, striking across the lake without a compass, without sight of land for eighty-seven miles, he made the crossing of Kewenaw Bay, and brought his crew and cargo safely to shore within six miles of Copper Harbor, the longest traverse ever so made in an open boat. In 1857 he piloted the first steamer into the old harbor of the Northwest Company at Grand Portage, the *Illinois,* which had also been, two years earlier, the first steamer to pass through the new locks at St. Mary's. And on one of his trips to La Pointe for James he stopped to explore the Pictured Rocks. The water was too high to permit of entering the great cavern by boat; John McDougall and two of his men stripped to the waist and swam under the stone arch, climbed up on a stony ledge which was raised some eight inches above the water, and found themselves in a vast chamber filled with frightened birds. Their voices sounded strange. They were afraid to penetrate far into the cave, for their feet were bare and the stones sharp, but John McDougall sent one of the men to the bateau for his flute. The man returned swimming with the flute in his mouth, like a dog with a stick, and standing there, barefooted and dripping wet, John McDougall played, while the swallows wheeled about his head, their harsh cries mixing with the sound of the flute and its multiple pure echoes.

He did not think of these things as achievements especially, but as the years went by they became things that he could say he had done.

In 1855 he went to Detroit at the request of Wayishkee, then in his eighty-seventh year, to check, for the Ottawas and Ojibways, the translations to be made by Cadotte, brother of Granny Cadotte's man, Charles. The Government was making one more treaty with the Indians. Cadotte was not known to be dishonest, but the Ojibways had of late been confronted with such unforeseen results from their treaties with the United States that they were grown uneasy and suspicious. Shortly before the time of Mrs. Jameson's visit the Indians had been greatly distressed because, in extending the limits of Fort Brady, the soldiers, digging new holes for the pickets, had violated a number of Indian graves. In July, 1853, greater desecration was committed when the first shaft for the State Lock was sunk through the Indian cemetery by the river. Henry Shegud had gone to Father Bingham, and in sorrow and indignation had protested that no treaty ever made with the Americans by the Ojibways had ever granted the Americans the right to disturb the Indian dead. Father Bingham pointed out to him the fact that although the Treaty of 1820 had been very plain about the Ojibway reservations, there had been many treaties since; they had sent delegates to Washington in 1836, to La Pointe in 1842; neither he nor Henry Shegud knew everything that was in those treaties; and moreover, he added sadly, even should the United States be now violating a treaty, it was too late for Shegud or for his Father in God to do anything to stop them. Shegud acknowledged the force of these observations, but his sorrow was not allayed. The State of Michigan continued to dig up the bones of his ancestors and fling them in a muddy pile beside the new canal. The next autumn there was another treaty at La Pointe. The Indian payments went on with regularity, each man, woman, and child of the Ojibway nation who took the trouble to present himself at the place of payment—Mackinac, St. Mary's, or La Pointe, as the case might be—receiving a blanket, a yard or two of strouds or calico, or a little pile of money; and still the Ojibways knew that they were losing without understanding how or why. Therefore when Commissioner George Manypenny called the Ottawa and Ojibway delegates to a conference in Detroit, Wayishkee asked John McDougall Johnstone to accompany them.

The new lock was opened formally the eighteenth of June, 1855, with great celebration. The village circus grounds southeast of the locks, the small bridge across the swift deep pool, were thronged with visitors. Miss Eliza was there, her dark aristocratic face shadowed by the green silk calash, a spray of sweet briar in her hand; and on the steamer *Illinois,* as she passed westward through the tandem locks, each with its lift of nine feet, its double wooden gates opened and shut by capstans worked by hand, were Father Bingham, Angie and Hannah, Angie's older sister, and General Cass. Each lock was able to take at one time three schooners and a tug, and each could be filled or emptied in seven minutes. The *Illinois* went up in the morning; later in the day the *Baltimore,* which had a few years earlier traversed the Portage on grease and rollers, locked down, with a cargo of copper. Beyond the locks to the north the stony Point still held a group of Indian shanties, and, north of these, Edward Oshawanoe's Island, still crowned with cedars, lay green and tranquil at the foot of the tumultuous white ascent.

In July the Treaty Conference began at Detroit. The delegates listened gravely, the big room full of the reek of their pipes, of their clothing, the air dense with their anxiety. Cadotte translated honestly, and for the Ojibways his explanation seemed to be adequate. An Ottawa, however, asked for a fuller statement of the matter. Cadotte, referred to, lifted his hands as a signal that he had already done his best, and the Commissioner inquired of the room at large if there were any one present who could improve upon Cadotte's translation. Feeling Wayishkee's eye upon him with a glint of satisfaction, John McDougall Johnstone rose from his place and mounted the platform, a spare, broad-shouldered figure in an ordinary gray suit with a black string tie, and retranslated Cadotte's speech to the greater comprehension of the Ottawas. He was about to return to his place when the Commissioner stopped him. "Stay here with us," he said. In this fashion was John engaged as interpreter for the commission for the rest of the time it was to be in existence.

The treaty provided for certain townships and sections, already speci-fied by the Treaty of La Pointe, to be set aside for each of the six bands of the Ojibways. From these lands, within five years from the date of the treaty, each head of a family might select eighty acres of land; each single person over twenty-one years of age, forty acres; each family of orphans containing two or more persons, eighty acres; and each single orphan, forty acres. And, "in consideration of these provisions and the payment of five hundred and thirty-eight thousand, four hundred dollars in manner therein specified, the Ottawas and Chippewas release the United States Government from all former treaties and the bands are dissolved except as necessary to carry out the treaty." Gone were the islands in the St. Mary's River and in the upper lakes, reserved by Henry for the perpetual use of the Ojibways, gone were the camping places at the foot of the falls, the perpetual right to fish in the rapids, gone Oshawanoe's Island, gone the Ojibway and Ottawa nations. Hereafter there were to be only citizens of the United States, having varying ancestry.

The first sawmill at St. Mary's had cut, as the first log through it, a maple, and the planks from this first log were made into a table for the agency. Henry Schoolcraft had used it in his study, and after his departure it had been called the interpreters' table, retaining its place in the agency office. As long as payments were made to the Ojibways, John McDougall sat behind this table, helped to undo the leather sacks and build up the piles of gold and silver coins, checked off the names from the list as one by one the Indians presented themselves and were paid, each his share of the tribal annuities. As long as it was necessary for "the White Father at Washington to speak to his red children," he translated. When, sometime during the seventies, the payments were completed and the terms of the treaty fulfilled, he completed his forty years or more of service with the Government. This was the last treaty and John McDougall Johnstone was the last interpreter. The interpreters' table fell to him, therefore, and he took it home as a memento of Henry and the Ojibways.

III

Meanwhile in the roomy study at Cambridge, with the June sunshine filtered cloudily through the long curtains, in the seclusion of summer air mixed with the domestic odor of carpet and upholstery, Mr. Longfellow meditated his long-considered plan of an epic of the American Indian. For three days he thought of the work as the *Song of Manabozho*. Then, finding that Mr. Schoolcraft had been able to identify the Ojibway demigod with an Iroquois hero by the name of Hiawatha, and being concerned about that awkward *zh,* he changed the title of his poem to the *Song of Hiawatha,* thus descending unaware from the mythical to the merely historical. Henry, taking his *Algic Researches* again in hand after his return from Europe, when he was settled in the Iroquois country and concerned principally with Iroquois research, firm in the belief that all things Algonquin could be reduced to a common term, had himself been deceived by this Clearer of Rivers, a man who had flourished in the days of the Six Nations, a hero indeed, but not a demigod. Manibush, Nanabush, Nenbozho, Wenabozho, Manabozho, Hiawatha—Mr. Longfellow considered them all, and chose the one which did not resemble any of the others, but which was a very pretty name. He had selected also the meter of the Kalevala, a simple primitive rhythm, as suitable for a simple primitive tale. There remained nothing but to read and indite. Late in June, 1854, with occasional interruptions of visits from Mr. Emerson, Mr. Lowell, from "two young Cubans with my friend Mr. Wales," of letters to be incribed to Charles Sumner about poor black Anthony Burns, of fits of indignation for the event and sentences of fiery praise for Sumner, he began the *Lament of Hiawatha for his Brother,* and in July took the manuscript to Nahant, where, within sound of the waves, the thin rattle of carriage wheels muffled in summer dust, crowing and cackling from the henyard, he went on with his fairy tale.

Should you ask me, whence these stories?
Whence these legends and traditions,
With the odors of the forest,
With dew and damp of meadows,
With the curling smoke of wigwams . . .

The three huge quartos of the *Algic Researches* were with him, not the little brownish, two-volume *Algic Researches* of 1839, but the enormous magenta tomes published at the expense of the Government, two inches thick, a foot and a half high, with elaborate plates, the result of Henry's lifetime of note-taking and grammatical speculation, Henry's monument in three volumes. Mr. Longfellow found in them "a mass of ill-digested material"; he endeavored to simplify, to rearrange, to suppress the "gross," the disagreeable, the too fantastic. He came across Neengay's little allegory of Winter and Spring, and used it almost without changing a word. Schoolcraft had attempted to place accents on the Ojibway syllables, a rash endeavor, and these Mr. Longfellow took at their full apparent value, fitting the Ojibway, with its light, hovering, and constantly shifting accents firmly into the rhythm of the Kalevala. Schoolcraft's orthography he had perforce to accept completely also; thus it happened that Maymay, the Woodpecker, went into literature rather oddly as Mama. But he was conscientious and sympathetic. The more he wrote, the more charmed he became with the Indian, his legends and his way of life.

The summer over, he returned to Cambridge; in the winter there was grand opera, Grisi in *I Puritani,* and in *Norma*. Lowell was lecturing on the English ballads, Sumner had arrived from Washington. Suddenly *Hiawatha,* which had not gone well through the autumn, began to move forward with grace and speed.

Mrs. Follen had a letter from Lady Byron which told of a dying soldier on the field before Sebastopol who was heard to repeat the line "Footprints on the sands of time." And in March *Hiawatha* was finished. In spite of his long hours of delving in the magenta tomes, he had used, in the end, practically nothing not to be found in Henry's first small volumes, material which had, as it were, been selected for him by Jane Schoolcraft. He began at once to copy the manuscript for the press, sending it off to the publishers page by page as fast as it was ready, and before the end of the year the *Song of Hiawatha* had been brought out in eleven thousand copies. Many a child had pages of it by heart before, in accordance with the Treaty of 1855, the bands were dissolved and the Ojibway nation ceased to be a reality.

Henry, who had been greatly confined of late years by a paralysis of the legs, wrote Mr. Longfellow a pedantic, mildly appreciative note of thanks for a copy of the *Song*. Mr. Emerson, more briefly, wrote that the poem was as sweet and wholesome as Indian corn. The nation in general, now that the West was safe for civilization, the Indian question having been solved by treaty, deportation, and other methods kinder not to mention, was delighted to contemplate the Indian as "a human being capable of the tenderest emotions."

IV

Miss Eliza died in poverty, in solitude, of old age, and without the comfort of those familiar walls in which she had spent her life. The house had been sold to a Colonel Wheeler, of the United States Government Engineering Corps, who covered the log walls on the outside with clapboarding painted a dull brown. A Mrs. Gilbert, of Grand Rapids, came to see her as she lay dying, the Angie Bingham of the days before there had been a ship canal, when the Soo had been called St. Mary's, when Miss Eliza, erect and taciturn, had walked down Water Street, twirling her sprig of eglantine, raising or lowering the folds of her green calash, according to the sun. Not the thrift, economy, and cheer of Mary Rice Johnston, George's wife, nor George's plans to recover the family prestige by copper-mine investments, nor John McDougall's steady years of intelligent service to the Government, had been able to retain for Miss Eliza the old log house, the garden of bachelor's-buttons, marigolds, and sweet william, the rows of currant bushes, the shade of the ash trees above the little portico with seats. George was dead at the Sault in '61, William in Mackinac in '66, Charlotte in '78 at Niagara. Even the children of the children—Jane's son Johnston Schoolcraft, serving in the Confederate Army because his father had married, some five years after his mother's death, a Southern woman, was dead. George's sons were killed in the Civil War—James, Sam, and Benjamin, Benjamin at the second Battle of Bull Run, as was the son of old John Tanner, the captive. Lying, and waiting, in a strange room, for the end of her eighty-second year, Miss Eliza felt herself part of a crowd, of a great procession, little concerned with what they were doing over by the edge of the rapids, or at the steamboat landing, or at the head of Portage Avenue; and eventually she joined this procession, green calash, blue-beaded bag, sprig of eglantine, and all, and Angie Bingham Gilbert, hearing the news later in Grand Rapids, sat down and cried because a bad-tempered old woman had quit the earth.

What had been going on at the edge of the rapids for eleven years was, precisely, besides the perpetual locking of vessels up- and down-stream, the building of the Weitzel Lock. The canal and lock were dug within the line of the State Lock, through the dry land, leaving the rapids untouched. When the State Lock had been built, almost every captain on the lakes had protested at the unnecessary size of the lock chambers, on the theory that there was no vessel then in use that could not easily be passed through a much smaller space, and that the extraordinary and fantastic magnitude of the proposed locks would prevent the project from ever being actually accomplished. Now they were building the Weitzel, with a single lift of eighteen feet, and a chamber five hundred and fifteen feet long and eighty feet wide, and no one was protesting. While Howard Lewis Johnstone worked at the State Lock, helping to operate the capstans that opened and shut the gates, or taking the hawsers of incoming vessels to be made fast before the water was set in motion, entering or leaving the lock chamber, his brother Will was helping to unload the face stone for the Weitzel that had been brought up on schooners from Kelly's Island in Lake Erie. Three years before Miss Eliza's death the Weitzel was opened, plans were being made to inclose the State Lock in a coffer dam and replace it by another modern work such as the Weitzel, and the channel of the St. Mary's was being uniformly deepened to seventeen feet. They were even designing a cut through the Middle Neebish Rapids. The Weitzel, with its long straight chamber narrowing at each end to seventy feet, with its double miter gates and manifold culverts, was considered the finest example of lock engineering in the world. Will was proud to have had a hand in building it. After the opening of the Weitzel, the Indians no longer camped on the "Point." Five hundred shade trees were planted in Lock Park, and electricity was used to light the park at night.

Kewenaw was still the Copper Peninsula, but there was more talk about iron, now, than there had ever been about copper. Through all the business of the upper peninsula, the word iron or the thought of iron echoed like the note of a great bell, constantly recurring, resonant, serious; the newspapers of the day were the *Marquette Mining Journal,* the *Escanaba Iron Port,* the *Iron Agitator,* the *Portage Lake Mining Gazette,* the *Negaunee Iron Herald,* the *Ontonagon Miner.* The towns were Iron Mountain, Iron River, Bessemer, Gogebic, Ironwood, and, later, Biwabik. The Sault was the great port of entry for all provisions for these towns, household goods, mining machinery, food, and the port of exit for thousands of tons of copper ore, iron ore, iron blooms. Yet, in spite of this new national importance, the close of navigation every year found the Sault as isolated as it had been fifty years before. The mail still came in from Saginaw once a month by train de glisse, and when it arrived, the town entered into a carnival of sociability for a day or two while every one called on every one and letters and news and papers were passed from hand to hand. Howard Lewis Johnstone carried the mail one winter, setting the record for the trip with mail, on foot, from the Sault to St. Ignace, three days and three hours, old John Busha, the Indian carrier, being runner-up, with a record of three days and five hours.

V

In the summers, while John McDougall Johnstone was yet alive, he and Justine had been in the habit of visiting Howard and Molly where they were homesteading the upper one hundred and fifty-five acres of Encampment Island. In the winters they returned to the Sault. Although greatly disabled by rheumatism, Johnstone could yet handle a boat more skillfully than most men. He and Justine came down the river, sailing or rowing by day, camping by night, making a leisurely journey of a distance that Howard had once rowed in five and a quarter hours, and, arrived at Molly's landing, set up a cedar-bark lodge or small house, such as the Ojibway family across the river had lived in. Molly had built a house, a long single room with a roof sloping one way, from front to back, faced with a long veranda. Later she added a couple of small lean-tos at the southern end. Virginia creeper, rooted in the corner between the new and old structures, soon bound the roof lines together, and showered the gray wood, in the fall, with leaves like scarlet feathers. John McDougall and Justine declined the hospitality of this building, Justine saying half in fun, "Mosquitoes never come into a bark lodge," but Charlotte and Howard lived with Molly. Eliza was married and living at Detour, her husband a Mr. Anthony, a man with a gift for small public offices—justice of the peace— an ingenious soul, addicted to bear hunts, a great reader and the best-informed man in the town. Molly had begun to take a few summer boarders from Chicago or the Sault. Howard made her a sign, O-Non-E-Gwud Inn, Pleasant Place, and met her guests at the slab landing below the sawmill, bringing them up past the Point to O-Non-E-Gwud. Black Anthony's house had passed into the hands of a Mr. Roach, stonemason for the Poe Lock, then being built on the site of the old State Lock. Below Anthony's house lived Miss Mabel Slocum, postmistress for the island, and below Miss Mabel's was the sawmill. On Neebish Island was the mill village, consisting of some forty families crowded into a series of low red shanties. Miss Molly's land was no longer valuable for timber. The river steamers, Major Rains, and John McDougall Johnstone himself had cleared from it the magnificent first growth of white pine, but it was still wooded with balsam and maple, ash and birch and cedar, hazel and alder, with vines and low shrubs, its shadows starred from May until October with wild flowers. Justine and John McDougall Johnstone celebrated their golden wedding anniversary at O-Non-E-Gwud in the summer of 1892.

In February, 1895, John McDougall Johnstone died at the Sault. Howard Johnstone was alone with his father the night of his death. He sat there, while the old man slept, watching the small round flame in the kerosene lamp floating just above the wick, golden and smooth, shielded by glass. The night was cold but not especially windy. As he sat there, he heard some one knock at the door, three taps, and he rose and crossed the room, opening the door in the expectation of seeing some neighbor, since every one knew that his father was very ill. The door gave directly upon the night, and there was no other visible presence. He shut the door, stopped a moment to observe the light, for the draft caused by the open door had drawn a thin thread of soot upward from the flame, and turned to his father's bed. The old man did not move, he would not move again. Howard, leaning over him intently, carefully, his hand lifted to be laid softly on his father's shoulder, knew this fact presently, and the hand remained poised in the air, dark and sensitive in an involuntary attitude of benediction. The quilt, checkered in squares of differently patterned and colored cloth, the white pillow and the sleeping head, all under the faint warm glow of the lamp, had entered into an eternity, a response to that light tapping on the door, the absolute, unostentatious summons.

Thereafter, Justine was happier to live with Molly at Encampment. In the seclusion of the woods she was less often reminded of the passing of all that had been familiar to her. She had stood, with others whose forbears were interred in that same earth, to watch the removal of the village cemetery in order to make way for the Armory Place; Shegud had stood so to watch the bones of his fathers disinterred for the canal, but the bones were not reburied. At least, these coffins would be placed in a new cemetery on the edge of town. The spades cut through the rind of sandy earth to the cold stiff clay. Where the pit was deep enough a workman threw away his spade and stooped to clear the clods with his hands, tossing them up on the bank of exhumed earth. Among these clods a plate of thin dark metal fell at the feet of Justine, who picked it up and wiped the clay from its face and read, "John Johnston Esq. Born August 25, 1762." It was the silver plaque which Neengay had made from the silver spoons. It was not replaced on the coffin, but rested now among the personal relics of John McDougall's family, with a dirk presented to John McDougall by Henry Rowe Schoolcraft and engraved on the blade, "Draw me not without reason, Sheathe me not without honor," and with a pitcher with a golden band given to Justine and John on the occasion of their fiftieth wedding anniversary.

In 1898 Howard built for himself a trim little house to the south of O-Non-E-Gwud, and in 1903 brought there his wife, who had been Miss Lucy Babcock. In 1898 also Mr. and Mrs. Purdy of the Sault built a house on the intervening lot, which they had bought from Miss Molly. As O-Non-E-Gwud acquired more fame, Howard began to put up a row of small shingled cottages for Molly's boarders, and one winter dragged down on the ice from Powder House Bay the old powder house used for storage by the men who were blasting out the new channel through the Middle Neebish Rapids. This he divided into rooms, built a double porch, for the building was two stories high, railed the porches with a lattice of birch boughs, and named it Birch Lodge. It stood near the Inn, close to a small sandy bay, sheltered, as was O-Non-E-Gwud, from the northwest wind by the thick woods. As the popularity of the resort increased, the labor increased, and Miss Molly, then in her early sixties, still with the slender body of her girlhood yet without her girlhood strength, sold the place to Augusta Kneipp, and withdrew, with Miss Charlotte and Grandma Johnstone, to a house built far back from the shore, but in sight of it, between Mrs. Purdy's and O-Non-E-Gwud.

Molly had sold a good many of her lots now, up and down the river. From the proceeds of their sale, and from that of the inn, she was able to live in a manner more fitting to her strength. There was leisure now for expeditions to Big Neebish with Miss Charlotte for berries, as in the old days, or across the river for visits with Owen Rains and his family, or to sit with Mrs. Purdy in a flat-bottomed boat in front of O-Non-E-Gwud, catching a few perch. On Sunday evenings an informal service was usually held in O-Non-E-Gwud. The cottagers came with kerosene lanterns down the shore path, extinguished them, and set them in a row along the porch. Miss Molly, with a candle-lantern in one hand, her dark gray woolen cape with the pineapple figures in light gray held together at the throat with her other hand, her head bare, came down the path through the deep grass, along the shore, followed by her mother and Miss Charlotte, walking single file on the planks which Mrs. Kneipp had laid here and there for paths; and seated in a group with the others, in her black silk dress with the high collar and the black silk ruching, sang, "There is a fountain filled

231

with blood, Drawn from Emmanuel's veins," or "Love divine, all love excelling," while Mrs. Deyoe or Mrs. Hanks or Mary Osborn played the piano. Miss Charlotte preferred not to play in public now. Her hands trembled a little, and she sometimes made mistakes if she was playing for strangers. She sat, her soft brown eyes framed by gold-rimmed spectacles, singing, and hardly glancing at the book which she held with Molly. Beside her on the cane table a kerosene lamp burned steadily, helping to warm the room against the evening chill, its globe covered with a green cardboard shade, its white wick curled down in the glass bowl filled with oil. On the porch a group of boys and girls, having come with their parents, whispered through the sermon, sang when they liked the hymns, and watched the lights on the freighters passing in mid-channel. In 1910 Mrs. Anthony came from Detour, after the death of Mr. Anthony, to live with Molly and Charlotte.

Never so massive in its bony structure as the face of Neengay, the face of Justine did not broaden with age, but remained a pure oval, the broad forehead lined, and framed with short locks of white hair combed smoothly down; at her cheek the small gold loop to which she had fastened, in her youth, the dangling ornaments of jet; her throat wrinkled and shrunk but still holding the beautiful old head gracefully above the unstooped shoulders. In a dress of finely striped cotton, gray and black, with a tight waist, long sleeves, and full skirt, and a small turndown collar of black sateen, a short string of jet beads about her throat, she sat in the cane-backed rocking-chair on Miss Molly's porch, watching the river, visiting with old French Ojibway women who came from Sugar Island to see her, or, on cold days, sat indoors between the stove and window, her head outlined against the dull red paper of the wall. Her hands were in her lap, folded one on the other, and in her eyes, except when she spoke, was an expression of great patience, not of suffering, but of waiting. Still the children who came to see her, who called her Grandma Johnstone, and to whom she gave Indian names, as Charlotte and Jane had given an Indian name to Mrs. Jameson, saw in her face only her age, and her dark, bright eyes. She was for them a symbol of antiquity. Loving her, and fearing her a little as one fears the primeval, they stood at her knee, receiving, for their summer hours and their childhood, the appellations of flower and bird, Opeechee, the Robin; Naynokahsee, the Humming Bird; Miskodeed, the Spring Beauty.

Miss Charlotte died in this house February 19, 1912. Because of the snow and ice it was not considered practical to transport the body to the Sault, and she was buried where she had been happiest, on Encampment

Island, under the pines beyond Molly's garden. In May of the year follow-
ing Grandma Johnstone died at the age of ninety-one, and in September
Mrs. Anthony followed her, leaving Molly alone. Both Mrs. Anthony and
Grandma Johnstone were buried at the Sault.

VI

Molly slept downstairs in the place that had been Grandma Johnstone's.
Upstairs, in the loft-like room divided into three parts upon occasion by
curtains of printed cotton hung on cords, the three beds were empty and
unmade, the blankets folded and laid on the bare ticking, or hidden away
in trunks. The windows, looking one on the garden and the other toward
the river, each with its white ruffled muslin curtain, were unopened, save
at such times as Molly, like a careful governor, made a visit to the upper
room to see that all was well. When she entered the loft, climbing the narrow inclosed stairway, the air smelled of wood. She opened the windows
then to sun and air the place, and the curtains blew gently inward, the
warm air was stirred and freshened. Life invaded the place but not, as
through the lower windows, a life immediate with activity, but life of the
upper air, the higher branches of the trees, the garden below seen from a
little distance, removed, as in a memory, the front yard full of daisies and
wild roses, the fence, the shore path, the river beyond the reedy shallows,
nostalgic, bright and calm. She stood there, letting the faint breeze stir
about her, a meager aging figure in gray calico, a blue-and-white checked
apron about her waist, her hair, thinning with age but still black, still waving, framing her face in the precise scallops, braided and pinned low at the
back of her head; her eyes opaque and bright, even in reverie, letting the
living quiet of the room touch her shoulders, her frail back, the hem of her
long skirts, "an aged virgin," as if the summer morning so inclosed by
walls, so mingled with furniture, the deep old trunks, the washstand with
its white china bowl and pitcher and flowered soap dish, the cane-bot-
tomed chair, the chest of drawers, were remembering for her the hours
spent there in winter or summer, morning or evening, with Miss Charlotte
and Mrs. Anthony.

Now she slept downstairs in the alcove under the staircase, shielded
from the room by a turkey-red drapery. There was no reason why anything
else in the house should be changed. Grandma Johnstone's chair stood in
its accustomed place between the stove and window; the desk, with her
father's letters and accounts of incidents in his life dictated by him and
transcribed in Charlotte's careful writing, standing within reach of the

233

chair. Across the room, the piano from Mathuschek, New Haven, held a little pile of hymn books, a silver cake dish engraved with the Johnston
crest, a crystal fruit bowl on a long stem that rang like a bell, when tapped,
a fragile note, glassy, high and pure. There were a great many bookshelves
for such a house. Above the piano was a portrait of Molly's grandfather,
John Johnston; it showed him with auburn hair, black eyes, wearing a dark
coat with a lapel of yellow satin. She had a miniature also of an Irish
cousin of her grandfather's, a McNeill in a red coat with a brassy epaulette.
The piano still belonged to Miss Charlotte, the chair by the desk to her
mother. Molly's particular province was the kitchen, or the edge of the
back porch, where she stood with a pan of grain, calling to her chickens.
And yet she tried to fill the house, sitting sometimes, when she was alone,
at the piano or in her mother's chair.

The spring and summer after Grandma Johnstone's death, Howard's
Lucy came often, Miss Mabel and Mrs. Purdy, dropping in with little
excuse, usually with some small gift, flowers or a loaf of fresh bread; and
Howard took Molly on the river whenever he could, knowing how well
she liked to be there. Lucy, always very crisp in her fresh cotton dresses
of pink or lavender or blue, came through Mrs. Purdy's garden to Molly's
side gate, and so through Molly's garden to the back door, where Molly
stood with a sunbonnet in her hand, wondering whether or not to work
in the garden that morning. Lucy turned her head quickly from side to
side, looked at Molly sideways with her big dark eyes, smiled and spoke
quickly, and her presence was enlivening. Miss Mabel, slower in her gestures, blue-eyed, pink-checked, with her gray hair going white about her
forehead, stopped on her way to the store, or Mrs. Purdy, snowy-haired,
with a lavender bow on her white dimity cap, old black silk gloves on her
hands with the finger tips cut away, came with bunches of pansies. Her
eyes were blue and unbespectacled in spite of her seventy-eight years, and
her face, minutely lined, was soft and white. Howard filled the water buckets and replenished the woodbox, and Lucy made an extra dish for Molly
of whatever she was baking. The chickens also, scratching among the
sandy rows of the garden or among the pine needles at the garden's edge,
white-feathered, commonplace, totally unconscious of any loss in the
scene, were company. All these Molly had in the daytime, but none of
these protected her at night.

While Grandma Johnstone and Mrs. Anthony had been there in the
house, she had not been afraid of Miss Charlotte's grave. Left entirely
alone, and missing Charlotte greatly, she became continually aware of
Charlotte's presence on the hillside under the pines. Without feeling that

she lessened her affection for the other members of her family by admitting it, after Grandma Johnstone's death she realized that she had loved Charlotte more than any one else on earth. Lying alone in the bed under the stairs, the red curtain drawn aside, the piano, the bookcases, the chairs and stove, all shadowy in the night, she wished for Charlotte, and, wishing, became afraid of Miss Charlotte's ghost. Not of her soul. Her soul, Molly was sure, was safe in heaven, and a heaven not thought of as a region, but as a divine serenity. Neither the body, moldering softly into earth, nor the soul, at home in the adoration of Christ, troubled Miss Molly, but the ghost, the jeebi, which perhaps did not exist, frightened her exceedingly. If there were such a thing as a ghost, that of Miss Charlotte would certainly leave the earth under the pines and return to the kitchen door, to the room upstairs where all her familiar little chattels lay undisturbed, or to the piano, certainly to Miss Molly, who was all that was left of Miss Charlotte's life. Night after night Molly lay struggling with this unchristian fear, having gone to bed, leaving, deliberately, the kitchen door unlocked, as she had always left it heretofore, and night after night she rose, a tall old woman in a nightdress of canton flannel that enveloped her from chin to heel, the cuffs folded down over the backs of her hands, and groped her way into the kitchen, touching the arm of the sofa, the back of a chair near the stove, the cold china knob of the door, and so across the kitchen to the back door, and drew the bolt in the flimsy lock. The front door she never locked. If Miss Charlotte's ghost came from the hill she would stop at the kitchen door, confused by the single bolt. Then she went back to bed and wept, thinking of Miss Charlotte locked out of her own home, thinking of her own behavior as unworthy of her Christian faith, thinking of her loneliness.

VII

A small open launch nosed its way carefully up the edge of the channel between Encampment and Sugar Island, going north. The fog was a gray wet vapor seemingly thin, but it closed around and above the small boat in an obliterating substance, and through it the put-put of the gasoline engine was both muffled and prolonged. Dr. Deyoe had removed his pince-nez, which the air bedewed, and laying the glasses in their case, had stowed them in the pocket of his yellow slicker. From under the edge of his soft tweed hat his eyes, a grayish green, peered into the fog, his upper lip with the short sandy-brown mustache lifted slightly, and the flesh about his eyes wrinkled in an effort to see what was not visible. His nose,

235

fine and pointed, and in expression suggesting that of a fox, sniffed the damp air, and he turned his head from side to side, the better to see or hear anything that might give him a clew to his whereabouts. His pocket compass lay on the wet wood of the seat close to his knee; his hand was on the tiller rope where it ran along the gunwale of the boat. He knew pretty well where he was, having made the trip many times, and as a red channel stake appeared in the mist and passed him slowly on the right, it, and its white-painted numeral and frayed base, where the ice last winter had rubbed it at the water line, receding, swaying slightly, into the fog, he corrected his course only a little, and imagined the Canadian shoreline beyond it, birches coming down to a stony shore and a stretch of shallow stony water. He was well above Coulter's. The launch ran on, saying, "Betcha-I-catchya, betcha-I-catchya," until above the sociable noise of it he heard the slow muffled throb of a big engine, and almost immediately perceived dimly ahead and to the left the bulk of a freighter. The large vessel made the launch seem a chip on a flood, as it proceeded ever so slowly, its propeller barely churning the water, its very mass creating a suction which drew the water up against it in a visible curve. The launch, hugging the edge of the channel, came nearer; the Doctor read on the high curve of the stern, swung out over the upper end of the rudder—for the freighter was going up unloaded—her name, the *Douglass Houghton,* of Buffalo, and as he passed her galley caught the hot breath of the engines mingled with the smell of cooking greases, all passing through the fog as a woman's breath passes through a veil. Bilge water was running from some small holes, each with a stained trail beneath it, down the side of the ship, and steam issued in a small white continuous spurt from a vent near the water line. Figures leaning over the railing above hallooed to him. Six o'clock in the morning, or very little later, and the month September. The Doctor was their first visitor for the day, and they greeted him as a sign of land, or, less metaphorically, as their first sign of the Sault, where they would be getting ashore in a few hours for a brief vacation from their ship. The freighter was marking time, her engines going mainly to hold her in position in the channel, and although she did move forward minutely, the launch ran ahead of her, passing the long blank side, the straight prow carrying the white pilot house out of sight above in the mist, and so on to the lower end of Sugar, the parting of the ways, for the ship channel went on to the left through the Dikes, and the Doctor was turning to the right on his way to Lake George, the sunken crib, and a try for bass.

As the launch ran on with its cheerful and ever-repeated remark, the Doctor was reminded of another view of the *Douglass Houghton,* or rather a partial view, for she was sunk in twenty foot of water off the Point. He had seen her since then, on her trips up the river, but her appearance from the fog, her name looming overhead in such an isolated and particular fashion, reminded him of the principal thing he knew concerning her, and that was her wreck. It was late in the year, and, as he remembered it, late in the day, for he was walking to the post office for his mail. The *Douglass Houghton* with a tow, a long red barge resembling herself save that she lacked the power of an engine and her galley smokestack was her only funnel, was coming up the narrow passage between the lower end of Little Neebish and St. Joe. The water rushed out to meet them and support them, leaving the sandy, stony beach sucked dry, the water retreating with foam and gurgle as if in a panic, as blood in a moment of great emergency for the individual rushes from the finger tips and brain to the heart. The Doctor noted the retreat as he had noted it many times before, and reflected that the Point was being cut deeper and sharper on its down-current side with every boat that passed. At the Point, the channel executing almost a forty-five-degree turn, the *Douglass Houghton* began to swing, standing on her propeller as it were, and bringing her long body around slowly. But as he watched, she stopped swinging, her propeller drove her forward, nose into the clay bank of the Canadian side of the channel. He heard her bells ring for stop and reverse, so close was she to the land at that place, but while the engines halted momentarily, the tow slid forward, unmanageable craft with no power or volition of her own save a little wheel in the pilot's house, quite unable to check herself, and with the power that her consort had imparted to her, rammed her consort full in the side. The *Douglass Houghton* sank, blocking the channel. The Doctor, lingering to watch the drama, heard from the coast guard that the steering gear had broken, and was requested, there being no telephonic communication from the station at the Point in those days, to show the Captain the way to the post office. The Captain went with him, saying nothing as they marched along over the sandy ground, over the sparse grass of the pathway, the leaves flying about their feet, and the gloom of evening increasing, suddenly chill about them as the path entered the woods. They passed the old Johnstone home, with its poplars, the tall Lombardies with heavily groined and corded trunks, each holding the cold breeze thick in its leaves like a sponge, passed Martin's low gray shack, the small terrace in front of it banked as always with bouncing Bet, now pale in the twilight, and before it, beyond the tangle of raspberry bushes, the piles of Major Rains's old dock, slimy and green, rotting coldly, almost completely submerged at the edge of the channel. The path entered the woods, which showed the gleam of the river intermittently to their left, although they were always within six or ten feet of the water, and presently brought them to the weathered cluster of buildings at the post office. The Captain glanced at the blue and white enameled sign hung from a corner of the post office building, indicating that there was a 'phone within, pushed through the door, let the Doctor guide him to the room at the back, where the 'phone was screwed against the wall, and there, standing with one foot on the teetering platform of a feed scale, with no light except a chance pallor from the river through the uncurtained small-paned window, he gave his message to his company. The Doctor had left him there. In the post office proper, the Doctor imagined the message. "The *Douglass Houghton* is sunk in twenty foot of water off Coast Guard Station Number One, St. Mary's River. . . . to tender my resignation." In his mind's eye, guiding the launch through the fog at the foot of Sugar Island, the Doctor surveyed the colored poster of Dan Patch, famous pacing horse, and his little black sully, on the post office wall, and wondered again about the wording of that message.

The sun burned away the mist before eleven. As it began to thin out, the men in the pilot house of the freighter saw the tops of the trees on the shore emerging, but looked down to an invisible river. When the white ranges, squares of whitewashed boards, arranged on their points and in line one behind the other in such a fashion that whoever sighted them one above the other knew he was sighting true along the channel line, when these appeared in the swathes cut for them in the low forest, the *Douglass Houghton* got under weigh again, and eventually reached the broad stretch of water beneath the locks at the Sault in a full blaze of sunlight. Tugs and ferryboats, ore boats, their stacks banded and blazoned according to their lines, small motorboats, a few rowboats, and an occasional dingy sailboat, crowded the slips and channels and the entrance to the locks. The water here rocked under a film of powdered soot and grease, clearing suddenly, for the current was swift and the channels were deep, but forming again inevitably, for there were many vessels. Seagulls sailed and swooped for trash thrown overboard, especially from passenger boats. The freighters hung below the locks, calling in deep whistles signals to the lock house, one long blow for the American locks, two for the Canadian. Flags, Canadian and American, sooty and draggled from being always carried aft in the full roll of the smoke, hung limp in the sunshine or flew gayly from white masts on the shore. The Canadian Sault, mounting the hill, terraced with flat bright facades, lay to the right, and to the left and ahead the water front of the American Sault was thick with business. The power house, a mile-long succession of dark arches over the water, surmounted by the two long rows of windows, shut off Henry Schoolcraft's Elmwood from the river. The deck hands lined the bulwarks of their ships and hallooed to the small craft skidding about below.

The Weitzel, the Poe, the Davis, all then operating, although in a few years the Weitzel would be closed as obsolete, incapable of containing the six-hundred-foot ore-carriers, and retained only for use in emergencies; the unfinished Sabin Lock, a deep pit inclosed yet by the great coffer dam, had absorbed Oshawanoe's Island, had moved the bed of the actual rapids farther to the north, had rearranged the whole scene in a new and rigid pattern. Most of the water which had formerly rushed down the remaining bed of the rapids was now detoured through the canal of the Michigan Northern Power Company; there was barely enough to cover the red and white freestone. North of the rapids, again, were the Canadian lock and lock canal.

Cold and green, translucent but not transparent, heavy with a vast chill inertia, the water lay in the canal of the Weitzel Lock, held in a wall eighteen feet above the level of the river. If the slow, barely perceptible motion of the water in the long vat had not been sufficient to indicate its heaviness, the bars and counterbars, and bolts and steel plates of the ponderous mitered gates, mitered toward the west, and locked shut, were another image of this innocent, terrific force, which, if loosed, would toss the *Douglass Houghton* against the farther gates and smash freighter and barrier as if they were the stuff of shingles. Deep in the lock chamber the *Douglass Houghton,* made fast by twisted steel hawsers to the blunt metal posts, waited while the water bubbled up about her, trickled down from the intricately barred inner side of the gates, seethed and eddied upward from invisible vents, and lifted her slowly, very slowly, between the sheer walls. Stains of iron rust, water stains, the faint lines of the stone seaming, were all that broke the monotony of the long, mathematically straight cliffsides of the lock. Standing on the cement walk beside the lock, passers-by could look down upon the red steel decks of the freighter, upon the long double rows of slightly raised hatch covers, the little swinging railing that ran the four hundred and fifty feet of the vessel's middle section, upon the winches, the capstans, could look into the open galley door. Gradually she rose, her name appeared above the wall's edge, and her anchor. Among the grassy lawns, the "graveled and cemented walks, the plumy autumn trees, she stood, appearing, from a little distance, as if she had no business there. Her weathered sides, a grayed red-oxide from the prow to the stern, hung there eighteen feet above the river where she had loomed to the

Doctor in the fog; her prow and stern a darker red, having been freshly painted at the beginning of the season. The bolts and plates of her shell were plain to behold. Bells sounded from the tower in the midst of the canals, a man ran out along the gate bridge to unlock the wrings, the great flanges, that folded back against the walls, moving slowly, ponderously, hardly daring to stir the water, moving against liquid weight as one moves in a dream against an unnamable impeding substance. The water from Superior, lying quietly in the long canal, mingled with the lock water, and the freighter, convoyed by her tug, went westward, free. From the locks one could see Superior, a larkspur blue, beyond the black web of the rail-road bridge, beneath the amethystine blue of the cold Laurentians.

VIII

The three boats lay drawn up part way on the narrow stony beach on the south side of the Hay Point, their deep hulls tipping, sails not yet furled. The old canvas stained with hemlock was the color of red clay, deep car-rot color, but more tawny, and was intensified by the sunlight, for it was late in the afternoon. The sails hung slack, swaying in a little wind. On one of the boats a line, stretched from the bowsprit to the tip of the mast, was hung with colored handkerchiefs, the morning's wash. A hum of voices rose above the boats, women's voices, light as children's, with the low round vowels and nasals of Indian speech in curious falling cadences. There were three women of varying ages, part of a family of Ottawas. Their rounded backs, under the faded cotton blouses, disappeared and rose beside the unpainted gunwales as they sorted and lifted out their belongings, now mostly very wet. They had come across from Lime Island to the lee side of the Point, quartering with a heavy north wind, and had shipped much water, both forward and stern. The prows rested above dry reeds, waterdrifted. Beyond the stones a thicket of tag alders with dense green leaves shut them from the birch woods. The sunshine was still and pleasant. There was a scent of sweet grass mingled with the odor of warm bodies.

The Hay Point ran out from St. Joseph's Island narrowly and ended in a blunt wooded tip. On one side of the point were quicksands. The rest was mainly swamp grass and cranberry bog, and in the grassy part of the swamp, Old John and Young John had been cutting hay. At the end of the day Old John sat down on the wagon to rest, while his son finished the last stack. The swamp stretched from his feet, golden and stubble where the land was dry, golden and waving where the marsh was real, over it all

240

the bleached radiance of fields at evening. Very far away a cluster of birches and poplars stood close around a house of which the gray front was barely visible, and Old John watched it idly. His pale blue eyes, like those of the cherubim, clear, translucent, and preternaturally untroubled, saw a little cloud of smoke rise gradually among the birch leaves, gather, and flash away in the wind, the apparition of a white wing. And thereupon he got up slowly, for he was troubled with sciatica, and walked out upon the marsh toward the house. Young John saw him go, but said nothing, and went on tying birch poles together in a tripod to weight down the hay.

The short gaunt figure in the snuff-colored shire moved out across the brilliance. He was an Englishman; he had been born in Ullswater, and he was seventy-three years old. Sometimes he took a little laudanum to ease him of the sciatica pains.

The house stood facing the swamp, its back to the west. It had no windows in the front, and the door was closed, which gave it an odd, inhospitable expression. The door was batten, hardly more than five feet high, and fastened with a piece of twisted wire. A small tin chimney projected from the board roof against which the branches of the birch tree swept and scraped this day of wind. From a distance the trees hid the house almost completely, but as one approached they seemed to disperse and stand away, leaving the gray walls visible, logs, slatted at the cracks instead of chinked. The ground about it was sandy. All through the morning a yellow-jacket had been at the door, advancing and retreating from the wire, as if it knew of something sweet inside. The trees to the left were poplars, with small pale green trunks. The round crisp leaves whirled and clashed upon each other.

As Old John came up, although he could not at first see the water, he had a vision of it, rushing in thin and foaming over the quicksands and the shallows to die among the upright green rushes, and strain back slowly. He knew the motion of it well. A great square haystack stood between the house and the shore. All the late afternoon the light had lessened over the swamp, with no appreciable shadows, for there were no interruptions. It grew slowly horizontal, and, the air cooling, the swamp and the stacks assumed the brilliance of sand. The house cast a shadow forward over ground littered with chips and loose hay. Old John trod upon blackberry vines as the grass grew shorter, and then stepped into the shadow of the house and trod upon the worn ground there. He heard, or thought he heard, a humming, and paused to hear it better. It was inside the house, voices in a foreign speech.

241

He knocked, the door was opened to him from within, and he entered. The room was full of Indians, in silhouette against the window at the far end, or seated with the light falling across their knees and giving them the appearance of a heavy substance, solid as marble. My God, he thought, for a moment, there was all the Indians of the country there! They had made a fire in the short pot-bellied stove in the center of the room. Old John made his way past the stove and sat down, where they had cleared a place for him, on the one-plank bench against the wall, stretching his game leg straight before him to rest it, letting his arms cross, wrist upon wrist, hanging loosely, his shoulders bent. He puckered up his mouth under the sandy mustache until it became like the mouth of a sucker. He was breathing hard, and his eyes, serene and abstracted, glanced from figure to figure. Then, as no one spoke, he lapsed into a trancelike stillness, gazing steadily before him at nothing.

One of the younger Indians, a short plump fellow with a great bush of hair standing straight out from his head, and tawny at the ends like the pelt of a bear, said very amiably, "This your house?"

Old John turned to him and nodded. The Indian beside the stove, directly across from Old John, with a black felt hat on the back of his head, promptly took off his hat and balanced it on his knee. He regarded Old John with bright, contented eyes. His lips were full and smooth, his mouth wide; a little fold of brown skin shortened his eye on the inner corner. Old John said, "Whence d'ye come?"

"From Manitouline," answered the Bear, sliding over the *r*, and added, "We go 'way tomorrow."

Old John shook his head. "No, my dear man," he said slowly, and with finality, "you'll not go away tomorrow unless you go right back where you come from. Nor the next day nuther."

"No?" said the Bear politely.

The man next the stove translated to a woman in the corner. There was a return of the humming Old John had heard from without, an eddy of protest, light, yet guttural, as the woman answered, and those behind her repeated what she had said, and the man with the hat on his knee repeated it all in turn to the Bear. The Bear put his hand behind his neck and rubbed it, and said beguilingly, "We got to go. We ain' go' no more bread." A pause. "We ain' go' no more bread sin' we leave Lime. They women, they tired to eating stick bread."

After this speech every one looked to Old John. The weight of the situation seemed to have fallen upon him, and no one said anything more. The man by the stove got up and tiptoed across the room to a pile of maple chunks that had evidently been there upon the Indians' arrival, and tiptoed back with one for the fire, while the sunlight poured through the one window, reaching even into the bunks in the corner, built in one above the other, sailor fashion, and filled with hay. The woman who had spoken was sitting on a bundle of quilts at the foot of the bunks, leaning back against the two-by-four at the corner. She might have been thirty or thirty-two, and was very large. She wore a black serge skirt and a pink blouse, and a short string of black beads around her throat to prevent the growth of goiter. When she smiled, she showed a toothless gum, and when her mouth was closed her lips had a mild, froggy complacency. She was wind-burned, and the sunlight gave her an added ruddiness under the ripe smooth brown of her skin. Her hair, drawn back close to her head, left clear the forehead and the pleasant modeling of the smooth flesh over the skull. Behind her, Old John could see the short bare legs of a little boy, who presently crawled out of the bunk and went to sit on the floor with his back against the door. Old John smacked his mouth with the sound of a toad catching flies.

"Yes," he said, "I give a look at yon water as I come up, and I said to myself that it wasn't likely nobody would cross yon water for some days, for when it hasn't blown like this for a long time after a sultry spell, it's likely to keep on blowing for two or three days.

"It blowed like this when Sundby and I come up here for the first time. Yeh, Sundby and I built this house. We built it in a week, and it ain't been touched since. That was, well, that was about fifteen years ago. We used to stay here, but a year or two ago some vagabones got in here and filled it up with bugs. So we ain't used it none since. John and I, we sleep under the wagon. So you can stay here as long as you like. And if anybody says you can't, you say John Porter said you could."

At this point he paused and turned his head aside with the movement of a man about to spit. He did not spit, however, and after a period of meditation he began to speak again. At any time when he had more than a single disconnected remark to make his voice assumed a narrative tone, slightly softer and more resonant than his usual speech. It was like the steady unseeing gaze of his eyes, and it produced a certain impersonality, on the smooth ground of which figures moved.

"Sundby and I, we built it. But I built my own house nigh thirty-five years ago, by myself, in less than a week, and the missus moved in, and we've stayed there ever since. And for that same period of time I've worked the ground at the Mountain, and pretty nearly every summer I've been down here to cut hay, to say nothing of the hours I've nigh broke my back and scraped my fingers to the bone picking these marsh berries."

243

"Mashkigimin," said the Bear softly.

"Before that time," went on Old John, "I was a railroader, and before that I worked in the stables. Yet I never laid no bet on any horse, and I never touched liquor, though I've been a barkeep in my day too."

The Indians were listening with great attention, the many pairs of dark eyes fastened on the white man, dark eyes with a film of blue over the pupil.

"I never touched liquor, and I never will. I was near to dying one day, and the engineer and another chap they took me into the roundhouse and they laid me out there. And they got the doctor, and the doctor said, 'Man, you need something quick, here swallow down this whiskey,' and I said, 'No sir, I don't touch the stuff and nothing will make me,' and I didn't, nuther. Nor I don't smoke nor chew. By Jiminy Blue, I come to some conclusions in my life, and I hold by 'em."

All this while the voice never altered pitch, but when the Bear lifted a small round pasteboard box from the table, he laughed. The box was a Copenhagen snuffbox, filled with granulated sugar, the big coarse flakes of the Canadian manufacture, and the Bear had found it in the house.

"No, by Jiminy Blue," said Old John, "that's Sundby's, that old Swede."

The Indians laughed, a soft ripple of amusement, though it was certain that no one but the Bear knew what the joke was about. The Indians were still laughing gently, the Bear shaking the box slowly and smiling down at it, when there came a knock at the door. The little boy took himself out of the way. For a moment, as he stooped to enter, the face of Young John appeared, ruddy, smiling to show the whitest of teeth, his stiff yellow hair alight with sun, his eyes blue and clear, his chin with a long clear sweep of jaw, slightly undershot.

"John," said his father, "these folks are staying here until the wind goes down. How many loaves of bread have we?" "Two," said John, "and some onions."

"Well, fetch 'em here. We shan't need 'em any more."

The face disappeared, and the Indian boy sat down on the doorstep, hands clasped about his knees. The dust on the floor cast fine, tall shadows. He could look far across the fields to the fringe of small bush where Young John was going, and above which hung the Mountain, a blue lake. To the north a heavy bank of cloud, blue like the Mountain, somber and cold, was gathering with speed, but left the sunset unobstructed. John's hair, like the stubble, burned with a steady gold.

The Indians began to move about. Pitonoquod had hung his felt hat on a nail. The women were spreading quilts over the hay in the bunks. There was a little talk, the pat and shuffle of feet on boards, slowly. Old John sat very still and felt tired. He was covered with light, like a very fine sand thrown over body and feet; among the darker moving figures he loomed, somehow, like far shores on still, sunny mornings. By the time Young John returned, the beds were made, cups and plates were on the table, and Pitonoquod had gone for water. The northern cloud, too, had drawn closer. Old John came out and joined his son.

The Indians watched them go. As they entered the small bush, where the wagon was, the first drops of rain struck sharply on the roof, and sang, like whips, on the tin of the stovepipe. The Indians shut the door.

IX

The forest surrounded the Magpie Mines with no intermediary fields or villages, the forest of the early days of the Northwest Company. The young growth struggled up between the fallen spars of pine, which hung obliquely entangled. Deep moss, velvety and sweet with damp, covered the enormous trunks dropping slowly closer to earth, rotting at the core to a fine even punk. The foot broke through and sank as in a bog to the knee. Moose, muskrat, wolf, and lynx and all the wild northern birds filled this wilderness with perpetual incident, and at the Magpie, the tubular kilns, eight feet in diameter, one hundred and twenty-five feet long, inclined one and one-half inches to the foot, revolved slowly, slowly shaking the mass of pinkish-white siderite and the black, more heavily carbonated metallic rock, until the heat, one thousand one hundred degrees centigrade, had volatilized the sulphur content and converted siderite to hematite and a fine Bessemer ore. At the Mesaba range they scratched away the surface earth and loaded the powdery red hematite by the shovelful directly into the waiting cars at the cost of less than five cents a ton. At Pewabic they were mining a lean silica ore to be mixed with the Mesaba iron. Lean magnetite, at Duluth, was being converted into a rich sinter by an electrical process, and the procession of ore barges through the locks at St. Mary's ran one ship to every eighteen minutes. Still the lake washed its cold water against metallic cliffs, hematite, siderite, magnetite, limonite, Indian red, pale yellow, black and gray, glossed with the action of waters, some of the earth or rock or rocky earth claimed, and the claim recorded in government offices, much of it yet unrecorded, almost unknown.

X

On the north side of St. Joseph's Island a small flourishing village, Richard's Landing, had grown up since the days in 1876 when Mr. John Richard, a merchant, had built a store there and sold lots cheaply, fifty dollars an acre, to prospective customers. Some distance off the international ship channel, east of Bear Lake and the cluster of stony islands known as the Blueberry Rocks, the town faced the Canadian mainland across a stretch of water, and occupied a triangle, two sides of which were water, the third the steeply rising, surfed and stony hills. The C-Line Road, beginning at a point opposite Encampment, ran across the island, west to east, and after a few winding miles near its end, intersected the road which came down from the hill, running northward into the town's main street, and ending at the government wharf. There were stores to the right hand side of the street, a bakery, a hardware store, Walker's General Merchandise, which had private wharves of their own at their back doors, like those of St. Mary's in the fifties, and across from them stood the County Hall, a few smaller shops, and a dwelling house with a low white picket fence and a yard full of lilac trees where people from out of town could order dinner. The Landing shared with Hilton the honor of being purchasing and shipping center for the island farms. On the red warehouse of the wharf the crown in white, and on the customhouse the crown and maple leaf in green, scarlet flags with maple leaf and the British cross, a monument of island bowlders cemented in a shaft, faced with a bronze plaque with the names of boys killed overseas, proclaimed the island's loyalty. Here the Canadian Red Cross established a small hospital, and here, early in August, 1928, Will and Howard Johnstone brought Miss Molly, for she had been failing rapidly all summer, and they were unable to give her at Encampment the care she needed.

In May the white lilacs were in bloom along the street. The young people built smudge fires because of the mosquitoes and played lawn tennis on the grass courts next door to the Anglican Church. The church was small, of stone, and covered with ivy as if it had been there a great while. The games went on after supper, long into the spring twilight, the darkness coming through the sweet air, the white ball flying back and forth, the smoke drifting from the smudge fires, the voices of the players echoing down the street. In July there were ball games behind the County Hall, political picnics in the maple grove west along the shore, Sunday evening concerts in the Hall, with the doors open and men and boys sitting on the steps, the street full of buggies and cheap cars, the stores dark. In August people drove from Encampment to see Miss Molly, the buggy wheels scattering dust on the goldenrod that had begun to line the roadside, or came in automobiles, or in motorboats around the head of the island. She would be eighty-four the twenty-fifth of October, when the leaves were red. She was not dying of any illness, but of old age. She said once, without petulance or protest: "I don't want to go. I don't want to go, but I suppose I must." A few winters of the last eight years she had spent with Miss Mabel in the house next the post office; the last winters of all she had spent with her brother Will in her own house. But she had long since ceased to fear Miss Charlotte's ghost. In her quiet room in the small hospital, the summer noises of the village outside her window, the young, pleasant nurses running in and out of her room, caring for her with affection, with her friends coming to visit her, she was almost happy.

She heard their voices outside her window, then in the corridor, as they came with flowers and small gifts. She received them lying with her head slightly raised on the white pillow, with a little motion of the hand and her old smile, the long lips drawing slowly back, faintly parted, and relaxing slowly, and listened with pleasure to whatever news they brought from Encampment. Her hair, still black, still framed her forehead in precise scallops, but the forehead was lined; the lips were pale, for the heart was not functioning strongly. Age had drawn the flesh tight over the bones of the face, narrowing the nostril, deepening the eye socket, revealing all the structure of the skull, and yet this flesh retained all the shyness, all the proud refinement and sweetness, of her youth; the black eyes with the film of blue were still bright.

So the days went by, carrying her nearer to Miss Charlotte.

On August 13 two visitors who asked if they might see Miss Johnstone were told that she had died a little after nine o'clock that morning in her sleep. A boat from the coast-guard service, the *Vigilant,* was sent from Encampment to bring Miss Molly home. The casket, not a heavy one, was placed on the after deck, and the small thick boat with the high prow, the black paint and brilliant varnish, moved out steadily through Bear Lake, passed the white lighthouse on the rock, passed the islands with their round sweet berries, the reedy lower end of Sugar Island, entered the channel which John Johnston had taken with his convoy of canoes on the way to Fort Mackinac, and so came down the river between St. Joseph's and Neebish Island. At Encampment Island the flags were all at half mast.

Of those who brought wreaths of cedar and scarlet bunchberries and white immortelles for Miss Molly, who waited in the yard for the burial service to begin, and sat down, finally, crowded together on the hastily improvised benches of boards and kitchen chairs, many had known her thirty years or longer, and all had loved her. They had brought their children to play among the daisies and long grasses, or to stand at Grandma Johnstone's knee, children that were now grown and married. At early morning, at noon, at dark, they had passed in and out of Miss Molly's gate, wearing the homely bars of peeled wood to a fine polish with the light touch of their hands. Now they sat, the daisied grasses bent beneath their feet, their faces lifted a little toward the porch, where the minister stood. Save Will and Howard, there were no persons present having Ojibway blood in their veins. Six years earlier, perhaps, there would have been friends from Sugar Island, but the French and Ojibway women who had come to visit Grandma Johnstone were now all dead; Showsh-ko-gezik, the Green Sky, was dead; the Indians who drifted up and down the river were mostly from the Canadian reservations at Garden River or Manitouline, Ottawas, or Potawatomis.

Beyond the gate lay the river, a calm flood which had carried bark canoe, bateau, schooner, side-wheeler, whaleback, tug, and barge; and beyond the river, the green fields of St. Joseph's shone in the sun. At intervals during the service, the freighters passed, going north, their engines muted across the water, moving slowly, the long red bodies sliding above the surface without breaking the stillness. The river was higher this summer than it had been in years. It had submerged the new docks, and reclaimed old beaches; the grass grew down to the water's edge without an interruption, and arbor vitae and Indian plum dipped their lower branches in the tide. Some of those waiting in Molly's yard remembered this replenishment as they listened to Mr. Bagnall, and joined in the prayer, and afterwards followed her in a narrow procession up the path through the garden, through the woods, to the pines on the hill, where they left her. Anna Maria Johnstone, the Woman of the Red Leaf. Born October 25, 1844, died August 13, 1928. O-miskabu-go-quay, unwaybin.